BATTERED

the monster among us

JUANITA RAY

TOXIC THOUGHTS

a true story series

BATTERED – The Monster Among Us

Summary: "When Ned Rose, widowed father of six children, falls in love with the
neighbor's wife, she moves into the Rose residence, destroys the family and tortures
Ned's youngest daughter for eight years, until Juanita who finds the courage to run away
is made a ward of the court—her father stripped of parental rights." - - Provided by
publisher.

For information regarding this publication contact:
SmorgasbordPublications@gmail.com

Toxic Thoughts Series #1
BATTERED
ISBN- 978-1-936954-17-9 (Paperback)
ISBN: 978-1-936954-16-2 (Digital)

Cover art and book design by Juanita Ray

Preface

Monsters do not lie under your bed. Monster do not live in closets. They go to church. They go to school. Some teach in schools. Some are mothers, fathers, sons and daughters. My monster was the married mother who lived two doors down. She moved in as the housekeeper and later became my father's wife. I was starved, beaten and held captive on our property. After eight years of torture, I survive and escape the monster.

When a story, like mine, hits the news, we are shocked.

Why would a child, attending school, endure eight years of cruel torture and starvation, yet not run for help?

Why couldn't an older sibling call the police?

Why didn't the children gang up on her?

To understand the answer to these and many other questions, you have to live the abusive, fearful lives we lived.

I once wondered, what fuels a monster? Greed, jealousy and control are three big factors. According to recent NCANDS data the majority of the perpetrators, half a century later, are still women.

The biggest question, is how could a Dad, not mutually engaged in the systematic sadistic torture of his children, allow it to happen on a regular basis? That answer is simple. Somewhere back in time, my father lost his spine. He too was a victim of the monster.

And yes, I will always be afraid of monsters, just not her.

Toxic Thoughts Series

a true story memoir series
about one woman's adversities and resilience

#toxicthoughts

Battered *the monster among us* (#1)
Stalked *the trials and successes of a child bride* (#2)
Intoxicated *a true story of an add relationship* (#3)
Charmed *a true story of a second secret life* (#4)
Shattered *'til narcissism do us part, a true story memoir* (#5)
Discarded *the throw away bride, a true story memoir* (#6)
Trapped *coming soon* (#7)
Hindered *coming soon* (# 8)

For information concerning release dates for paperback, ebook, or audible formats, in regard to this series, or inquiries about any other books or series authored by Juanita Ray, contact SmorgasbordPublications@gmail.com.

Contents

Two roads diverged in a wood, and I—I took the one less traveled by, And that has made all the difference.

– Robert Frost

The Party

Aunt Patty flings open the window and cups her broken fingernails around her mouth. "Drive slower before ya kill someone! Yer plumb crazy. I liked that house better when nobody lived in it." Her lipstick smudged mouth curls into a smile as I pull my fingers from my ears. I hate it when she yells. The last time I heard anyone yell that loud was when my brothers set fire to the babysitter's pantyhose.

"Hello me ducky. I hear somebody just turned six today. So tell me what yer wish is. Oh, and tell yer sister she can keep the candles."

Every year I make the same wish and I make it more than once. I've wished on stars and even fought with my brothers to blow out their candles for extra wishes, but so far nothing's worked. Candles don't have magical powers.

"My wishes never come true, so you can have your candles back. I don't need them."

Aunt Patty smiles at me and yells, "Try praying. Your mudder loved the Lord." She rolls her eyes. "Joe git dat damn phone." She blows me a hurried kiss, and smiles at Sharon. Her eyes soften.

I decide to change my birthday wish. I want someone's eyes to glow, like hers, when they look at me. Today I'll wish for a new mom.

"Honey, treat your cousin real nice and don't forget today is all about her. Love youses." Her pink rollers disappear behind the red checkered curtains and the window slams shut.

"How come your mom talks so weird. What's youses mean?"

Sharon shrugs, "It means both of you. All my aunts from the bay, talk like her. Sometimes Mom embarrasses me, but I'm still glad I got one. It would suck not having a mom who loves you."

"Just because my mom is dead, doesn't mean she stopped loving me. Besides, Marie acts like a mom. She loves me when she's not too busy. And your mom can't even braid hair like Marie can."

"Sister's aren't the same as a mom. You know that, right?"

"You know we're not really cousins right? And I don't like how your mom says mother—sounds like she's talking about a cow. Mudder."

Sharon turns toward me. "Why are you acting so mean?" The elastic snaps and flies through the air. "And what was that?"

I shrug. "It was fast. Sounded like a fairy to me."

Sharon turns, folds her arms tight against her chest, and frowns. "Mom told you before, tons of times, fairies are not real."

"They are too, and they grant wishes. Three wishes."

"Mom always says if you want something you have to pray for it, not wish for it." She dangles a new elastic band above her head. "And I know what that sound was. Don't you dare break this one."

I twist it around her hair three times. "You're wrong Sharon. I tried praying. I prayed every single night, for a whole year. I prayed for God to send mom back, but no, God just wants to keep her all to his greedy self and not share. So, for your information, your mother is wrong. Prayer doesn't work. Not for dead people, and not for me." I tug her braid through the last loop and yank on it extra hard.

Battered

"Ouch! Stop yanking my hair." She massages her scalp with both hands, while weird wincing noises hum from between her clinched teeth. She twists and gives me her finest scowl.

"So-or-rr-ry," I lie.

Bullet sounds ricochet from the fence in front of us. My hands fly outward. Sharon's braid catches in my ring.

"OUCH! What is wrong with you? You never act like this."

Pebbles fly through the fence. The stench of burning rubber swirls under our nostrils, while the sound of screeching tires is followed by a loud horn blaring in the distance. "Did you see that? The thing almost came crashing down. You guys need to fix it."

"Mom's right about that woman. She's going to kill somebody one day." Sharon points above the old, decrypted fence, at the small vacant house. Its dirty windows, and peeling paint, gives me the creeps.

"Mom is praying, whoever lives there, beats down the fence, so we can make them pay for a new one."

"What type of person moves into a haunted house?"

"I don't know. Maybe a witch? I saw them move in yesterday." She points to the right side of the fence. The loose gray boards, riddled with splits and holes, reminds me of our old barn back in Heart's Delight.

Sharon cups my ear and whispers, "Through there, that gap, I saw two boys. One is our age, and the other must be younger, maybe four, and he cries all the time. Last night he was screaming blue murder." She pulls a long blonde strand of hair from my ring. "See, you did pull out my hair! It's tangled through your—where did you get that ring?" Sharon's eyebrows straighten. Her finger pokes at my chest. "You stole your mom's wedding ring from Marie, didn't you? If you're smart, when you blow out your birthday candles, your wish should be that you don't get murdered."

"It's not stealing because Mom is dead and Marie didn't buy it. And I'm not a thief but you can tell your mother God's is and prayers don't work. My Dad told me, Mom was too good to be here on earth and that's why God took her. But that's stealing, because he didn't own Mom. And Marie is no better than God. She's doesn't know how to share either. That's why

Juanita Ray

I like you better than her. We share all the time. We're more like real sisters, right?"

She crosses her blue eyes. "I don't think so. We don't even look related."

"So? Not all my brothers look related either. We could be sisters. We're the same height, we're in the same class, we're both the youngest, we both have a bossy older sister and bossy brothers. That's five ways we're alike. Oh, and we're both six, because I'm six today." I slide down one step and sit beside her. A screw on the railing snags the frill of my dress. The more I try to break free, the worse it rips.

"Yeah but that would make us twins. Twins look alike and we don't."

"Not always," I examine my torn frill and wind it around my finger. "Let's go meet the new neighbors. I want to see what they look like."

"They look cute. Really cute and—"

"JUANITA. JUANITA."

I press the toes of my shoes into the holes of the chain link fence, climb to the top, sit and pivot backwards. The fence rattles and vibrates as I slide down into my back yard. I stumble across the lawn uprooting clumps of dirt and grass. They stick to the toes of my shoes.

The more I wipe them, the greener they get. I slip them off and scrape them against the concrete steps and hide them behind my back the moment my sister's shadow falls across the porch.

"I'm impressed. I only had to call you once." Marie leans against the door frame and points towards the kitchen. Then her hazel eyes narrow, her smile disappears, and her hands fly high above her head. "Tell me those things are NOT your new shoes. Not your new saddle oxfords."

I slip them back on. "Okay. They're not my new shoes." I race past her apron, up the steps, and dash down the hall.

"Hey Trouble, the kitchen is that-a-way. JUANITA!"

Out of breath, I stare out my bedroom window. I can't see anything. The only way I'm going to catch a glimpse of those boys from here is if they're fixing their roof.

"When do you suppose you might start acting like a lady?"

I turn around and grin at Marie. "Never."

Battered

She shakes her finger. "You won't be grinning when Dad sees your shoes. Oh my god! Look at that dress. It's ruined. Already?"

Marie is fifteen going on eighty. She was only thirteen when Mom died but when Dad announced she was in charge, she forgot she was my sister and started acting like a grandmother.

Adam is the second oldest and thinks he's the boss of everyone in the house, including Marie.

"Adam said my job is to be a kid, so I'm just being a kid. We make messes and stuff." I stare at her from the closet mirror and mimic her by crossing my arms. "Besides, it's not so bad. My dress looks better without frills anyway." I rip at the dangling lace. "See?"

"Stop that before you totally ruin it," Marie grabs my wrist. She's too late. The lace frill dangles from my fingers.

"Now you've done it."

"Done what? You're the one who said it was already ruined." I tug at the two small pieces of lace above the pockets, but before I can tear them off, Marie cups her hand around the back of my neck and propels me toward the kitchen. She sits me in a chair.

"Close your eyes."

I spread my fingers apart and peek between them. My brothers are flocking around the table like vultures. Aunt Patty, Uncle Joe and Sharon appear out of nowhere and slip into chairs.

Through my ring finger and pinkie, I see Dad tiptoe toward me, carrying a chocolate frosted cake with six yellow candles. The ring! I slip my finger in my mouth and clench the ring between my teeth.

"Happy Birthday to you . . ." Ryan's voice is the loudest. "You look like a monkey and you act like one too." He takes a deep breath and pretends to blow out my candles.

I stick my tongue out at him and try not to swallow the ring. "You suck Ryan. Dad please don't let Ryan blow out my candles. I really need my wish to come true and he's trying to ruin it."

Dad bends down, kisses my forehead, and lifts me up over his shoulders. He picks up the cake and places it on top of the fridge. I smirk at Ryan while Dad lights the candles.

I cross my fingers and say, "I wish for Ryan to disappear." One deep breath later, I uncross my fingers and make a real wish. With the ring nestled under my tongue, I blow back and forth across the cake until my breath runs out.

Dad slides me down his back and puts the cake on the table. Two candles flicker back to life.

Ryan pushes me away and blows them out. "Ha-ha! You wasted your wish!" he snickers. "Neener-neener-neener."

Aunt Patty leans forward and kisses Dad on the cheek. "Ned, this party gave Joe and me a great idea. We've been thinking it's high time you started circulating again. You know, find yerself a good woman."

They look so odd together, Dad with his receding hairline and Aunt Patty with bangs shaped like rollers.

Uncle Joe punches Dad in the arm. "Bein' my best friend gives you no rights to me woman. Patty you keep dem lips to yerself, and speakin' 'bout lips did Patty tell ya we were yappin' 'bout throwin' ya a housewarmin' party?"

Dad slides his hand back and forth across his head. "No point in it. Don't know anyone to invite except you guys."

Joe slaps Dad' shoulder. "That's why we have ta have dat housewarmin' party! God, I miss a decent wake. Nar a one—"

Aunt Patty coughs and throws Uncle Joe an ice-cold look. He bows his head and mutters something that sounds like an apology.

Aunt Patty rubs Dad's knee. "A party would do you a world of good, Ned Rose. No need to worry. The youngsters can spend the night at our house. Marie is old enough to learn how to serve the odd snacks and drinks."

Marie shakes her head and whispers in my ear, "Who do you suppose Aunt Patty thinks the housekeepers been for the past two years?"

"I can help too." Bruce grins. "And I can supply a few flowers for free."

Battered

Dad lifts one eyebrow. "Flowers? Free? From where? The graveyard?"

"No Dad. I don't do that no more. I buy them."

"You buy flowers? With what?"

"My allowance."

"Why would you spend your allowance on flowers?" Dad pulls the mangled toothpick from his mouth, examines it, and sticks the good end between his front bottom teeth.

"I sell them to the neighbors. Triples my allowance."

Dad leans back on the chair and rubs his chin.

"Remind me why you get an allowance?"

"So I can buy flowers."

"Since when is selling flowers a household chore?" Dad tilts his head toward Bruce. His eyeballs move to the left corners of his eyes and rest on Marie's face.

"He clears the table, and puts out the trash." She points at Aunt Patty and says, "I cook and clean. Done it for three years now." Aunt Patty pats her heart. "Did it before Mom died too." Then Marie points back at Bruce and says, "He also vacuums. And when you were away, and we ran out of money, he bought the groceries."

Dad looks shocked. "Ran out of money? When?"

Marie picks some crumbs from her lap and places them on her empty plate. "When I had to use the food budget to get them school supplies."

Dad faintly shakes his head, tilts it to the right, and nods at Adam.

Adam's smile is gigantic. "Controlling the horde and doing laundry."

Drake grins, "How do you think the lawn gets cut?"

"And I make the messes so everyone can get an allowance. Now that I'm older, I get a raise, right?" Before Dad can answer me, everybody talks at the same time, asking for a raise.

"Hush! You know the rules. You get your raises on your birthdays."

Ryan grumbles, "No fair. I gotta do dishes and she gets almost the same allowance as me for doin' nuttin'. She don't deserve a raise, or a birthday cake."

Dad pats my head. "Oh yes she does. Living with the four of you is a hard enough job in itself, and for that alone, she's earned a raise."

"Ryan is a big fat liar. I don't do nothing. I sort socks, right Adam?"

Adam laughs, "Yes she certainly does sort socks. And I make her do it before they're washed."

"Dad, do you have any extra odd socks in your drawer?"

"Extra? If extra means mismatches, yes. Why do you want them?"

"I was using them as sleeping bags for my dolls but now I need some for the brownies. They get cold at night"

"Juanita, I don't suppose you've seen any of my mismatches?"

Drake smirks. "Brownies? You put food in socks?"

"Not food brownies, the other kind. The fairy kind." I smile from ear to ear. "They love socks."

Dad's mouth twitches. "And exactly how do you know that for sure young lady?"

"Because they take the socks, every time I leave them out."

Bruce grins. "I collect odd socks too, but I like to stuff them with snow and keep 'em in the freezer. Nothing beats a snowball fight in July."

Aunt Patty frowns. "That child will never learn one decent thing if you let her believe in all this nonsense. If I've told her once, I've told her twice, there are no such things as fairies."

My smile evaporates. "Are too. Just because you don't like them and can't see them, doesn't mean they're not around."

"Listen here ducky, it isn't that I don't like them. Us grownups don't believe in things we can't see."

"They only show up for people who like them, not grownups like you. Besides, you believe in God and you can't see him either."

"That's different."

"What about the tooth fairy? Dad, you believe, right?"

"Yes, I certainly do. I believe they came to our house and switched out your brothers at birth."

The boys howl.

Dad gives me a very serious look and whispers, "They think I'm kidding but I'm not. Fairies do that sometimes."

"Dad you're the best." I wrap my arms around his neck and whisper, "So how much is my raise?" I kiss his forehead, lean back and wait for his answer.

He glances at Marie. "Why are you so quiet? Get your butt over here." Marie's sad smile fades. Dad pries my arms loose from his neck and sits me on his left knee. He wraps his right arm around Marie's waist. "I don't need any warming up party. Why would I want another woman when I already have the best two in town?"

"Because children need a mudder."

Everyone gets quiet. For the next minute, all I can hear is Aunt Patty sighing, while her fingers rapidly tap the space between her two breasts.

Adam is the first to break the silence. "Why don't you tell Juanita what you told me, last time I asked for a raise?"

Dad cocks one eyebrow at Adam. "And that was?"

"You offered me a kick in the butt."

Dad cocks the other eyebrow. Three long wrinkles flow across his forehead. "No. I don't think so. That doesn't sound like me."

"Yes you did. Back when we had that sitter, the third one that quit, and you put Marie and me in charge. The one we called Moolah. What was her real name? Anyone remember?"

Bruce curls his fingers against his forehead, "Moo-ooo-lah. She's the one that chain-smoked right? Beu-moo-lah."

Dad shakes his head. "Going through five sitters in two months had to set a new world record."

"Yeah, that's it. Beulah." Adam shrugs at Bruce, "I liked her. She changed her brand of tea just so I could collect bird cards."

"Oh, that reminds me. I brought you these." Aunt Patty takes several cards out of her apron pocket and hands them to Adam. Her voice sounds hesitant. "Or have you stopped collecting them?"

Adam flips through the cards, "Never. I'll always collect bird cards. I'm glad Mom started me on it."

Juanita Ray

Apparently, Mom started all of us on new hobbies before she died. She knew Dad wouldn't make us go to church, because he was never home, but that was the only thing that we did together. Everyone got some sort of kit after she died. I wasn't sure what I got, but if it was something good, Ryan probably stole it.

"Ryan what did you get when Mom died?"

Ryan glares at me, slams his fist into my cake and runs to his room.

Marie pushes Dad's arm away. He pulls her back. "Let him be. It's not his fault his mother's wake was on his birthday."

Suddenly the conversation is centered on Mom.

I half-listen, while Uncle Joe talks about how great and beautiful Mom was and how Dad will never be able to replace her.

"Ouch," he yelps, and moves his chair away from Aunt Patty.

Dad twists and untwists his napkin until it breaks apart.

Uncle Joe says, "Shame we had to be stationed away and gone so long, like we were, especially when the cancer ate her up." Aunt Patty coughs at Uncle Joe.

He ignores her and continues to talk about Mom. I remove all the pepperoni from my pizza and carve a big thirty-four into the red stained crust. Then I draw a cross around it.

Aunt Patty coughs louder, jerks Uncle Joe's chair and turns my piece of pizza upside down on the plate. "Juanita and Sharon, go outside and do something. Bruce, be a doll and go git me some paper to write on." She glares at Drake and Adam, "You two stop eating all the frosting and go clean up this holy mess. Marie, stay here child, you and I need to make up a hardy party menu." She takes a deep breath and looks me square in the eyes. "Outside I said!"

"What's a hardy menu?" I ask.

Aunt Patty turns to Dad, "Bet your kids haven't had a hardy meal in ages. That's one good reason they need a mudder around!"

"We don't need a new mother," I say.

"Did I not just tell you kids to go outside? Do what I say."

Sharon and I bolt for the front door but Sharon stops dead in her tracks. "And do what Mom?"

"I don't know. I'm sure you'll find something. Just go . . . go find those fairies Juanita is always talking about."

"What for? You said there are no such thing as fairies."

"Well go find one so I can change my mind. Besides, if Ned says there are fairies out there then it must be true, so go find some."

"And do what with them?"

"How in God's name would I know. Juanita is the fairy expert, not me. Ask her. But ask her outside." She opens the door and shoves us out.

"Mom is acting too weird. She just shooed us out like flies."

"I know," I laugh. "Your mom is funny. Are all moms like that?"

"Yeah all moms are the same . . . sort of."

We run down the sidewalk. The shiny new gate slams into the side of her house, revealing the weathered, creepy back fence. Sharon races for the biggest hole. Her voice sounds disappointed. "The car is still gone. Guess it's fairy hunting time."

"It's too windy out for fairies. Only angels come out on windy days."

I stretch my foot toward a lose board and kick it sideways. It creaks back and forth. The board beside it is half missing and cat fur is caught on its jagged edge. Others have large knots missing. One hole is almost the size of my fist.

"Hear that? The car is coming back!"

"Stop pushing. Use that other hole." Sharon points to the jagged board that has the bottom half missing. I shift to it. I see a car door open and a worn red shoe step to the ground. Two slim bare legs stomp to the passenger side.

"I said NO and no means NO. Get out. NOW." The smaller boy is sobbing. She drags him by the shirt collar. He loses his balance and falls. She curses, bends over, grabs his wrist and drags him across the ground toward some steps. He holds the crotch of his pants but can't stop the pee from flowing.

"You filthy little pig!" she yells. She grabs the boy by the wrist and drags him up and over the front steps. He stumbles and losing his footing—his feet thumping against the boards until they disappear past the front door.

I jump up and whisper, "Oh my god! Did you see that?"

Her shoes click-clack back down the steps. She slides on the urine and stumbles. Her two arms stretch out in front of her and her hands slam into the side of the car.

"Look what you made me do!" she screams. The rear car door flings open. A boy about my age steps out. He has huge eyes and a red snotty nose. The woman lifts her arm and whacks him in the head with the back of her hand. "Shut up and get in the house!"

Sharon's fingernails grip my wrist. She whispers. "He didn't even talk. What a monster."

Everything turns quiet.

"I think they're gone." I stretch up and try to reach a bigger hole, higher up. I lose my balance. The broken board snaps. I hit the ground with a thud. A flapping noise grows closer. I crane my neck toward the gap. Her shoes are a foot away from my face. A gust of wind whips her skirt through the crack and it catches on the big splinter above my head.

"Hello? Hello?"

Sharon crouches beside me and makes a small barking noise.

"Good idea," I whisper. I make a low growling sound.

"Hello. Who's there?" Her voice sounds like broken glass.

I pick up a rock and scratch it against the fence. I bark twice.

A small black shoe kicks my knee away from the gap. "Mom it's just a dog."

I hear a loud slap. "Didn't I just tell you to shut up? Are you stupid or what? Get inside and check on your brother before I murder both of you."

Her skirt rips free of the board. She turns back, curses and kicks the ground. Rocks spray toward me. The loose board smacks me in the face. A genuine yelp escapes from between my lips.

"If I have to listen to that stupid mutt bark all night, I'll have your father shoot it. Go get the hose and clean these steps."

"But—but you said to check on my brother."

Slap. "ARE YOU DEAF OR WHAT? GO GET THE HOSE."

We run across the yard, though the gate, slam it shut and crumble against it. Sharon gasps, "I'm just glad I'm not her kid." She squeezes my hand. "Next time you get sad and miss your mom, pretend your mom was like her."

"My mom could never be like that. Besides I think I'm better off without a mom."

Sharon's eyes pop open. "Oh my god. Your nose is bleeding."

I wipe it with my arm. Blood drips onto my lap.

"You must have done it when you fell. Pinch it tight. Like this." Sharon twists toward me, grimaces and pinches the bridge of my nose. "When my nose bleeds, Mom holds it tight like that. Try it. It only works if you tilt your head back."

I tilt my head back and pinch it. I can taste blood in the back of my throat. "Yuk!" I pull up some grass but it sticks to my bloody hand. "Help me rip the frills off my dress."

"What frills?"

"The pieces above the pockets. Hurry."

I pinch my nose while she yanks at the frills. By the time she hands them to me, the bleeding has stopped. I roll up the lace and stick one in each nostril, just in case it starts again.

Sharon bursts out laughing. "You look so funny. Let's walk to a window so you can see yourself."

The more we look at my reflection, the harder we laugh. The harder we laugh, the more I have to pee, but I can't stop laughing. My stomach hurts so bad I can't stand it. My laughter sounds more like yelps of pain, which makes us laugh even more.

"What are you two up to?" I turn around to face Uncle Joe. "Holy Mary Mudder of Christ! NED! NED! NED!" Uncle Joe scoops me up into his arms and runs toward my house.

I protest and tell him to let me down but he ignores me and races up our steps two at a time. Dad pushes open the door. The house turns upside down. Then it tumbles three times.

Sharon looms over me. "Are you okay?" Uncle Joe and Dad zoom into view.

"Good lord. It's only a nosebleed Joe."

"Well it looked to me like someone half-murdered her." Uncle Joe sits up and rubs his elbow.

My brothers appear out of nowhere, come to a screeching halt and roll on the grass laughing.

I reach up and pull one of the frills out of my nostril. It looks like a red worm. Now everyone is laughing, everyone that is, except Aunt Patty.

She slaps Uncle Joe upside the head.

"What's wrong wit' ya women?"

"What the hell are you trying to do? Kill her? And you, yer no better Ned, are you going to pick her up or just stare at her all day?"

Dad picks me up. Aunt Patty yells for Marie and follows us to the bathroom. I look at myself in the mirror and smile. "Dad before I get cleaned up can you take my picture? It's my first nosebleed!"

Aunt Patty raises her hands and waves them in the air, like she's trying to shake something off. "I don't know how any of your kids managed to survive without Elsie. I swear on her grave I am having that pardy because if I don't, those kids won't have a hope in hell of being normal without a mudder."

"If Dad doesn't want a party you can have one for me," I yell at her, as the door slams shut.

—————

The last time I smelled shortbread was the day of Dad's party. "Is Dad having another housewarming?"

Marie closes the oven door and smiles. "Not that I know of. But he said the shortbread was such a big hit that this morning he wanted me to make a double batch."

"Can I have one?"

"Once they cool."

"How long will that take?"

"Long enough for me to make some cocoa."

I sniff the cookies. "Today the kitchen is my favorite room in the house."

Marie laughs and tousles my hair. "What was your favorite room yesterday?"

"The playroom. It's mostly my favorite, except when we have to do laundry, then I like the living room best. What's your favorite room?"

"The kitchen."

"I only like the living room when cartoons are on or it's Christmas. I only like the playroom when it's not laundry day but I always love the kitchen so maybe it's my favorite too."

The smell of shortbread cookies and hot cocoa drift through the house. My brothers raid the cookies faster than Marie can bake them. While she chases them off, I confiscate the mixing bowl and eat globs of raw batter, then I hide behind the living room recliner.

The metal bowl clangs. Marie screams, "DADDDDD. The boys ate all of the batter!"

Dad spends several minutes chasing the boys but he's no match for them. They're used to being chased and I've never known them to ever get caught. He doesn't look grumpy or angry. He saunters back into the living room and for some weird reason he's smiling at not catching them. He turns up the stereo, lies on the couch, and when the song is over, gets up and plays it again. When he attempts to play 'put your sweet lips a little closer to the phone,' for a fourth time, I jump from behind the recliner and yell, "I did it. I ate the batter." But, Dad doesn't get mad. Instead he yells at the top of his lungs, "Who wants milkshakes and burgers?"

I don't get involved in the scuffle for the front seat. I know my place. I'm last. I shuffle into the passenger side back door. One of the benefits to getting car sick is getting a window seat. I usually only get sick on long drives or dirt roads, but sometimes I fake it on short trips, so I can look out the window.

Marie sits next to me. She's wearing the ring I stole. "Dad how come Marie gets all of Mom's old stuff?"

"Because she's the oldest, AND, because your sister has been looking after you guys, since she's been thirteen. She's earned it."

"I don't like being the youngest," I grumble. Marie rubs her hands through her short hair. Her long nails are precisely manicured and painted a pale pink. She doesn't look fifteen. She looks like an adult. Everyone says she looks like Mom, just plumper. If I were almost fifteen, I'd have at least one boyfriend. But she's only interested in us. Nobody else. I squeeze her hand three times. Only Marie, Dad and I know it means I love you.

My stomach lurches a little as Dad turns into the parking lot, but I don't complain, because I want a shake. Dad doesn't ask any of us what we want because it never changes.

"Adam, I'm warning you, do not move this car one inch. Stay out of the driver's seat." Dad leaves the keys in the ignition to keep the heater running. Adam nods, but as soon as Dad walks inside, he scoots behind the wheel.

Marie taps Mom's watch. "Does it still work?" I ask.

"Of course, why else would I wear it?" Marie unbuttons Mom's outdated jacket and fans herself.

Adam changes the rearview mirror. "When it breaks can I have it? For my collection?"

"It's not going to break, and if it does, I'll know you did it. So, no." Adam adjusts the mirror back in to place. Marie covers the watch with her hand. "I swear if you touch this watch, I'll tear up your entire bird card collection."

He reaches over the front seat to get a closer look but Marie hides her arm behind her back. Drake gangs up with Adam and pulls on the arm of her jacket. "Juanita, bite his hand." But before I can open my mouth, Dad swings the door open. He passes everything out except my shake. He takes a long sip of it, and winks at me. I hold out my hand.

"After you eat half of this burger, you can have it."

"No fair. I love milkshakes."

Battered

Dad holds it hostage until I stuff the last bite into my mouth. By now we're almost home. I tap his shoulder, pass him back my half-eaten cheeseburger, and hold out my hand for the shake. Adam passes it back to me. The outside of the cup is waxy, wet and slippery. The ice-cold chocolate splatters over my lap. It looks like diarrhea. Without warning, my stomach churns and the cheeseburger comes back to say hello.

I can't stop gagging.

"HUUURG. HUUURREGGEHH."

"No! No! Not in the car. I just cleaned it. Cover your mouth."

Cars honk and skid as Dad swerves toward the curb. I uncover my mouth and yank hard at the door handle. It flies open. Splat! I lift my head from the snow and vomit. The sight of vomit swirling in slush makes me gag again. My clothes are sopping wet. Two arms swoop me up.

"Holy Christ, are you okay?" His laugh sounds nervous. He gives me a slight shake, "Never do that again. Don't ever jump out of a car before it's stopped. I nearly had a heart attack. I thought I ran you over." He throws me onto his shoulder and grunts, "Adam, pull it up into the garage."

"Dad, I'm getting sick again."

Minutes later, I'm sitting on the bathroom counter getting my face washed. "Don't you think I'm a little old for this? I'll be seven in six and a half months." He ignores me.

"MARIE. GET IN HERE." He pulls off my boots and throws them in the sink. "I've been meaning to have a talk with both of you." I can tell by his tone of voice it's going to be one of those talks. I shift my eyes to the Christmas ornaments sitting on the shelf. A few of them look strange. I don't recognize them. They look old yet I haven't seen them before. Dad yanks at my shoulders, "Did you hear a single word I said?"

"I heard you. We are getting a new sitter and I—"

Dad cups my face toward his. "I didn't say sitter."

"Fine, we have a housekeeper coming." I move my face away from his onion breath. He stares deep into my eyes and slowly says, "She is not just any old housekeeper. This one is special. I don't want anyone driving this one away. Understood?"

17

"Then how come you're not having this talk with the boys? They're the ones that drove all the other housekeepers crazy. I'm not the one who put worms in slippers." Our sitters could never move out fast enough. The fifth and final sitter dumped a pot of stew on the floor and used a red lipstick to leave a message across the wall. 'If you're going to act like animals, you can eat like animals.'

No matter how hard they scrubbed, it would never wash off. Marie said there were only two choices. The boys could paint the kitchen with two coats of paint, or leave it there for Dad to read. When the boys told Marie the only thing they were ashamed of, was ruining a good dinner, Marie refused to let them paint the wall. So did Dad. He left it there until two days before we moved, as his reminder to never hire another sitter and to keep Marie in charge.

"Earth to Juanita," Dad flicks at my ear.

"What's the point of getting anyone here? I bet she ends up quitting."

"She's not just anyone. And this one is no quitter. I already warned your brothers, if anyone leaves around here, it won't be her."

Marie is panting. "The boys said you called me."

"What took you so long?"

"I didn't hear you. I was using the other bathroom."

"Dad wants you to clean me up, but after that the new housekeeper will clean everything because you need a break."

Marie glares at Dad. "I told you I don't need or want a break. I needed a break when I was thirteen—not now. Besides, it's not like the boys aren't pulling their weight."

Marie folds her arms and backs up against the wall. "I don't want some woman living here. Especially when she lives so close to us and can walk back and forth in two minutes."

"She's going to live here? At our house? Why does she have to live with us, Dad?"

"Because...she...er... because I said so, and last time I checked, I was still the boss around here."

The Room Downstairs

This is not how I wanted to spend my day. I toss the last snowflake into the box and wipe the sparkles from the dresser. If I see one more forgotten decoration, I plan to keep my big mouth shut. I don't get why Dad bought new decorations when we had so many already, or why he's donating our perfectly good ones to the Salvation Army.

I put the box in my room, next to the one marked M & M. The mattress is still leaning against the wall and Marie's dresser doesn't have any drawers in it. The only noise in the house is coming from a vacuum.

I follow the sound, past the kitchen, through the living room, and into Dad's bedroom. A strange woman in a pink uniform is cleaning his carpet. I pull the vacuum plug from the wall.

"Are you our new housekeeper?"

"I'm the maid." She looks annoyed.

"Did you already move in to live with us?"

"No. But if that's an offer I'll be glad to accept it."

"Then why are you here?" I, run past her, and flop onto Dad's bed. His ugly blue room is now a pretty sage green.

"Who repainted this room? You?" I run my hand across his new bed frame, while I wait for her to answer me.

She sniffs the air. "No child, I don't do paint."

"Why are you here cleaning instead of the new housekeeper?"

"Because your father hired me for a one-time spring-cleaning of the kitchen, living room and bedroom." She plugs the vacuum into the socket.

"But it's not spring," I yell. She pretends not to hear me.

Back in my room, I find the four boys carrying Marie's dresser out in to the hall. They complain it weighs a ton, even though the drawers are missing. I make a face at them and chant, "I know something you don't know."

"Stay out of the way before we drop it on your foot," Drake grunts.

"Or you'll feel something we don't feel," Ryan mimics my chant.

I move down the hall, sit in the corner and frown. I stay out of their way while they track back and forth like an army of ants. When the boys lift the last of the boxes, I follow behind them.

Drake stops in the middle of the stairwell and grunts, "Set it down for a second."

I squeeze past them. Ryan stumbles, regains his footing and takes a swing at me as I dart by.

"You did that on purpose!" he snarls.

"Leave her alone. She didn't do anything, and if she did it was an accident." Drake shoves the box toward Ryan and tells him to start moving. Ryan loses his grip.

Thump. Thumpity. Bang.

The box topples over the steps, slams against the wall, bounces back onto the landing and stuff flies all over the place.

Drake shrugs at Ryan. "You dropped it, you pick it back up."

Ryan's face is fiery red. "It's her fault. She can pick it up."

"Drake's right. You dropped it Ryan, I saw you drop it."

Battered

Drake sits on the steps and exaggerates a yawn. "Let me know when you two are done cleaning up this mess."

"I'm not helping her clean it up. She's the one that caused it."

"I did not! Stop lying Ryan." He lunges toward me.

Marie's cries, "No! Not this box." We stop and stare.

"Geez it's only a box," Ryan bends to pick up some jars.

"STOP. Don't touch a single thing." She pulls it upright. It's the box marked M & M. I look closer. It's an O. The box is marked MOM. She frantically gropes around collecting the scattered contents. "It's okay. I'm not mad at you. You can be my helper. Think you can find the matching earrings to these?" She smiles but her bottom lip is trembling. She wipes her eyes. "Think you can help me find everything?"

"Yep. I'm really good at finding stuff." I hug her, rest my chin on her shoulder and make a face at Ryan.

"You little pest. You're such a suck!" Ryan spits at me.

"What's going on down there?" Dad hollers from the top of the steps.

"Nothing," several of us answer in unison.

"Juanita what's going on."

"Nothing."

Dad scrutinizes us for a moment, winds his watch and whistles that stupid song he always plays. "I'm heading out for pizza. By the time I get back I expect you to have that upstairs bedroom cleaned spotless for the new housekeeper."

"Ha-ha-ha. Haahahahahah." Adam slaps his leg. "Us clean up for a housekeeper? What's the housekeeper going to all day? Chew gum and fart?" My brothers crack up.

Ryan is laughing so hard he can hardly talk. "Hey Juanita, if you're so good at finding stuff, why don't you go find Dad's brain."

The boys crack up again.

"That's not funny. You guys have finally driven him nuts."

They laugh harder.

"It's not a joke."

I gather up lipsticks and perfumes. Finding earrings isn't as hard as finding the lipstick caps that rolled away. It takes me an hour to find some of them. I drop the last one onto Marie's outstretched palm.

"Marie, makeup makes you look too old, you should stop wearing it."

"I'm not wearing any."

"Yeah and you look younger."

"That's why I wear it. I want to look older."

"When you get older can I have any leftover makeup?" I ask.

"I doubt there'll be any left. If there is, I'll need it to look younger."

Maybe I'm wrong. Maybe she's the one who drove Dad nuts. A glitter in the corner of the stairs catches my eye. A diamond stud is caught in the carpet. I tug at it and hand it to Marie. "I found another earring."

"That's not my earring." Her voice is flat. "Give it to Dad."

"Maybe it was Mom's."

"Nobody in this family has pierced ears."

The boys exchange looks. Adam chuckles, "Oh my, how could I have lost that there?" He takes the earring and shoves it in his pocket.

"I bet it belongs to that woman. The one Dad took on a tour of the house. She clung to Dad the whole night." Drake smirks at Adam. "You know the one, right?"

Marie slumps down on the stairs and stares at her bare fingers.

"I'll find your ring. I promise," I whisper and cross my heart.

"You won't. Dad took the ring back on New Year's Eve."

"That's a weird mean thing for Dad to do."

Marie squirms and groans, "Dad's been nothing but weird since that stupid party. I hate Aunt Patty."

We sit in a circle while Adam gives us a blow by blow of what happened the night of the housewarming party. Marie slumps further into the shadows. Her shoulders are shaking. I run to Ryan's room, steal back a handful of Marie's Twinkies, and drop them in her lap.

Ryan doesn't seem to notice. He's too busy asking questions. "Why would Dad show someone this basement? Why would Dad want Mom's ring back? Why is Dad turning into an Indian Giver? Has anyone noticed

Dad disappears every second day and when he does, he doesn't come back home to sleep?"

My brothers all shrug and mumble about how strange he seems since the housewarming party.

Marie is the only one not talking. Her blank eyes stare past us, while she unwraps her second Twinkie.

"Maybe she was casing the joint," Bruce nudges Adam. "Or maybe she's scheming to marry Dad, do us in, and murder Dad in his sleep, so she can have everything all to herself."

Adam rubs his hands together and rapidly raises his eyebrows at Bruce. "Yes, that must be it. Or maybe she's an evil demon, about to possess Dad and destroy the Rose family."

In that moment, I hate him. "Why would you make up such horrible jokes? You're making Marie cry, stupid."

"Because it is a joke. She's practically half Dad's age. You guys should give Dad a bit more credit than you do."

Marie smiles. "Adam's right. Someone almost as young as me would never want someone with six kids." Her smile looks genuine. "Maybe we should ask Dad to explain all of this."

We vote to go upstairs and confront Dad about the earring, but he's already gone. The boys scatter.

Marie yells, "Everybody get back here now! We need to grow up and stop acting so silly. Dad has never given us a reason not to trust him. Not once. If he wants the room cleaned, I say we clean it."

Marie delegates tasks, for each of us to clean a portion of our old upstairs bedroom. I'm in charge of trash. She takes the vacuum from Bruce and tells him and the rest of the boys to scrub one wall each. I finish first. Bruce finishes last because his wall has a closet. For fifteen minutes, we sit against the clean walls in the empty old bedroom and wait for Dad.

"What's up with Dad being gone so long?" I ask.

"Damned if I know. He should have been back here two hours ago, easy," Ryan grumbles.

"If he's not here in another fifteen minutes, I'm ordering Chinese food," Adam says.

Drake jumps up from the floor, "I'm sick of these cleaning fumes and I'm starving. Let's go order some food now. Who's got money?"

Everybody looks at Bruce. He yells "Pocket search!" and runs out of the room. Everyone jostles to pass him.

"First one in gets to search his pockets for money. How much is Chinese food?"

Adam twists his mouth to one side. "I'm not sure. We'll find out when we order it."

"Dad wouldn't want us to go through his pockets," I say.

Adam grins at me. "We're not. They are." Adam grabs the phone book and hurtles onto the bed. The bedspread and pillow slips smell new.

"His pockets are empty." Bruce calls from the closet.

"Make sure you check his inside pockets." Adam flips through a few more yellow pages. "Don't forget to check the closet floor. That's where I always find some. It falls to the ground when he hangs up his pants."

The boys dive onto the bed, empty handed.

"If there was any, that housekeeper took it."

Adam taps me on the head. "She hasn't moved in yet. Give her a break."

"Not that housekeeper, the one that was here earlier cleaning the rooms for spring." I point to the wallet on the night table behind me. "Why would Dad go for pizza and leave his wallet here?"

Adam rifles through the wallet, smiles, phones a number and orders Chinese food.

By the time it arrives we are starving, and none of us seem to care what happened to Dad. Adam fills his plate for the second time. Four bent heads eat sweet and sour chicken. I suck the sauce from my chicken and stroke Drake's hair.

"What?" Drake squints at me. "Why are you staring at me like that?"

"Why is your hair blonde? How come you don't have the same hair color as us and your eyes aren't brown either?"

"Because I'm better looking than the rest of you."

Battered

Marie breaks her silence. "He turns after Dad's mother, the rest of us turns after Mom, except Bruce. He looks like Dad."

"Did Mom own those perfumes?" I ask.

"What perfumes?" Marie cups my chin in her hand. "Where?"

Adam bites at his lip. "I don't think so. They look too new."

"What perfumes Adam?"

I race back to Dad's bedroom. This time everyone is chasing me. Adam pulls the earring out of his pocket. It matches the one on the counter, next to the tallest perfume bottle.

Marie's voice is glum. She holds out her hand. "Give me that earring."

"Which one? This one, or the one I just put in my pocket."

"Give it Adam. Give it up now!" Adam frowns and reluctantly hands it to her. "And put that other one back on the counter. I hope she spends every moment here, looking for the missing one."

"What missing one?" I ask.

Everything is quiet except for the sound of drawers opening and closing. She wraps a bunch of toilet paper around the earring until it resembles a golf ball. She drops it in the toilet and flushes. I watch it swirl out of sight.

"Come on Marie." I tug on her hand. "The boys are tearing up Dad's room and raiding his drawers."

Her stone-cold stare remains fixated on the toilet. "Good for them. I hope they set the room on fire."

The boys chatter while they rifle through every drawer, every shelf and every suitcase. Ryan dives under the bed. I bounce up and down on the mattress, trying to touch the ceiling.

Ryan yells, "If she doesn't stop, I swear I'll break her neck."

I ignore Ryan and keep jumping. Adam gathers up the receipt for Chinese food, and the change, and places them in Dad's wallet. He tosses the wallet on the night stand.

"Dad's up to no good." Adam nods at the wallet. "Why else would he leave it at home?"

"Maybe he forgot it." Drake grins. "Maybe he's getting Alzheimer's. Wouldn't it be great if Dad lost his memory? We'd get allowances all the time, and imagine how many birthdays we could have each year." Everyone laughs, except for Marie. I can hear her in the bathroom, muttering to herself.

"Having fun, are we?" The laughter stops abruptly. Dad is standing in the doorway with his hands on his hips. I run to the bathroom and yank on Marie's hand. She's sitting on the toilet staring at the counter.

Adam turns beet red. "How long have you . . . you—"

Dad says, "Long enough. I forgot my wallet. Can't buy pizza without it, now can I?"

"You were gone three hours Dad. We were starved so I ordered Chinese food. We left you some. It's in the fridge. I got the money from your wallet." Adam reaches for the wallet and hands it to him. "The receipts in it."

Dad skims over the receipt.

"What didn't you order?" He jingles his pocket change. "Here's the deal. You pilfer my room and I get to pilfer yours. You stay out of my room and I stay out of yours. Deal or no deal?"

He points to the door.

Marie immediately heads for the Twinkie box. It's a sure sign she needs some space. I decide to check out the boys' room and find Adam sorting his bird cards.

"Don't you think Dad and Marie are both acting weird lately?"

"Yes, and I like it," Adam beams. "Yesterday, Dad told me, he wanted me to start taking driving lessons."

"To drive what? Dad only has one car."

"Good point." Adam cocks his head to one side. "He seems to be in a big spending mood these days. Maybe he's buying a new car and giving me the old one. He did say he wants me to drive the five of you guys around and do errands, so he can have more free time."

"You drive the five of us? Free time for what?"

Ryan walks in with a fistful of cupcakes. His cheeks are stuffed. He looks like a chipmunk. Food crumbs spray from his mouth, "Nope. Adam meant to say four not five. You don't count. You're not part of us."

"Shut up. And I'm telling Marie you're eating her snacks."

"Go ahead. But you're wasting your time. She told me she didn't care if I took them all. So, I did. She needs to lose weight anyway."

"Fine! I'm telling her you called her fat."

Adam gathers up his cards. "Knock off fighting. You guys fight like an old married couple."

"Is thirty-four old? Did Mom and Dad fight?"

"Dad wasn't home long enough to fight with Mom." I follow him out as he bends and disappears into the dark opening under the stairs. "But on TV old couples always fight about money or relatives. What are you squealing about?"

"Something cold wiggled across my forehead."

"It's a chain for the light. Pull on it." I stretch for the chain but it keeps swaying back and forth. "Forget it. I'll do it."

The light shines down on what resembles a metal coffin. The sides and top are bronze. The edges are a tarnished gold color. Two worn leather straps dangle over a set of rusty latches.

"Lift it open."

I shake my head and back away.

"If you can open it, I'll let you borrow something from it."

The lid weighs a ton. I drop to my knees and grunt and heave. "I can't, it's too heavy," I complain.

"Try again."

"No. I don't want to. I told you it's too heavy for me."

"Good. I just wanted to make sure you couldn't get it open."

A satisfied smile crosses his face. He pulls up the reluctant lid. It groans and moans and slowly reveals the contents of the trunk.

"What's in here?" I whisper.

Adam ignores me and methodically places the boxes in a row. He rearranges a towel over the top, shuts the lid, locks it and says, "In here is everything I hold near and dear to my heart. Well almost everything . . ."

"For real? Are you serious?" To me it looked like a big pile of junk. Nothing but old books and broken watch parts. "Can I use it to hide some of my stuff from Ryan?"

"No," Adam says. It isn't a maybe, it's a flat-out NO. "And don't ask me again."

I pull on the light chain and leave him in the dark. He chases me to my room. Marie and the rest of the boys are standing in the middle of the bed with their heads tilted upwards toward the ceiling. He grabs my shirt collar and motions for me to keep quiet. He creeps over to the bed, and scares the living death out of half of them.

Bruce flaps his arms and says, "Ssshhh." He points to the ceiling. "It sounds like Dad's got a woman upstairs."

"Maybe it's Aunt Patty" I say.

Bruce shrugs, "I bet it's the one in the picture he had on his night stand. I don't know her name but I've been in her house and sold her flowers. Her house is crappy, so she probably likes this one better."

"When?" Marie climbs off the bed and pulls on Bruce's leg. "Get off the bed and tell me everything."

"I already told you everything."

"How many times were you there. When did she start buying flowers from you? How often?"

"Once. Last week. She bought flowers from me and acted really nice, like she knew me, but I never laid eyes on her before."

Adam frowns. "Knew you how?"

"She asked if I was Ned Rose's son."

"How would she know Dad's name?"

Bruce shrugs at Adam and says, "All I know is when I said yes, she gave me milk and cookies and asked me stuff about Dad."

"What kind of stuff?" Drake taps his finger against his teeth. "Like what?"

Marie yanks on Bruce's arm and asks, "What's she look like? I'm the oldest. Answer me first."

"Fair enough," says Adam. "That means I'm next." His eyes look dark and intense. "And I want to know where she lives."

Battered

Bruce turns toward Marie. "She's not near as pretty as Mom, if that's what you're askin' but she's not much older than you. She's the same height as you but not skinny and not fat."

Drake shakes his head. "I think you guys are making something out of nothing."

"When I asked her how many flowers do ya want, she said she would take all of 'em. Don't that seem strange to you?"

"How many flowers did you have left?"

"All of them. She was my first stop."

Marie's eyes grow bigger than oranges. "Liar."

"Truth. That was my first stop. I'm telling you the truth. And it's her picture I saw by Dad's bed."

Marie says, "How come nobody but you saw it? Why didn't I see it?"

"Because you can't see Dad's bed stand from the toilet."

"Shut up Juanita. I'm talking to Bruce, not you."

"It's my room too. I'll talk if I want."

Marie gives me a warning look and turns back to Bruce. "Why would Dad keep a picture of a neighbor by his bed?"

"Because they gotta thing goin' on."

"SSSSHHHHH." Adam hisses. "Listen. Hear that? It sounds like Dad is moving furniture around. Maybe the voice is coming from the television and he's up there by himself. I don't know about you guys but I don't want to get roped into doing more work. I'm going to bed."

Drake whispers, "Me too. I'm tired of being recruited today."

The boys scatter like dust leaving Marie and I alone.

That night, all night, I awaken to thumps, bumps, and voices. Maybe the boys decided to help him after all, I think, as I drift back to sleep.

"Good morning, Sunshine." Marie kisses my forehead. Her wide smile looks forced and sad. I yawn and turn my back to her. "Get up sleepy head. Time to shower."

My eyes take a moment to adjust. Marie is dangling a black velvet dress above my face. "Dad bought a new dress for you to wear."

"Wear where? What's with all these dresses lately?"

"He thinks you're too much of a tomboy and I agree."

I trudge past her to the bathroom. Her voice trails behind me. When I get out of the shower, I find the dress hanging from the doorknob. It looks like something suitable to wear to a wedding.

On my way upstairs, I glance toward Adam's bedroom, take two steps back and stare at an impersonator. He's wearing a tie, has slicked back hair, and his shoes are polished. "Are we going back to church?" I ask.

He leans toward the body of his guitar, listening to the same note over and over again. Finally, he says, "Nope. Just upstairs to the living room."

"Did someone die?"

He strums his guitar and sings me a song, "On a weekend past, I wouldn't have time, to get home and marry, my ebony eyes."

"Who taught you to play? Dad?"

"No, he was always away, at work. I taught myself. Besides, the only thing Dad can play is a stereo."

"What are ebony eyes?"

"Dark eyes, like ours, like Mom's."

"What was it like when Mom died? Were you scared? Did I miss her?" I ask.

"Everyone was scared. But mostly for her. She didn't look like herself. The radiation caused her to go bald and every day she lost more weight until she was too skinny and too weak to fight."

"That's not true." Bruce leans against the wall. "Mom got up every morning and lit that stove so we would be warm when we got up. She did it every day, no matter how sick she was. There's only one quitter in this family and it wasn't Mom. Anyway, Dad wants you two upstairs." Bruce scowls and disappears.

Mom died a month before Christmas. I heard bits and pieces, mostly from Marie. Once I heard Dad talking to the school principal, explaining how the boys became defiantly wild and out of control ever since they lost Mom. Adam was usually the instigator but Bruce was the head troublemaker.

Battered

Adam said it was easier on Dad because he was always stationed away. Marie said Dad was more heart broken than any of us but he just hid it better. All I know is, toward the end, Marie and Adam were the ones who took care of Mom. Sometimes Mom's best friend, Aunt Nita, another one of my fake aunts, would leave her family to come over and help out.

I can remember living in two story houses with a long banister, before Mom died. But I always got to come back for visits. The only steps in our house were steep and led to the dark basement. Once when I fell down them, she had to crawl down to save me. That was a few months before she died. That's when they sent me away for good.

"Where did I live right before Mom died?"

"A bunch of places. With Aunt Nita, and a few more of Mom's friends, with Grandmother Reid, and then at Aunt Sally's in St. John's. Once in a while at home with us."

"Was Aunt Sally real or fake?"

"She was a real aunt. Dad's stepsister."

"How come I got sent away and you didn't?"

"Mom wanted you to be safe. Marie looked after you inside the house and I looked after you whenever we went anywhere. Our favorite spot was near the mouth of the river," his mouth twists into a smile, "at the stream. You loved the water and I loved watching you slip and slide over the slimy river rocks."

"You made me cross rivers?"

"only up until Ryan almost drowned. Before then it was just funny. When Ryan fell over the bridge and nearly drowned, you wandered off, and Mom freaked out. That's when all those fake aunts took you in."

"When did I come back? Before or after Mom died?"

"You came back after Mom died. Her wake was on Ryan's birthday. That's why he hates birthday cakes."

"Tell me more. I want to know everything."

"There's not much more to tell. By then, Marie was in charge of the house. Dad felt she did a better job than anyone else could and he made a promise to her that if she kept the family together and stayed until you reached age fourteen, she could have all of Mom's clothes and jewelry, and he would pay for her college, buy her a house and practically anything else she wanted."

"Why would she want Mom's old clothes?"

"The clothes help her remember Mom before she got sick. Cancer changes how people look. It's how Marie copes."

"Marie said Dad's a quitter. And Bruce just said it . . . well sort of said it. How come?"

"They're right. He is a quitter. We're almost at the finish line and Dad's quitting the race. All he had to do was wait three more years but I guess he got too lonely."

"Why three? I wouldn't be fourteen in three years."

"No, but Marie would be in college. and wouldn't have to see Dad replacing Mom."

"I don't get it."

He stops tuning the guitar and rests his arms on it, "It's got something to do with you calling her a monster."

"Me? I never said one word about the housekeeper. I don't even know her."

"Really? Well that's not what Marie told me."

"Well Marie is telling a fib." I brush my velvet dress and watch the color change, wiggle my toes, and examine my new glossy black shoes.

"Ready to go upstairs?"

"No. I have to change my shoes."

I massage my crunched toes, but they don't hurt as much as my feelings do. Why Marie would tell such a lie? It's true I tell Marie all my secrets but the only thing I ever said about the housekeeper was that we didn't need her.

I hear Dad playing with coins in his pocket a full minute before he appears around the corner.

"Put your shoes back on. It's time for you to meet someone special."

"Where are we going?"

"Upstairs."

Battered

"Then I don't need shoes."

"Yes, you do. And be on your best behavior. You only have to wear them for a few minutes."

At the top of the stairs, my old bedroom door is ajar. It's filled with cardboard boxes. Dad jerks me toward the living room. The coins in Dad's pocket jitter and jangle, louder and faster.

"Juanita, say hello to Irma."

I freeze.

Sitting on our couch, with her two kids, is the monster.

A Special Housekeeper

Dad yanks my arm. "She's shy," he lies. My brothers snicker. They wouldn't snicker if they saw what I saw that day through Sharon's fence.

"Don't force her to meet me Ned." Her plastic smile doesn't move and her teeth are stained with red lipstick. "Would you rather go back downstairs?"

I say, "No thank you," only because she suggested otherwise.

I sit by the bar and watch her two boys cringe. The cuter one seems to be the size I was two years ago. His hair is a montage of curls. His long, wispy eyelashes flutter between shut and half-open. His sleepy head rests against his mother's chest. Next to him is a boy, my age, dressed in the same gray suit as his little brother. He looks better than the last time I saw him. His nose isn't red today but his eyes are nervous and jittery. They drift from his shoe to mine. I remember the shoe, and half-smile, then I shiver, jump off the stool, and dash toward the kitchen to find a safer place, beside Marie.

"How rude. Children should wait to be dismissed." "Go back. Be smarter. Do it for me." Marie whispers.

Battered

All eyes are glued on my face. My brothers look like sitting ducks neatly lined up on the couch. Their smiles look forced. When Drake smiles his mouth twists up on one side, but today it looks straight. Adam's smile is always a wide oval, but his looks like a rectangle. Dad must have bribed them to behave like frozen mannequins.

Marie is the only one acting half normal. She always polishes the kitchen counter, but she never polishes it three times in a row. Nobody in this house is acting like themselves, not even me, because I never go anywhere, I don't want to go, and the last place I want to be is here. I climb back on the stool and watch the carpet because the carpet expects nothing of me, unlike all the eyes still peeled my way.

The silence is deafening. I can't stand it any longer. I point to the gifts. "Who owns all those?" I really don't care about presents, and couldn't care less about the answer. I want them to stop staring at me and it works.

Dad motions for me to come over to him. I hesitate and ask,

"Can I watch from here?"

"Watch what?" he asks.

"I dunno . . . you guys?"

Everyone laughs, even the housekeeper. Dad looks relieved. "Juanita this is Irma. And these handsome young men are Jacob and Justin. Irma and the boys will be living with us as part of our family. She is not a babysitter or a housekeeper, or your new mom. She is simply Irma."

"Then if she's not the housekeeper, why is she here?"

Her smile fades. Her eyes darken. She doesn't like me, but that's okay, because I don't like her either. I doubt anyone human could ever like her.

"Why? Because we like each other." Dad says.

I try not to roll my eyes when everyone is ordered to go over, shake hands with the three of them, and introduce ourselves. Her hand feels limp and her smile looks plastic. And Dad is acting a little weird. He's not being himself either.

Jacob is the older boy. He doesn't look anything like his brother. His skin is olive. His dark hair is wavy. Normally I would feel shy around a boy so cute but all I feel is pity and lucky I have no mom.

Dad smiles at Jacob and says, "Why don't you help Juanita hand out some presents?" Jacob slides off the couch. Our eyes connect. I'm not sure what his are saying, but they remind me of my dog and how he looked during thunder storms.

Jacob hesitates, and waits for his mother's permission. Once she nods, he kneels down and picks out the smallest present. He struggles to read the tag. He looks up and shrugs his shoulders at Dad.

"Help him read the tags Juanita."

"Jacob can read very well Ned, can't you Jacob?" her voice has a threatening undertone. "Your daughter's help isn't required."

"The tag has my name on it," I say.

Her stare is glued on Jacob. Her sooty eyes look dull, like rotted wood. I don't get how my Dad could like her. I look back at the present and reread the tag. "Yep it's for me."

"Irma, spell Juanita for me," Dad says.

Irma hesitates a second, "W-a-n-i-t-a."

"You're wrong my dear. It's J-u-a-n-i-t-a."

Dad smiles at Jacob, "Even great spellers can't get that one right. Carry on. You're doing a great job," Dad pats Irma's hand. In a split second, contempt flashes across her face and flickers out. I try to convince myself it was only my imagination but I know what I saw was real.

She pats Dad hand and says, "Yes that's a tough one to swallow."

She meant me. Not my name. I scan to my left and find Marie hiding in the corner. She points to the basement door, walks her fingers in the air, points to her eyes then her chest. My eyes shift from Marie to Irma and back to the kitchen. Dad points at my present. I shake it, wondering what we're celebrating. "Am I supposed to open it?"

"No, you eat it." Ryan is actually funny for once. Dad leans behind Irma's back and casts a warning look toward Ryan, who immediately puts his hands in his pockets. I see it shape into a fist. I knew it! Dad bribed them with money. That's why they're so quiet and polite.

I rip the wrapping from my gift. A shiny red leather wallet tumbles onto the carpet. It has all kinds of pockets with zippers and snaps. Inside the billfold is a ten-dollar bill. I grin at Dad and murmur a thank you. Dad nods and smiles, while Irma gasps.

"What?" Dad tilts his head toward her. "Isn't that a little over generous, Ned?" Irma asks. He raises her hand and kisses it. "Get used to it. You won't be darning worn socks in this house." My eyes are riveted on Irma and Dad but my thoughts are on Marie, but when I glance back toward the kitchen, she's gone. I snap the wallet together, scoot next to Adam, and cup my hands around his ear. "Is she the one from the party?"

He whispers back. "Yes."

"She's mean to her kids and I don't like her. Can I sit by you?" Adam shifts to make room for me.

"It's really rude for children to whisper Ned!" Irma stares expectantly at Dad.

"She's right. No whispering. If you have something to say, talk out loud so everyone can hear it," Dad says.

Adam clears his throat. "She is asking if I know what the presents are for or who they are from."

Dad smiles and points at himself. "Me. I decided we should have a family day. What better time than today when Irma, Jacob and Justin are joining us."

Irma whispers something to Dad.

"Juanita go back and help Jacob by handing him the presents."

I move the presents from the bar to the floor beside Jacob. There are only six left. "Some seem to be missing," I say. "I don't see any for Marie."

"Don't worry, it's taken care of. Marie helped me wrap and she has opened hers already."

"What about her?" I point to Irma.

He stands up and offers Irma his hand, "Show everyone your presents, so they can see what a classy old man they have."

Irma blushes as Dad twirls her in a circle. The second time he twirls her, she tugs on her shirt and flips her arm. I assume that means Dad gave her the outfit she is wearing. She flips around her left hand and dangles her ring finger. The ring looks exactly like Mom's missing wedding ring. The one I stole from Marie.

She sits back down and whispers something to Dad. I want to say, 'Now who's being rude?' but I don't.

"You tell her," Dad urges. "You've got to start showing them who's boss sooner or later." The boys and I exchange looks. Jacob picks at his shoe lace. Dad lifts Irma's hand to his mouth and kisses it. "Go ahead. Don't be shy."

She's locks eyes with me. "Obviously your mother was too sick to teach you any manners." She frowns at me. "What do you have to say?"

"Yes."

"Yes what?" She leans away from the couch and waits.

"Say what?"

"Say what—what kind of English is that? Don't you mean to say pardon? Or, I beg your pardon?"

I have no clue what she is taking about. She looks exasperated. I decide to shut up until she makes more sense.

"You do know the word thank you? Right?"

"Yes I know the words," I say.

"Well? What do you say?" Irma purses her lips and waits.

I feel stupid and confused. At this point I have no clue what she is talking about. Something about mother and manners. "What do you want me to say? Thanks?" I ask.

She looks at Dad, waits a few seconds, slants her eyes at me, leans forwards, and says, "Thank you."

I hesitate a few seconds. I feel stupid. I notice a wine glass on the end table. Maybe she's drunk. "You're welcome."

My brothers burst into loud laughter. Irma flashes them a curt look.

"Manners are not a joke," she says, and glares back at me. "Thank your father for the wallet," she orders.

"I did already. Right after I opened it. You heard me, didn't you Dad?"

"I heard her," Adam says.

Drake nods in agreement.

Dad's face turns red. He stammers, "She did thank me Irma."

Battered

"Ned, I didn't move in here to be outnumbered and out argued by you and a bunch of kids." She flings his hand onto his lap, stalks into his bedroom, slams the door, opens it and slams it harder.

Dad scurries after her.

We roll our eyes at each other for a full five minutes before Dad reappears with Irma.

He takes my wallet from me, and removes the ten-dollar bill.

"But Dad!"

"Irma thinks you guys need to learn some manners. She also thinks you should earn money. Not be given it for nothing."

"That's not fair! That's mean! I hate you and her."

"Are going to let her get away with that?"

Dad sighs, "Irma what do you what me to do?"

"I don't know. Act like a man? A little discipline wouldn't go astray. My children don't talk to me like that and if they did, I certainly wouldn't reward them with ten dollars. If they got anything it would be several slaps upside the head, right, boys?"

Jacob nods. The younger one answers, "Yup. A bunch of 'em."

Dad taps my knee with his foot. I don't want to look at him but I do. He winks at me but his voice is stern, "I'm taking the ten dollars back. Irma is right, money has to be earned, not gifted." He turns toward Irma, "Now will you relax?" She gives him a dirty look.

"Irma, sweetheart. Try not to be so tense. I know you didn't sleep all night and your nerves must be shot after what you've been through. You've had a helluva time this past week, but for Christ's sake today is a celebration. Sit back and enjoy it. God knows you deserve it."

This has to be the weirdest day ever. There is no doubt in my mind that Dad has finally lost it. He's bribed my brothers, is being bullied by a woman none of us know and we're exchanging wrapped presents for no good reason.

"Can I go now?"

"No." Dad lifts one eyebrow and orders Jacob and I to continue handing out presents. Irma maintains the look of a sourpuss the entire time. I don't see how he can like this Irma.

Jacob points a finger at his own chest, smiles from ear to ear, and rips the wrapping to shreds.

"Jacob you know better than that," Irma says with a frown. "You know not to tear the paper."

Dad pats Irma's knee. "You need to relax. Ripping wrapping paper is what makes opening presents fun. Rip away Jacob!"

"I thought we said we would compromise and not contradict each other? In my house we save wrapping paper," Irma says.

"Irma. You are not in your house now. You are in our house and—" Irma storms back into the bedroom and slams the door three times. Dad scurries after her. "Irma, I didn't mean it that way. Ours includes you three too."

Adam swings an imaginary bat. He holds up three fingers and points to the door. We grin from ear to ear. Our grins fade when they return, sit on the couch and snuggle.

Jacob looks down the barrel of his fake gun and pulls the trigger.

Irma nudges Dad. "My boys aren't allowed to have guns." Her voice is firm and curt. My brothers squirm. They glance at Dad. They not only own and play with toy guns but they get to shoot the real ones when Dad hunts for moose or deer.

"Dad can I have a dog for my birthday. Like Dork."

"Dork," Irma laughs and turns toward Dad. "What kind of name is Dork?"

"His name was Pal. Ryan nicknamed him Dork," Dad points to Ryan who smiles from ear to ear and raises his hand.

"The dog tried to save me, so we had to shoot him. Dad buried him in the back yard," I volunteer.

"Good thing you did Ned. It would have been me or the dog." Irma looks apologetically at Dad, "I'm sorry Ned but I hate animals."

Battered

"Guns are worse than dogs." I mumble and stare at Jacob's toy rifle. "I'm glad you don't like them, Irma."

"Juanita, I didn't say I didn't like guns. I said my boys aren't allowed to have any type of gun at their age."

Jacob obediently places the gun on top of the bar, waves goodbye to it, and resumes handing out gifts.

Drake unwraps guitar picks and crams them into his pocket. Adam holds out his hand. "You owe me three!" He reaches toward Drake's pocket. Drake grabs Adam's two hands and holds them tight.

Irma stands up and says, "Excuse me," taps her pointy shoe up and down and waits for the boys to clear the way. When she returns her lips are a brighter red and her perfume smells stronger.

Jacob twists the torn wrapping paper into a long rope until Irma gives him a nod. He reaches for the last gift. "To Juanita love M." Jacob tosses me the package and says, "It feels like socks."

I untie the string. The paper springs apart revealing a wad of toilet paper. I laugh. It reminds me of the earring she flushed.

I unroll enough toilet paper to wipe the nose of every kid in my class. A gold chain dangles from a heart shaped locket. I open it. On the left is a picture of Marie and on the right is a picture of Mom.

I glance at Irma. She's glaring at me. Question marks are pulsating from her pupils. Bruce was right. Irma doesn't hold a candle to Mom. Irma's face is stern looking and the big fat mole on her jaw looks like something I saw in a cartoon about a witch.

I slip the chain over my head, examine my short stubby nails, one by one, until I run out of nails. Nobody's staring at me. They're staring at the mound of toilet paper. Will Irma save it for Dad to use when he cuts himself shaving, or make him use it to blow boogers in?

I burst out laughing.

"What's so funny?" Dad lifts his eyebrows.

"The toilet paper reminds me of something funny."

"Like what?"

"What if it's only funny to me?"

41

Marie appears out of nowhere and says, "I know what she's laughing at. She's laughing at the time I used your shaver to shave lint from her dress, then you used it and had to cover your face with little bits of toilet paper? I think that's it."

"How did you know I was thinking about Dad shaving?"

Adam laughs. "Now that you mention it the toilet paper does remind me of that. We took a picture of it didn't we?"

Irma turns to Dad, "Can I see it?" She pushes him off the couch. "Don't be bashful Ned, go on, go get it. I'd love to see it." Dad reaches into the coffee table opening, pulls out an album, slumps back beside her and flips through a few pages. Irma taps his wrist and points at a photo. "Was that her?"

"Who?"

"Their mother." "No. That's my stepsister, Mable." Dad smiles and continues flipping through the book.

"Oh. Is that her?"

"No. That's Patty, she lives next door."

"Well which one is her?"

"This album is full of pictures from Stephenville. Elsie died in Heart's Delight."

Irma leans away from him, straightens her back, and glares at Marie. "The point is the toilet paper reminds me of a big waste of money." Marie smiles politely, excuses herself and leaves. I squirm my way from behind the bar and sit in Mom's old rocking chair. It's the only piece of furniture that looks warm and inviting. Everything else is marble, glass or made of cold leather. I stare over at the big TV and watch Dad and Irma's reflections. When I first saw Irma, she looked poor but not today. Her white satin blouse has sheer sleeves with fine gold lace trim. Her long black skirt touches her foot when she swings it back and forth. I've seen shoes like hers before, in Marie's celebrity magazines. Irma's mouth frowns as she continues to complain about the waste of toilet paper and her frown grows bigger as Dad tells her a package of twelve rolls of toilet paper is cheaper than one roll of wrapping paper. "It's a bit ridiculous to use an entire roll, on a gift that small," Irma states in a prim voice.

"Irma you know I'm not poor. I made that perfectly clear to you the first night we met. You know I stopped counting pennies years ago. So why are you dwelling on this?"

"I detest waste and there's nothing wrong with counting pennies. They turn into dollars. Having money and wasting money are two different things altogether." The real reason Dad doesn't count pennies is they disappear too fast. My brothers swipe them. After Adam checks the dates and confiscates any old ones to save in his trunk, the rest go in a jar to bring to the railroad tracks for the train to flatten. Dad's response to Irma is a kiss on the cheek. He caresses her hand and gives it three quick squeezes. My eyes feel too big for their sockets. Did Dad say a secret I love you to Irma? A repulsive feeling flows through my body. It gets worse when she rises from the couch, kisses Dad on the lips and yanks him toward his bedroom. Dad hoists Justin over his shoulder and follows her.

Jacob pokes me in the ribs. "Stop staring or she'll get mad." I poke him back. He pulls a ball and glove from behind his back. "Ryan's so cool. He traded me for the gun."

"You're lucky he likes you."

Jacob moves over to the loveseat and plays catch with himself. He's sitting right across from Dad's door. I hop onto the seat beside him, and check out what's going on in Dad's room. Justin is sprawled across Dad's bed. Irma is sitting on the floor near the end of the bed picking at her nails. She notices me watching and pushes the door half shut. "What happened to your Dad?" I ask Jacob.

He slams the ball into the glove. "Mom said he's dead, but I know she's lying. He told me he had to go away for a few days to fight a big forest fire over in Clarenville." Jacob's eyes gloss over. He starts to sob. "Mom said the fire killed him and without him there was no money and we had to move here, because we're poor."

"When people die there's a funeral. Did he have one?"

"No because the fire's still burning."

43

"Then how do they know he's dead and not just missing?"

"That's what I asked Mom."

"And what did she say?"

"She hit me with the belt and said to never to challenge her or bring it up again."

"What's your Dad like?"

"He's big and strong and really nice. Way nicer than Mom."

A movement in the bedroom catches my eye. "Why is your mom putting Justin on the floor?"

"Probably for a nap. Your Dad gave us a new sleeping bag. We slept in it last night. Wanna see it?" I nod.

Together we head toward the door. Jacob raises his hand to knock, but I push the door open and barge inside. Dad has a big smile but Irma greets us with a cold hard stare. She stomps toward Jacob with an open hand. He cowers as she raises it. Her hand grazes the top of his head and hits my shoulder. I tumble on top on Justin. Dad's mouth hangs open. He stretches out his hand in attempt to catch me.

"Irma that was uncalled for."

"It's her fault for not knocking." Irma folds her arms and stares defiantly at Dad. He returns her glare. "I swear it was an accident but if she had knocked, you know none of this would have happened, right?"

"Irma, I have an open door policy in this house. Always have."

"That is so stupid. I could be getting dressed, or be naked."

"Well you didn't live here before and I didn't have other women, naked or not, in my room. My kids are not mind readers and you can't expect them to break old habits overnight." He shakes his head twice. "And why would you hit Jacob for something she did?"

Irma shoves Jacob out of her way. He falls on top of Justin who screams out at the top of his lungs. Irma turns to me and scowls. "See what you've done now? For the second time? Get out." She shrieks, "I said get out! Get the hell out of my room. Get out right now!"

Her Dead Husband

Marie is usually preoccupied with eating, which is why she's always the first one upstairs but today she won't leave the basement. The house is quiet and except for our gurgling stomachs, you could hear a pin drop. The last thing we expected was Dad to materialize in the doorway.

"Having another powwow?" Marie refuses to answer, so I don't either. "Give her time she needs to adjust. She's young and this isn't an easy decision for her. Anyway, I want to take you guys for breakfast."

Marie folds her arms and asks, "Is she going?"

"No, she needs her space right now."

Marie's lips hardly move. "Good."

He grimaces and says, "You need to give her a chance." I yank Marie's hand and race past him, while he talks to thin air. My idea of a great breakfast is a donut but Dad drives to a place near his work and the breakfast special is bacon and eggs. The boys dash for a small booth and spread their knees apart. Dad's choose a larger curved booth in the far corner that has room for all seven of us. Before he sits, he reaches into his back pocket and hands me a ten-dollar bill.

I examine it and hand it back. "I want the one Irma made you take from me. The one with the creases."

"I don't have it. What difference does it make? A ten-dollar bill is a ten-dollar bill." He sits beside me, and cups my hand around it. He gives my hand three squeezes and says, "I suggest you hide it."

"From Irma?"

"And your brothers."

The waiter is slender and short. The hair at the sides of his head is shaved close but above his right eye is a greasy three-inch curl, flattened against his forehead. He fills our glasses with ice water while his left hand flips menus out from somewhere behind his black apron. I browse through the pictures. The food selections all include eggs and there are no muffins. I order a hot chocolate and suggest they hire Marie as their chef. The waiter disregards me and focuses on Dad, who is instructing him to ignore my brothers until they join us. The waiter glances around nods then glances my way. His plastic smile reveals his top teeth, "I'm sorry did you say something earlier?"

"I'd like a hot chocolate, please." He doesn't write it down, instead he looks at Dad for approval. Dad nods and raises three fingers. I raise three too. One is just a little higher than the others are. His lips twitch into a one-second amused smile.

"Sir would you like me to have those boys come join you?"

"No. Not yet. I'll get them in a bit."

Marie elbows me and hisses, "Who taught you that?"

I shrug and point at the boys table.

Marie turns in time to see Adam snatch two menus from another table, waves them at us and scoots back beside Drake.

Dad taps my head, "Juanita, there's something you need to understand." His eyes are intense. He doesn't blink or smile. I know he's about to drop a bomb so I scrutinize the egg dishes on the menu. He pulls my ear and says, "Put down that menu and pay attention. We need to talk about yesterday."

"I don't want to." I shrink lower in my seat.

Marie's face is stone-cold and her eyes are motionless during Dad's lecture and for a minute I'm not certain if he's talking to her or me. At the end, he tells me to imagine being such a young woman and how overwhelming it would be to inherit an instant family of six kids.

I cock one eyebrow at him. "I'll ask Marie. She knows."

The water topples over the top of her glass. Between coughs she says, "Maybe you should have waited for somebody older. Somebody who could handle six kids. If I could do it at age twelve, I don't see what her problem is and she obviously has one. You'd have to be blind as a bat not to see it."

She slaps the menu at him and struts out the door. A bewildered Adam races after her. Moments later, they return arm in arm. Adam takes a deep breath and says, "Juanita, tell Dad what you saw." I glance at Marie but she's too busy glaring at Dad, to intervene and save me.

"Tell me what?" He waits a few seconds taps my hand and says, "Now." Dad's slack jaw tightens before I get halfway through. "Maybe Irma is right. Maybe you are an ungrateful spoiled brat, trying to sabotage our relationship."

Mortified, I plant my face against Marie's chest.

"She's telling the truth Dad"

"Were you there when it happened? No, you weren't, were you? So, don't say she's telling the truth when you don't know for certain what did or didn't happen."

Dad's hand covers the top of my head and twists it until my nose is facing him. "Next time you tell another whopper like that, I'll do what Irma does to her kids."

"What? Beat me?"

"No. I'll wash your mouth out with soap. And it won't be clean soap either."

"I'm not lying! Ask Jacob. I swear on Mom's life, I'm not a liar. I know what I saw. You can even ask Sharon. Irma's the big fat liar, not me."

Dad twists my ear, "Enough. Your mother is dead and—"

"No, she's not. She's alive in heav—"

"You will not start, or spread, rumors about Irma. If you guys think any one of you is going to sabotage my relationship, you've got another thing coming. It's not going to work. Got it?" While I sit with my mouth hung open, Marie stalks toward the boys table. They shift closer together and make room for her.

Adam stays and does the unthinkable. He says, "Maybe you were sick of Mom by the time she died, but we weren't." Dad leans back and frowns. Adam strikes again. "Marie and I have hung around the house looking after everyone like slaves. Tutoring Bruce, doing laundry and cooking. And I can tell you Juanita might be a handful but she's no liar. And after she swore on Mom's life how could you call her one?"

A tiny bead of sweat forms on Dad's forehead. "Swearing on a dead woman's life means nothing," Dad's voice is flat, almost sinister.

Adam's voice is deliberate, slow and steady, "We are not talking about some dead woman. We are talking about the mother of your kids, the woman you married. You might find it easy to forget her, but we don't and I hope she haunts the living shit out of you for the rest of your life. And Irma too. Especially Irma."

Dad looks shocked, angry and confused, but Adam stands his ground. "It's day one and she's used you to intimidate the entire family. Face it Dad, she's nothing but a money hungry monster who hates kids."

Dad grabs Adam by his ear lobe and stalks out the door. The waiter appears with a tray. His eyes sweep the room. "Where's . . ."

"He's gone outside. He'll be back in a minute. Did you add any marshmallows?" I ask.

He places the mugs on the table. "I did, because that's how we make them. Oh, I'm sorry, of course you are too young to read aren't you?" His sarcasm reminds me of Irma saying, don't you know the word thank you.

I reach into my pocket and take out my wallet. I hold up the crisp ten-dollar bill. "See this. I was in charge of your tip." I tear it slowly in half and put it back in my wallet. He stalks away.

Marie shakes her finger at me, "Great, Juanita. Now he's going to spit in our food."

"I don't care. I'm not hungry anyway."

"It's not his fault Irma ruined our day," Marie whispers. She calls to the waiter, "Excuse me. Excuse me. Please excuse her. She's not being herself, her Dad died recently."

"Well, who's that man with you? Isn't he your father?"

"No. He's a delusional distant relative. Our parents are both dead. So, give her a break, okay?" The waiter murmurs some sort of apology and slips away.

He returns with a concerned smile, "How delusional?"

"Delusional enough to give you a huge tip," I say.

He kneels by the table and giggles. "How huge?"

"You'll be glad I tore up the ten."

"Really?" he flips his head back and looks at Marie. "Please tell me she is not joking."

"She is definitely not joking and trust me, by the time we all finish eating you will have undoubtedly earned it."

"Oh my god! You have no idea how many people never tip." He slides into the seat telling us about some of his cheap customers. Once the boys come over to join us, the waiter leaves.

"Can I have your hot chocolate?" Ryan takes a swig, jolts forward and spits it back out into the cup. Marie's lips twist down in disgust. She pushes the mug away.

Drake shakes his head at Ryan. "That's why it's called hot chocolate idiot,"

Marie us a halfhearted wink, takes Dad's hot chocolate and places hers, with the spit in it, on Dad's placemat. "Here you guys can have the good one."

I'm too grossed out to drink anything. Outside I find Dad and Adam arguing inside the car. I yank the door open, yell, "You're the rottenest Dad in the world," leave the door ajar, and run back inside the restaurant.

"Where did Marie go?"

Drake points to the bathroom. The door is heavy, so heavy, I doubt anyone frail or old, would get it open. Marie is standing behind it. The corners of her lips turn upwards into a smile. Her face is dry, her makeup fresh and her puffy eyes are the only telltale sign of how she feels. She clasps her hand around mine and leads the way to a new table. "I have money. Let's pretend we're here alone."

"Who's going to watch them?" I jerk my head toward the boys.

"I don't know. But it it's not me. I've been fired from the job."

"Well I didn't fire you. You're not abandoning me, right?"

"God no Juanita. I'd never abandon you. Come here you." I glance over her shoulder. Dad's sheepish smile grows closer.

"Look what you did! You fired Marie and made her cry. You're just as rotten as that monster you brought home."

Dad ignores me, bends down and whispers something in Marie's ear. She keeps her head turned away from him. He shifts to see her eyes. She twists further away. He pulls me out of the seat and sits beside her. He puts his arm around her and whispers something else in her ear. Her chest rises and sinks. A deep heavy sigh escapes from her lips. Her head makes a slow turn in his direction. He pulls her toward him and kisses her forehead and says, "I'm really, really sorry."

"You should apologize to me too. I'm the one you called a liar."

Marie sighs again. This time it has a broken beat to it. Dad kisses each of her eyes.

"Juanita, go tell the boys to get in the car." I turn the corner just in time to see the boys run out the door. Their booth looks like a bomb hit it. The tablecloth is a sopping mess. Pools of hot chocolate, gooey marshmallow and semi-melted ice cubes drip on the seat. I walk backwards until I reach Marie. Dad smiles and says, "Good job Juanita."

"Bet you ten bucks you won't be smiling when you see the table cloth, and I hope it ruins your day, for calling me a liar."

He tugs on my collar and yanks me closer. "I'll make you a deal. You stop inventing stories about Irma and I'll stop calling you a liar."

Dad stands up, eyeballs their booth and lets out a loud painful groan. He slumps back down, scoops me into the seat beside him, yanks me by the waist, and asks the waiter to get the manager. The waiter appears with a bony old woman, dressed in black. Dad hands her a one-hundred-dollar bill. He motions toward the table, nods his head at the waiter, and says, "Give the kid twenty bucks. Anything left over should cover the hot chocolate and linen."

He apologizes twice while she walks us out the door. I wait for my apology but it never comes. Before Dad has a key in the ignition, Bruce says, "Let's go eat. You promised us food and we're starved."

"After that mess you made, you deserve to starve to death."

Drake grumbles, "You know we had no dinner last night, right?"

Dad sighs, shakes his head, and says, "Based on what I saw here, I'm thanking my lucky stars we skipped that meal." He drives to a burger place and refuses to order any drinks for the boys. He holds the food hostage until we arrive back at home, parked in the driveway. Everyone is quiet. No one reaches for the door. Dad twists toward the back seat and says, "The boys . . . her boys, do not want to be here because they miss their home and I'm sure you've heard them crying all night but I want you to know they are not being punished nor is she beating them."

"You're not always here, how would you know what goes on?"

Dad puts his hand on Marie's' shoulder and squeezes it three times. "Because I trust Irma and in time, you will too. It's no different than her boys not trusting or liking me. Over time they'll see I'm a nice guy, nicer than their Dad, and over time you'll see Irma isn't the monster you've made her out to be, but until then Irma wants me to put locks on the doors to keep them from running away. So under no circumstances are you guys allowed to help them get outside. Understand?" He glances from face to face. "Juanita you and Ryan will need help getting out, because the locks will be too high for you to reach, but it won't be for long . . . not too long."

Ryan asks, "How long is not too long?"

"Until the boys stop having a tough time."

"That'll be forever," I say. "I'd have a tough time too if I was stuck with her for a mom."

Ryan bolts out of the car while Dad bangs his head on the steering wheel. Dad mutters something, opens his door and tilts his shoulders back toward me. His voice is a loud warning whisper, "That's enough out of you today young lady. You need to stay quiet. And I'll grant you this, if the boys are asleep, and you wake them up, you certainly will see a monster in our house, and it won't be Irma." He taps Adam on the shoulder. "Try to talk some sense into your sister." He leaves the door ajar and struts up the steps.

Marie groans, "Dad's lost it. He's gone one hundred percent insane." She swears twice, and follows him toward the house.

I point at Marie and grin. "Adam, I'm sure he meant that sister, not me." Adam shuts and locks the car door and five of us sit inside, crunch our food and share thoughts about Irma and her dark toxic intentions. Before we finish our food, Ryan reappears with a big bulge in his pocket and taps on the door.

He pulls a jar of pennies from his jacket pocket and says, "Let's go. Dad and Irma are arguing again, so we should run now." We scramble down the driveway and race down the hill.

I pant and try to keep up. "Where are we going?"

"Just hurry," Adam cautions, "walk faster. As a matter of fact, run and whatever you do, don't look back, especially if they call us." I have no clue why we're running and when Dad yells and I pause, Adam yanks my hand, "Pretend you don't hear him. Let's go this way." He pushes me over a fence, through someone's yard and lifts me over another fence.

"This isn't the right way," I say.

"Oh yes, it is. We're taking a couple of back roads because I heard Dad start the car." I'm about to collapse when my nose recognizes the unmistakable smell of fish and seaweed. In that second I feel lost, like a stranded mermaid. The smell is familiar but everything looks different. I take a deep breath and taste the salty air on the tip of my tongue. The last time I smelled this smell, was at Aunt Sally's house and it's the only familiar thing I've smelled in two years. We visited a harbor similar to this, every day, when I lived with her in St. John's. We'd walk out on the pier, she'd barter and buy nothing, and then we'd head to the spot where they sold fresh lobster and crab at roadside stands. The smell of fish on those carts, didn't smell like the ones at the harbor. They smelled like rotting dead guts.

Battered

Empty broken clam shells, crunch under my feet. A bed of slimy green grass curls and winds, like cooked spinach, around blue shells and wet pebbles. A cluster of closed clams are clinging to a flat rock. I stomp them until their rosy pink guts splatter and ooze from the cracks of their broken shells. "Stop it! You can't do that."

"Ouch. Let go of me."

Bruce yanks it harder. "Stop or I'll carry you back home and dump you straight in Irma's lap."

"Fine, I'll stop."

I climb a large jagged rock, sit on it, and watch my brothers engage in a coin-skipping contest. Most of them get swallowed by the waves and never skip. The rumble of waves rolling and crashing against the shore is deafening, but somehow, above it, we hear the sound of a honking horn.

We trudge toward his car. "Adam how did he know we were here?" I ask.

Adam shakes his head, "I think he has built in sonar."

"Great timing Dad we ran out of pennies," Adam says.

Dad stares past the ocean spray, past the pier and exhales a deep sigh. He leans his arm over the seat and shifts the car into reverse. A horn blares, metal crunches and Dad yells, "Holy Christ!" He tilts the rearview mirror at us then tilts it back. Some stranger taps on the window, exchanges some words with Dad and suggests they each take care of their own damage. The man goes to the back of his truck, tightens the ropes on some bikes and drives away. Dad pulls back into the parking lot and shuts off the engine. "That's called compromise. Do you guys remember what it was like to learn to ride a bike, right? That's how our journey will be. The trick is to get back on after we fall. Yesterday was Irma's crash and burn. Today was mine, and I predict we will all have a lot more. The remedy is to keep trying, and never give up." His voice drones in and out but when he finishes, nobody says anything. Dad coughs, takes a deep breath, and continues for another twenty minutes, until I interrupt him.

"And what's so good about riding a bike?"

Ryan answers, "It's great. If you lean into the hill you can beat some of the cars." He glances at me and adds, "Unless you're a chickenshit who is afraid to ride her bike because she fell once."

"The only reason you never fell is because yours had training wheels, dummy," Bruce says, "and her bike had none."

"Yeah and it had no seat either, so I rode standing up! Ha!"

Dad's voice is elevated, "You guys just don't get it, do you? Why do you have to make everything so hard? It's not about bikes. It's about the ride. The point is Irma will get better with practice."

"Better at what?" I ask.

"Better at being a mother. She needs more time to practice."

"Dad how do you take back birthday wishes?"

Ryan grins at me. "You tell someone what you wished for and then it never comes true."

"I wished for a mother, but I wanted ours back, not her."

Dad's shoulders drop. He turns his head toward the sky. "Looks like a storm's headed our way. We best get back."

That night I dream I'm riding a bike and singing at the top of my lungs. I pass Irma's old house, hit a rut and fly through the air. I close my eyes but open them when I land on something soft. It's Irma's belly. I stare at her closed eyelids. She hisses, and they open to reveal two flattened pennies. "You're sweating," Marie whispers, and fans my face. "Ssshhh, Ssshhh, it's okay, I promise, it was only a dream."

"I'm afraid to go back to sleep."

"Don't worry you probably won't. They've been at it all night. I've not slept one wink. It's been a war zone upstairs." Marie yawns and pulls the blanket over her head.

I pull it from her face. "Sing to me."

Marie promises to sing if I answer a few questions about the first time I saw Irma.

"But I told you everything already."

"I wasn't paying as much attention as I should have. Tell me one more time and don't leave a single detail out." When I finish, she says, "Dad's lost his mind," she pauses, "listen . . . they've finally stopped. They must have passed out from fighting so hard."

As hard as I try, my eyes won't stay open. Her minty breath is vibrating near my ear.

Until . . .

"Juanita! Get up here," Dad's voice is urgent. Sleepy-eyed, I follow him upstairs to the front entry. Dad has a chair propped up against the door. "Stand on this chair and see if you can reach that lock. Try as hard as you can."

I stretch up on my tiptoes. "It's too high for me, get Adam or somebody taller to try."

"You'll do just fine. Five bucks if you can figure out a way to get outside." This time I put more effort into it. I fail. He tucks a dollar in my hand. "I'll trade you a five for that. Try harder. Try to break it." He waves the bill in my face.

"I'm still too short." I grab the handle and shake the door violently. The weird thing is it actually works. The lock falls from its clasp.

A voice behind my back shrieks, "Are you retarded or what?"

Is she talking to Dad, or me? He ignores her, hands me five bucks, and says, "Good work I'll fix that and thanks to you the boys won't escape again."

Again?

Irma has a disturbed look in her coal black eyes. She snatches the five bucks from me, and snaps at Dad, "It's high time you smarten up or I'll be the one running away. I can reach the lock anytime I want."

Dad motions for me to leave and follows her toward his bedroom saying, "Next time I might not be working out back." That night we skip dinner again but after it gets dark, my brothers raid the freezer and we have a feast of leftover Christmas turkey, heated up with an iron. Marie tucks me in bed and leaves to rewrap the used foil around some other frozen leftovers. It seems as though only two minutes have passed when Marie's alarm blares in my ear. I dread going upstairs. Even though Irma stays in the room and never comes out, everything feels different. It doesn't feel like our house anymore and for the first time ever, I can't wait to go to school today.

"Adam, Adam, wait up. I need to button my coat."

Ryan twists around and says, "Hurry up slowpoke. A turtle with three legs, would be faster than you." He quickens his pace. I stop fumbling with the buttons and race after them, but not one of my siblings slows down or waits for me.

Determined to beat them to school, I take a shortcut. I open Sharon's gate and climb over the backyard fence. Two feet from the fence, I hear a rip. My belt has broken through one loop and the buckle is caught in the other. I yank the belt free, and run past Irma's old house. The wind bangs the screen door against the porch railing. I skid to a stop and walk back toward the steps. Is it locked? The knob twists. A man is standing in the doorway. I turn and half run, half slide down the icy steps.

"Whoa. Whoa. Slow down before you crack your skull."

At the bottom of the steps, I turn and say, "I thought nobody lived here. I thought it was empty. Who are you?"

"A better question, is why did you think it was empty?"

"Because the people that lived here moved."

"Don't go anywhere. I'm getting my coat. I'll be right back." His eyes look wild and his hair looks like he hasn't combed it for a week. He steps two feet back, keeps his eyes glued on me, throws one arm into his coat and rushes out the door. I flee down the driveway and pass three houses before I run out of breath. When I try to stop, I step on my belt, skid on a patch of ice, slide toward the center of the road and tumble on my back. A car veers out of control. I open my mouth wide. Screams catch in my throat. Jolts of fear shoot through me, paralyzing every inch of my body. A second car stops beside me. I recognize the boots. His hand grabs my coat. I dangle in the air, then slide across the car seat. His stinky breath is only a foot away. "You okay kid?"

I shake my head no.

"Stay put. I'll drive you to school."

I gulp and say, "I'm not allowed to ride with strangers."

Battered

"If your parents knew I just saved your life, I don't think they'd consider me a stranger. You're damn lucky I saw you. If I stop talking, will you stop trembling."

"I'll try."

Five minutes pass before the car slows to a stop. "I assume this is where you were headed?"

"How did you know?"

"Only choice in town and you look about my son's age and this is his school." He shuts off the engine. "I want you to come by my house after school. To talk about my boys. I'll show you pictures. Maybe you'll recognize them. Now get out before you get into trouble for being late."

"I can't," I say.

"Can't what? Come by?"

"No, my coat's stuck. I can't reach the handle."

He leans across the seat. His smelly underarms hover above my face. "Oh, it's caught in the door." He opens it.

"I can go?"

"What did you expect? To be kidnapped?"

"Sort of."

"Sorry to disappoint you kid, this isn't your lucky day. And please don't tell your teacher a stranger drove you to school. The only reason I came after you, is because you know something about my kids moving. Hey, don't look so scared. I'm not a monster. My name is Dave Hogan and I'm just a guy looking for his wife and kids. She took them both, and disappeared without a trace. I need them back, and it seems to me that you might know where they are."

A Monster Rears Its Ugly Head

My teacher interrupts my daydream. I blink at her. The entire class twists in their seats. Rows of bulging eyeballs stare at me, while Mrs. Jefferson wags her finger in front of her beet red face.

"Don't play deaf with me. I know you heard me." She stomps towards my desk. She has a garden patch of sparse hairs growing under her chin. Her thin mustache moves and partially disappears, as she rolls both of her lips inside of her mouth. The only thing I've heard are my own thoughts and questions. They've been repeating themselves all day. Who is this Dave Hogan? Is he telling the truth? Why isn't he dead? Does Dad know he survived? Does Irma? My teacher wraps her hand around my shirt collar and walks me to the office.

Principal Wells says, "So what have you to say for yourself?"

My thoughts disappear. "For what?"

"Young lady have you ever heard of ADD?"

"You mean like the opposite of subtract?"

Battered

"According to your teacher, you have had the attention span of a flea. What is going on with you today? Care to share your thoughts?"

"I feel really sick."

"Well, you're not alone. You're the ninth one today." She feels my head. "You're not hot but you are white as a ghost. I would send you to the nurses' station but she's up to her ears in sickies. Do you live close by? Within walking distance?"

"I live really close. I can walk. I always walk."

"Anyone at home?" He stops writing, and raises one eyebrow.

"Yes, my Dad."

"Okay kiddo. I'll call ahead so he knows I'm dismissing you. Collect your books, and head home."

I hurry outside, to a nearby bus stop and sit down on the bench to wait for my brothers. There's no way I'm walking home alone. I stare at the frosted semi-frozen water puddle below my feet. I press my boots on it. It moans, groans and creaks but doesn't break. A strange shadow looms across the bench. I recognize the smell of him before I look up. "Miss me? Scoot over," he chuckles and sits by my side. "Is it okay if we talk?"

"I wasn't going to come by."

"I assumed as much." He wrings his hands and asks, "How was spring break? Good?"

"No. Not in the least. It wasn't much fun at all. Neither was the month before. So yeah it was bad."

"I hear ya loud and clear. It wasn't so good for me either," he sighs. "Truth is I had a rotten time. Want to hear about it?"

"I got in trouble today because of you. My teacher sent me to the principal's office because all I could think about was who you were and why you weren't dead."

"Oh, so I'm dead huh? Says who."

"Just someone who knows Irma, and Irma told that somebody that you were dead."

"She wishes," he mutters and cracks his knuckles. "Oh, don't get me wrong. I'm a good guy. I work hard, twenty-four-hour shifts and sometimes

59

in an emergency getting forty-eight off doesn't happen. Last couple of months I was gone too much. I took on some extra shifts to . . ." He blows at the air in front of us. "It was for extra money to buy her a special anniversary present."

"What was the present?"

"A ring. One like she always wanted. But I didn't buy it."

"Why not?"

"Because she was gone. Just like that. Poof. No kids., no her, nothing." His voice breaks. He wipes his eyes and covers his mouth with his hand. I reach out and pat his other one.

"Never saw it coming. Haven't slept a wink since. Maybe if I knew the boys were safe, or if someone I knew, someone like you, could tell me the boys were safe, maybe I could get some shut eye and keep my job. God knows I need it." He stares up at the clouds and mutters, "What I really need, is to find a good lawyer."

"And a shower. You should get a shower."

"That bad huh?"

I fan my nose.

His laugh sounds broken. "Listen kid, I'm not a big Christian but the day you ran through my back yard, I was praying for a sign." He points his finger at me. "And I think you're it. Our paths crossed for a reason. It's a sign alright. You were sent to help me."

"I'm just a kid. I'm too small to help you. Maybe you can call the police or something," I say.

His eyes lower. He rubs his hands together. His wedding band slides up and down his finger. "The police never get involved with this kind of thing, especially when the children are with their mother. They call it a domestic dispute. My only choice is to go to court and duke it out."

"Then maybe you should be there instead of here."

"They can only help me if I have more facts. That's where you come in. And dealing with it there, takes time, too much time. I can't wait that long and neither can my kids."

"What's your job."

"The same as any other Dad. Feed them, protect them—"

"No. The job you might lose."

"My job is to protect the public in emergency situations. I'm a fireman. I save people, like I saved you." Dave Hogan's voice is filled with torment. "My kids are probably frightened to death right now. I guarantee it. Their mother is not the nicest person in the world. She can be scary. She takes things out on them."

He fumbles behind his coat and pulls out a wallet "Once she punished the boys just because their shirts were hanging out." He opens his wallet and pulls out a photo of the four of them. "I just want to show you I'm not some nutcase making stuff up. And . . . and I'm hoping you've seen them . . ."

In the photo everybody is smiling. Everybody looks happy and younger. I've never seen Irma or her kids ever smile like that. Now I know for sure her smile is fake. Now I feel an urge to help him.

"It's not like she wants them because she loves them. It's a control thing." He rubs his hands back and forth across the knees of his pants. "Anything you've got, no matter how small, can make a big difference. Anything? I know you've got something for me."

His eyes remind me of Dork's, when he used to beg for dog treats. And they also remind me of Jacob's eyes. Mostly because they look so sad. "I know your family, a little," I say.

"How? A little is better than nothing."

I tell him what I saw through the fence. Unlike Dad, he believes me and asks, "Have you seen hide or hair of them since?"

I nod. "They're the ones who think you're dead."

"Why would they think that?"

"I think they heard it from Irma. But why would she lie about that?"

He takes a sharp breath and says, "Because the woman is insane. I think she has a mental illness."

"But you live so close. Wouldn't they find out you weren't dead, sooner or later?"

"Exactly. How sane is—so close to where? Kid tell me what you know. Look at me." He grabs my shoulders. "I know, you know where my kids are and you have to tell me. For Christ's sake you have to tell me."

"If I tell you, don't ever say I told you, promise?"

"I won't tell anyone. I promise."

"If you do, I'll get in big trouble. Humongous trouble"

"Listen kid. I'm a good guy. I'm a good dad. I promise I won't get you in trouble and if you help me and ever get in a bind, I promise I'll get you out." He loosens his grip on my coat and says, "Kid. I cross my heart. Swear on my mother's grave."

I take a deep breath. He leans in closer. I talk faster than I ever have in my life and say, "Your kids and Irma are at my house."

He crushes me with a hug. My ribs hurt. He buries his head into his hands and his shoulders shake.

"Is your Dad okay?"

"Yep." I say to the two kids passing by as I pat his back.

He looks up at the sky, "Thank you. Thank you Jesus." He shakes his head like a wet dog, and presses a finger against the corner of each of his eyes. He sniffs, leans back against the bench, and stares at the clouds. I blow steam out of my mouth and watch it disappear. "Your mom and Irma been friends long?"

"My mom's dead. Died three months after I turned four."

I watch my breath for another full minute.

"Dead?" he swallows hard. "I see. Look kid I don't give a rat's ass about Irma anyway. You can keep her. I just want my kids back."

"No way! I don't want to keep her. You can have her back."

"You may not want her, but your Dad does, so my guess is you'll be stuck with her for a while, at least until she shows her true colors. How far from me do you live?"

"Why?"

"Don't worry, I'm not coming over. I just need to know to figure out a rescue route. Is it the house behind me?"

"No. The one next to it. The blue one."

"I know that place. Now it makes all the sense in the world. By the looks of that house your Dad can afford a team of good lawyers and I can't afford one from a cracker jack box."

"But you have your ring money."

"Yes, I suppose I do, but it won't go far." A snow ball flies past our bench. His eyes scan the cluster of boys.

"They're not there. She keeps them locked inside."

His eyes widen and freeze. "I knew they wouldn't stay away from me if they had a choice. Listen kid. I've got some thinking to do. Go home and act normal. You don't know me. Agreed?"

I am three feet away when he yells, "Hey kid, can you meet me here tomorrow, during your lunch break?"

"Maybe … okay."

"And don't tell my boys I'm alive—at least not yet."

I take the longest route home. Our house isn't that much fun anymore so I'm in no hurry to get there. Acting normal gets me into nothing but trouble lately. Act normal! How the heck am I supposed to act normal now when I know Irma isn't a widow and Dad is a home wrecker? I trudge up the driveway and find Dad standing on the front steps with the door ajar.

I hang up my coat, but it falls off the hook. He picks it up, drapes it over a nearby chair and asks, "What's up? You look like you saw a ghost."

Stop acting weird, I tell myself. Say something normal. "I felt sick so they sent me home early. There was a line up at the nurses' station so they sent me home a little early." Stop repeating stuff.

"What else?" Dad scrutinizes my face.

"Some weirdo followed me so I sat on a bench and waited, but the boys, they never showed up."

"Followed you? Was it a man or a boy? What did he look like?" His brow furls up with beads of sweat.

"Didn't I already say it was a boy?"

Relief floods across his face. I learn two things in that moment. If I leave out some words, Dad fills in his own blanks, and I can avoid lying by answering a question, with a question.

Over the next few days, Irma holes up in Dad's room, Dad acts like a stranger, and I feel like a traitor. I spend some lunch hours and most afternoons meeting up with Mr. Hogan, at the bus stop bench.

He's tapping two rulers on his knees. "Yesterday you said you were too short to reach the lock." He hands me the two rulers and a roll of tape. "If one's too short, tape them together."

"We own chairs, and one ruler will be enough."

"You can keep them just in case."

"In case what?"

Instead of answering my question, he tells me he's changed the locks on his house to keep Irma out but he's nailed a wooden ladder against the outside of the house, below the small open bathroom window.

"The room must be freezing. Is that why you don't shower?"

"I shower. I just need to do some laundry. I also loosened boards on all three fences at the corner posts between your house and the neighbors to give the boys extra options to use. And I crawled into George McDonald's back yard and loosened a few of his fence boards and a few more behind your garage. That's the route the boys should take if they get the chance to run. They can't run down any roads. They'd be too easy to catch."

It serves Dad right. If he hadn't killed Dork, Dave Hogan would never have gotten near any fences, especially ours. Maybe God is finally punishing Dad, for murdering my dog.

"Your eyes are cloudier than the sky, what's wrong."

"What if Irma recognizes the rulers."

"She won't, I bought them for you. Are my instructions clear enough for you to pass on to my boys?"

I suck the snow from my mitten and nod. I don't have the heart to tell him I never get to talk to his boys and the last time I saw them was the first day they arrived.

"What if I don't get a chance to tell them your plan?"

"You will. The big question is when. If I'm not home, tell Jacob to call 911. I'll be at work and hear the call. The fire and police departments share the same building." He bites his nails. "I'm on leave right now but my leave is almost up."

He glances at his watch. "Kiddo, I suggest you run home."

The last time I ran I had to make up a story about why I was out of breath. Dad believed me. Irma didn't.

I walk but take a short cut home by crawling through the boards he loosened. I barely fit through.

The front door is unlocked. Irma's voice is coming from the kitchen. My mouth hangs open while she bangs the phone repeatedly on the counter. She bends her neck and yells into it. "Ned! The flour is by the sugar." She picks up the phone, shakes it and holds it to her ear. "No, I haven't shopped there before, but baking aisles are all the same."

I can't believe she is trying to describe baking supplies to Dad, over the phone. Good luck to her. Dad doesn't even know what a baking aisle is. His idea of grocery shopping is waiting in the car, until one of us taps on the window, to have him pop the trunk.

She snaps, "Just forget it. I said forget it Ned." She slams the receiver twice before I reach the basement steps.

I change out of my school clothes, climb a chair and hide my rulers on the top shelf of the closet.

"Juanita. Come to dinner."

"Coming Dad." I knock on the bathroom door. "Marie did you hear Dad?"

"I told him earlier I have an overload of homework."

Miraculously dinner tonight includes Irma and her kids. The table looks longer because Dad has added the leaf. It's the weirdest dinner. The only sounds are forks scraping against plates.

"Irma, she was near ninety. I thought her advice would be good."

Irma looks at him, "Have you gone senile? Since when did you think cornstarch was the same as flour?"

"She swore by it. Said cornstarch was better."

"Better? That would be like me telling you to put cornstarch on fried fish? Ned Rose, I know you can fry fish. And I know you use flour. So, you do know what flour looks like."

Bruce and Drake exchange looks. Are they thinking the same thing as me? Dad always bottles fish. We haven't eaten fried fish since the summer, before the housewarming party. If Dad cooked fish here, we'd smell it for a week.

"Maybe you should have picked something else to cook."

"Like what Ned? The pantry is blocked solid with nothing but salmon and an entire herd of moose are in the deep freeze. Besides I already had it cooking for an hour before I realized you had no flour."

Dad flicks his moose stew back and forth across his plate. "They don't hang out in herds." He drops his fork across his plate.

"Don't blame me if you don't like it. Blame the cornstarch."

"There's a twenty-four-hour grocery store up by the crossing. Tomorrow, before dawn, it'll be empty. We can—"

Irma coughs. Her eye's flicker to her boys and back to Dad. He shuts up. I seem to be the only one who can hear my heart thumping. My hands are clammy. I can barely hold my fork. I keep my head down and focus on eating my stew.

"What's wrong with her?" Irma asks Dad. "I don't like the way she's acting."

"The nurse sent her home early the other day. A bunch of kids at school came down with something or the other."

"Then what the hell is she doing at this table? Get her out of here. The last thing I need is us getting sick."

"Irma, she's not finished eating and she's probably not contagious."

"Really, but everyone at school has it? Think about what you're saying Ned. Do you really want to risk my two boys having to visit their family doctor or go to the hospital? Then what?"

"Christ, she doesn't have the plague. But if you feel that way, maybe the boys should eat in their room."

Battered

"Like hell. Forget it. Those kids have been locked in that room day and night. They have every right to be in this kitchen as much or more than she does." My throat feels dry. My hands are trembling. She picks up her plate and slams it at the table. Peas, carrots and gravy splatters everywhere. Seconds later, my milk spills over the cloth and splatters onto the floor.

"See what you've done?" she shrieks, and pulls the cloth from underneath the dishes. Cups and plates topple over. Some crash to

the ground. She grabs her two boys and stalks away saying, "And don't expect me to clean up your filthy mess."

I hold my breath. It takes a moment to absorb what just happened. The kitchen looks worse than the last time the boys had a food fight.

Adam raises his eyebrows, and chuckles nervously, "Does this mean no dessert?"

Dad bends down on his knees to pick up broken glass. I try to help him. He cups my wrist. "I don't want you to cut yourself. It'll be better if you go downstairs," he whispers. "Go get some rest."

I curl up in bed but I can't sleep a wink. I lie still and wait for morning to come. Before it does, the floor above me creaks. The garage door rumbles open.

Marie's hand is lying across her stomach above the bed sheets. Should I wake her up, or let her sleep? What if Irma didn't leave with Dad? The faint patter of running feet, catches my ear. I stand on the chair in my room, and wait until the beam of headlights curve out of our driveway. My heart hammers against my chest. What if Irma's still here, or they come back and catch me? My excuse will be I couldn't find any toothpaste. Armed with my toothbrush, I creep up the steps. Each time they creak, I hold my breath and wait. I do this five times before I reach the top of the steps.

I tiptoe down the hall. Jacob sways back and forth. The broom handle clunks against the door frame, then gets caught in the gap between the chain and the wall. He takes a deep breath and tugs on the broom. I creep toward him and tap his leg.

He yelps, teeters and collapses on the chair. "Please don't tell."

His brother Justin wobbles against the wall and slides to the floor. He seems to be sleeping.

"Is he okay?"

"She gave us cough medicine to make us sleep but I only swallowed half. I spit the rest of mine into the toilet." He points to his groggy brother, "He swallowed all of his."

"Where are you going."

"Back home. Somebody's at my house. The lights change from off to on." He's talking eighty miles an hour. His sentences don't make sense. I tell him to calm down and talk slower. He doesn't.

"Jacob your Dad is alive and—"

Jacob punches me. "You're a liar!" Tears fall down his face. "A big liar."

I cover his mouth. "Stop or you'll wake everyone up. Who else would it be at your house?" I wipe my snotty hand on his pajamas.

"Relatives. Getting Dad's stuff. That's what Mom said."

"Your mom's the liar. You need to listen, before they get back, or you'll never see your Dad again, EVER. If I never met your Dad how would I know he's a fireman and he has a picture of you wearing a blue sweater with red and gray diamonds on it? He's been meeting me every day waiting for me to help you escape."

His chin quivers while I tell him his Dad's plan. He blinks repeatedly. It's the first time I've seen anyone smile while they cry.

I climb up the chair and reach for the chain. I can't touch it, not even with my tooth brush. "I'll sit. Try standing on my lap."

He totters away every time the tip of his outstretched fingers come near the chain.

The living room tables have marble tops, perfect to put a chair on but too heavy to move. I take the toothbrush and hold it between my teeth. I straddle each edge of the chair. "Jacob, climb between my legs, hold the back of the chair and roll up into a ball with your knees against your chin. I'm going to stand on your back okay?"

His boney spine arches up. He grunts and groans. All I manage to do is rattle the chain. On the second try I almost get the chain to jiggle off.

Battered

"Jump."

"No, I might break your back."

"I don't care."

The clunk of the lock releasing the chain sounds deafening. The toothbrush slips between my fingers and falls to the floor.

"She took our coats and shoes with her," Jacob says, and yanks his brother to his feet.

I swing open the door. "Run."

A cold gusty wind hits my face. It's snowing like crazy. Jacob takes a step backwards into the house. I push him outside. "Run, run, run and don't look back."

Jacobs drags Justin through the snow, towards the back yard.

Panic sets in. The door closes in slow motion. Should I put the chair back? What would Jacob do? I leave everything as it is and creep downstairs. At the bottom of the landing, I realize I forgot my toothbrush. I dash back upstairs. Headlights bounce off the kitchen wall. I race toward the door and hunt for the toothbrush. The garage door rumbles open. My heart is pounding. I crawl under the chair.

The toothbrush is balanced upright against the inside leg. I clutch it and run downstairs as the garage door rumbles shut.

I dive over Marie, pull the covers over my head and hold my breath. She murmurs, "You're cold," and cuddles me close. I gasp for air and suck in another deep breath. Screams fill the house. Livid screams. Footsteps stomp across the floor. Doors slam. The footsteps get closer.

I hear the boys panic stricken voices. By now I'm toasty warm. I pretend to be asleep. Marie is snoring in my ear. The blanket makes a loud snapping sound as it's ripped away from the bed.

"GET UPSTAIRS NOW!"

First, we are interrogated as a group. Then we get questioned individually. They try to trick me. At first, they treat me nice, then Irma turns mean. She says the boys told her they saw me. I act stupid and keep with my story. I talk about the dream I had.

"SHUT UP. I DON'T CARE ABOUT YOUR STUPID DREAM."

Nobody knows the truth but me, so I lie repeatedly and say I was asleep the whole time.

"Calm down Irma."

"CALM DOWN? CALM DOWN? I'll calm down alright, AFTER I KILL WHOEVER DID THIS."

Dad sighs and says, "One of you must know something."

"One of those little bastards knows something alright. They're damn well not deaf and there is no chance in hell that my boys did this on their own." Irma's eyes are filled with hatred. She despises each and every one of us.

I look Dad square in the eyes and ask, "How come you guys didn't hear them?"

The jolt to my jaw sends me reeling.

My eyes instantly fill with water. Irma pounds me with her fists. Dad pries her off. She kicks her feet at me.

"Irma stay out of this. This is my house, these are my kids, let me deal with this my way."

Her eyes are seething. "I bet every one of you knows something," she says through gritted teeth. "Every damn one of you deserves to get your heads knocked off. My boys are too stupid to do this on their own." She slams the chair against the wall. "And they're too damn short."

"So is she," Dad says. "It's not fair to take this out on her, or any of them for that matter." I'm not sure if Dad is calling me stupid or short and I don't care and don't dare ask. All I know is my face has stopped stinging and I don't want to go through that again.

My brothers swear on their lives they are innocent and after hours of hysterics, Irma gets her way.

Dad agrees to punish each of us.

My beating is not the worst because Dad believes I'm innocent. Each of us stays away from the other. The house seems like a morgue and it feels like our lives have changed forever. Will Dad always let her get away with whatever she wants? How can he choose her over us?

Battered

Monday seems so far away but it finally does arrive but it goes by too quick. The dreaded three o'clock school bell makes everyone in class happy, except me. It's piercing ring sounds threatening. It means I have to go home and walk past the kitchen.

Irma has been as cold as ice and each day she creates more rules to follow. No TV on school nights. No going out after school. No having friends over. The house feels like a prison. My only reprieve is school. All six of us never agreed on anything in the past but we all agree last weekend was the worst weekend of our lives.

Because today is the start of parent-teacher week, and all the older kids have to clean classrooms for an extra thirty minutes after school, I walk home alone. Once I see the roof of my house I feel an urge to vomit. I stop and turn around hoping to see Marie or my brothers.

"Psssst." The bushes beside me rustle.

"It's me. Don't look around. Pretend you're tying your shoe."

"I don't have laces. I'm wearing boots."

"Then pretend you're taking snow out of them."

I crouch and balance myself from falling. I sit down and dig at my boot with my snow-covered mitten. White globs fall into my boot. The more I try to dig out the snow the worse it gets.

"I want to thank you kid. You're a brave girl. Did you get into any trouble?"

"Yep. Lots. We all did."

I tell Dave Hogan what happened.

"Are you scared?"

"Yes. She's a monster."

"Listen kid, the best way to diffuse Irma is to apologize. But be careful because if you apologize for the wrong thing, she will feel justified to reward that with one severe wallop."

Somehow, I expected better advice from him. I stop messing with my boot and straighten up.

"Whatever you do, never ever admit to helping my boys or me. She'll flip out."

"She already did. I'm sorry for helping. She's mad at all of us."

"Kiddo you did the right thing. She's just showing her true colors, sooner than later. Your Dad will see her for who she is and if he has any sense, he'll kick her out. I thought she could change. But now it's plain as day that I was wrong. A wrote a note for your Dad."

"Why?"

"This note will help you. But you have to give it to your Dad, not Irma. If she gets her hands on it, she'll destroy it."

"What if he asks where I got the note?"

"Tell the truth. Say some man jumped out of the bushes and gave it to you but you have to lie and say it's the first time you met me. Kid, this next part is going to be hard to do and it's something I should have taught my boys years ago. Irma is going to examine every expression on your face and read between every word you say so when you tell her a lie don't look left or right, or up or down, look her straight in the eyes. Got it? Sometimes a lie can save your hide and when that time comes, look her in the eyes and stick to the lie no matter what and never take it back. See you in a few minutes."

"But what about the note."

"Not yet." He disappears behind the brush.

I'm glad he's gone. I feel relieved and safe. I count every footstep before I reach the front of the driveway. I'm dizzy and weak and I'm afraid if I stop, I will flat-out faint. I count ten more steps.

Dave appears out of nowhere.

"Kid. Hey you, kid."

Sharp pangs of fear rip across my chest. If Irma sees me with him, I'm as good as dead. I try to run up the driveway but he catches my arm. My feet fly out from underneath me. I scream and try to get away. I yell as he grabs me by the collar and stuffs a note in my hand. "Make sure you give this to your Dad not Irma."

I dash in the house and slam the door. I lean against it trying to catch my breath. Dad is not home and Irma is pacing the floor like a lunatic half-crying half-ranting. Her smile is twisted. "If you and your sister think you can outsmart me you are both dead wrong."

She grabs me by the neck and squeezes harder.

I can't breathe. I panic and gasp, "Some strange man is outside. He grabbed me and gave me—"

She runs to the window. "That son-of-a-bitch." She pulls the curtains shut and slaps my face. "And he gave you what?" Her head tilts to one side. "GAVE YOU WHAT?" Her fingers curl around my neck. I can barely talk. My eyes bulge out of their sockets. I hold the note in front of my face. She releases her grip. I gag for air.

She reads it, and threatens me to not move a single inch and disappears into the bedroom.

Thuds and bangs fill the air. It seems like forever before she comes back with two bags of clothes in one hand. I can see shoes sticking out near the top. The same shoes that saved me last year.

She waves a note at me and flicks it at my face. Her voice is frantic. "Did you read this? Exactly what did he say to you when he handed you this?"

Her eyes are smoldering. "Tell me, word for word," she shrieks.

I open my mouth. At first, nothing comes out. I look into her crazed eyes and say, "He said give you the note."

Irma slaps me across the face, "Don't lie to me. Tell me what he said, word for word." She slaps my face harder. Tears run down my cheeks. She shakes me repeatedly. The crumpled note falls from her hand down my shirt. It pricks my chest but I keep looking in her eyes. The more I look the worse she gets. She opens the door, and snarls, "Pick up those bags and get the hell out."

I grab the bags. One shoe topples to the floor. I bend to pick it up. She boots me out the door and her foot lands square on my face.

I bend back up. She raises her arms backwards and shoves them against my chest. I twist around, tumble down the steps and trip over my own feet.

I collect the scattered contents, and run to Dave's house.

Dave is pacing back and forth at the end of the driveway. I drop the bags at his feet. The same shoe falls out. I pick it up and hold it against my chest.

He reaches for it. My fingers curl around it tighter. He gently pries it away. Blood drips onto his thumb.

"Please don't send me back."

He pulls me toward him and hugs me tight.

"Who did this to you? Him or her?" His voice is ice-cold.

"Her," I say. "I did what you said. I lied but it didn't work."

"Kid sometimes nothing works. Sometimes she goes off the deep end no matter what you say. When she gets on a rampage, there's nothing you can say to stop her. Hopefully the note helps."

I point to Dad's car. It slows as it passes by Dave's house then it screeches to a stop. "That's his car. He wasn't home. So, she got to read the note."

Dave groans.

Dad backs up and rolls down the car window. "What the hell is going on here?"

"My bruised-up kids—your kid's bleeding. Do the math man."

I stand in disbelief as Dave walks up his steps and slams the door shut. Part of me wants to run after Dave but the other part wants Dad to run over him. "Get in the car." Dad holds the door ajar. His voice breaks, "Did that son-of-a-bitch do this to you?"

"Irma did it. She went crazy again for no reason."

Dad chews on his bottom lip, parks in our driveway and says, "Don't worry. I'm going to put an end to this."

He stomps to the front door and turns the knob. It's bolted.

By the time he fumbles with his keys and inserts one into the lock, the door swings open. Irma is holding it ajar smiling.

Dad tilts my face upwards. "I was told you did this to her. I was told there was a note written for me and you read it and did this."

"She's a liar," Irma yells. "There was no note. Tell him the truth you little liar."

"Dave told me, the same story."

"Can't you see that little bitch is trying to break us up?" She stalks toward me. I crouch in the corner. Dad yanks her by the elbow.

"Let go or I'll call the cops," she hisses through clenched teeth.

Battered

My rowdy brothers bang on the front door. Dad releases Irma's arm. She runs to the bedroom, and slams the door behind her. Dad hits the wall. The boys come to an abrupt stop. Everyone stands still with frozen faces and open mouths. Marie pushes past them and kneels beside me. She glares at Dad. "I swear she will rot in hell for this and so will you."

"I wasn't home, Marie. I had nothing to do with this."

"Yes, you did. You brought that animal in to our home. This certainly is your fault." Marie springs up, races to Dad's bedroom door, beats on it with her fists and screams, "If you dare come out—" she chokes on her spit twice, "even for a second—I will kill you! I swear I'll kill you the minute you come out!"

Dad pries Marie away from the door. She pounds on his chest, "Let me go. I said let me go. This is your entire fault! You made this happen."

"Calm down. Your sister needs you. I'll take care of this, I promise."

Marie turns quiet and still. She backs away from him. Her voice is low and slow. Her words are like bullets. She shoots them one by one.

"You-are-not-fit-to-be-a-father. You weren't worthy of my mother. I will hate you until the day I die. DO YOU HEAR ME? I will HATE you until the day I die."

Dad slowly removes his belt. "Boys get downstairs."

The boys don't need to be told twice. He turns toward the bedroom door and uses the buckle pin to unlock it. He twists his fingers and grips the knob. The door only moves an inch. "Open this door or I'll call the police myself. THIS IS MY DOOR. OPEN IT."

Marie wraps her arm underneath mine and pulls me against her chest. Her arm tightens against my back and she carries me to the bathroom. She sits me on the edge of the tub and flips on the tub water. The water flows down the open drain while she holds me and hums.

"Stop. I don't want to be up here. I want to go downstairs, please, Marie."

The bathroom door swings open. It's Dad. His shoulders are slumped. He looks shorter than normal. "You need to talk to your sister about lying. She's making matters worse than they need to be."

75

Marie makes a scoffing sound and turns her back to him.

He grunts, bends over and picks up my scattered clothes. The note falls to the floor. He stays in a bent position for almost a minute, his eyes riveted on the note. He reads it, while the color drains from his face.

Child Services

A weird whistling sound comes from outside my room. A sheer shirt wiggles midair, and disappears. I sink further into my bed and pull the covers over my face. This is nonsense. Grow up. I peek above the blanket. It comes back from the other side, sways high above the floor and glides across the entrance to my room and vanishes.

I shove my blanket away and hang one leg over the edge of the bed. Suddenly it returns. It's transparent and has no legs. A blood-curdling scream fills my room, I dive back under the sheets and scream again. I scream repeatedly when it tries to grab the blanket from over my head.

"Ssshhh before you get in trouble." Marie pulls me toward her. I cling to the headboard. Strong hands pry my fingers loose.

"Good lord your strong as an ox," Dad grunts. "Let go before I break your fingers off."

"Is it there?"

Dad and Marie both ask, "Who?"

"The ghost. I saw a ghost." Long sobs rack my body.

"It was just a nightmare," Dad says.

"No. I-I-I wasn't asleep. I s-s-saw it, for real. I'm not lying."

Dad's sigh is long and loud. "Yes Juanita, I know you're not lying." He kisses my forehead and walks back upstairs. Two minutes later, I hear muffled laughter coming from the boys' room. I creep toward their door. It's slightly ajar. Adam is laughing so hard tears are pouring down his cheeks. He has a fishing pole in his hands. Drake is doubled over holding his stomach. Adam reels in the fishing line while Drake tries to unwind the other end from around his gloved hand. A shirt is lying on the edge of their bed. I shove open the door, grab it and run. Before I can reach the foot of the stairs, a hand covers my mouth. Adam steers me to his room

"What the heck happened to your eye?"

Drake says, "The ghost socked her."

Adam's mouth opens wide. He tosses his head back. Veins pop out on his neck. Laughter bellows from deep down his throat. I have an avid desire to pull his tonsils out. Instead, I chomp down on his hand. He finally uncovers my mouth. "Go ahead. I dare you to go upstairs and tell them it was nothing but a big joke."

"Stop laughing at me. It's not funny."

"Oh, but Juanita, it is funny. See. Everyone, but you, thinks so." He points to Drake who's rolling on the floor. Even Marie is giggling.

"You hung it by the shoulders to your fishing pole string using safety pins. Then you reeled it back and forth. I'm not stupid but your joke is and you can have your dumb shirt back."

Drake catches it and grins, "Nobody called you stupid."

"Where did you get those pins, Drake. You stole them from my sewing basket, didn't you?"

I tug at Marie. "What sewing basket? Can I see it?"

Marie holds out her hand while the boys drop six safety pins into her palm. "Sure you can, after Adam hands it back."

A sheepish look crosses his face. He lifts his pillow and hands her the sewing basket. "Touch it again Adam and I'll sneak in after midnight, and sew your eyelids shut."

Battered

I sit on our bed while she shows me everything in Mom's old sewing basket.

"I guess that's the benefits to being older when your mom dies. You get to keep what you want," I blurt out. I pick up an empty spool. "Why are you keeping this?"

"In the end I had to help Mom sew. She couldn't hold the needle by herself. That was the last spool she touched." Marie caresses it reverently.

We hear the upstairs arguments escalate into a thud followed by silence. "Maybe she's dead," I whisper.

"No such luck. But if she was, we would let her rot and feed her stinking carcass to some vultures," says Marie.

"What if Dad's half dead," I whisper.

"Then maybe, just maybe I'll call 911." Marie shuts the sewing basket. A crash is followed by a shattering sound. "And that's a very small maybe."

I twist the spool and read the top. "E.M.R. RIP 1960."

Marie says, "Mom's initials never changed after she got married. She used to be Elsie May Reid, and after marrying Dad she became Elsie May Rose. Mom was strong. Mom was brave. Don't ever forget who Mom was. Don't ever forget you can be just like Mom. Here, you can keep the spool."

I tuck the spool inside my pillow. Irma's rantings and ravings echo through the furnace vents.

"How can we get her to stop?" I ask.

"Pray. Pray for peace."

I frown at Marie and ask, "Will it work?"

"I swear it will," she says. "Mom prayed all the time. Prayer works."

For the next several days, I pray to God but God doesn't listen. Irma doesn't leave and Dad doesn't kick her out. Maybe my prayers are too vague. I make them more definitive. "Please Lord let Irma fall down hard, hit her head, lose her memory and wander away, never *ever* to be found."

But she doesn't.

She spends the better part of most days in Dad's room and as time passes by we all come to the same conclusion, Dad has fallen under some sort of evil spell. When she does venture out of the room, she kicks us all downstairs and over the next few weeks takes full control of the house. The last time I asked to watch TV she snarled at me and said, 'This is the last time I'm telling you. Nothings on. Get downstairs before I wring your neck.' That was two weeks ago but it feels like ten. The weeks continue to drag by until finally the day comes, when something hopeful happens.

A dog joins the family. A dog that looks exactly like Dork our last German Shepherd. The dog sits beside me towering over my head. He is huge. He puts a paw on my head and starts licking my face feverishly. His wet tongue feels like sandpaper, and even though it hurts, I let him lick my wounds.

"Let's call it Dawg," Ryan is beaming from ear to ear expecting a yes.

The dog looks like a big fox. "How about Foxy."

"That's a girl's name. Pal is better. He has a wiener," he scoffs.

"Fine, we'll name him Pal because he'll be our best friend. Bet he bonds with me first."

"Bet he doesn't." Ryan yanks at the dog's collar.

"I'll bet Ryan is right," Dad says, appearing out of nowhere. "He's a guard dog, not a pet. He's not here to play. Stay away from him until he learns to guard the place. Drake come help me fix the fence."

He must have found the loose boards and that's why he got the dog. The boys argue about who gets to sleep with Pal. Dad whistles loudly with his fingers between his teeth. The arguing instantly stops. Dad folds his arms and says, "All of you can sleep with the dog, as long as you shovel yourselves a snow bed and join him outside."

"The dog isn't for any of us. It's for Irma. He got it to keep Dave Hogan away," Ryan mutters as we head downstairs. I find Marie curled up in a chair in the laundry room, flipping through a heavy looking photo album. She points to a picture and tells me it's Mom. She's wearing a sailor dress. She looks healthy and pretty.

"I thought she might look older like Aunt Patty."

Marie turns the page. I point to the photo of a slightly older woman sitting on a rock. She looks like a model. "Marie isn't that the sitter who rescued me when I was trapped in the barn."

Battered

"What barn?"

"Our old barn back in Heart's Delight."

Although I can't remember too much about those years I do remember playing inside the barn whenever it wasn't locked. Crowley, our cat, loved lying on the roof. The roof was covered with weeds, dust and chunks of Crowley's fur. Our cat was black as tar and half feral. The roof had a hole in it and occasionally Crowley would emerge from the hole with a rodent between his jaws. The barn had two rows of tiny windows that ran along both sides. Some were cracked from rocks that pelted from passing cars.

I reach to turn the page to see if there are any photos of the barn but Marie grasps my wrist.

"Juanita this isn't a sitter. This is Mom. What else do you remember from back then?"

I smile at the next photo. It's Crowley.

"I remember Crowley, on the roof stalking birds and remember trying to throw a rock to scare them away, but I missed and hit him."

"No about Mom. About being rescued."

I close my eyes and think back. The boys were building a cart, using two broken wheelbarrows as parts. The cart was upside down and Bruce was trying to attach the wheels. My rock missed and hit Crowley, but it did cause the birds to fly away for a second.

Adam and Drake pulled their slingshots from their pants and started shooting rocks toward Crowley. I pulled on Drake's arm to stop him, and made him accidentally break the first window. The next shot was deliberate. A dead aim by Adam. The rock went in one side and out the other, breaking two windows simultaneously. Drake thought it only fair if Adam broke two windows, he should do the same. His first shot was weak but broke through one. The second shot went through both sides. Now Drake's score was three. Bruce joined in the fun. Eventually after all the windows were broken and the boys turned back toward the cart, I was throwing the last cartwheel down the lane. Bruce tucked the sling shot into his belt and ran after the wheels while Adam grabbed me by the waist, threw me in the barn and latched the door. I beat on it until I got a splinter in my fist.

"Well?" Marie waits for an answer.

"I fell asleep in the barn," I say.

"That happened when you were so young," she says. "What else do you remember?"

"Falling down some steep narrow steps into a dark basement."

Marie laughs, "It wasn't funny at the time but you would always lean against that door and fall down. It took Dad months to discover that the boys had jimmied the door so it didn't close right. I'm amazed you're not brain damaged."

"She probably is brain damaged," Ryan sneers. He looks over our shoulder to see what we're looking at. "Never mind I take that back. You can't be brain damaged unless you have one . . . Boy oh boy, do I miss that old barn. That's where I found a whole box of jujubes, and where Adam found his trunk."

I ignore Ryan and stroke the picture. "She's beautiful," I say.

"Mom didn't look like that when she died," Ryan says. "She had to wear wigs and her funeral was on my birthday."

"She died that same year, the year she found you in the barn. It was freezing outside and snowing the day she died and . . ." Marie's voice trails off her eyes turn dark.

Ryan's says, "Yeah and Dad invited all these people over and let them eat my birthday cake and we—"

"Dad told me she died from chasing you guys around the house."

Marie sighs, "I doubt that, but it didn't help any. Mom died from radiation poisoning and cancer." Marie strokes the picture's face, and then she strokes mine. Her fingers feel like feathers. "You look just like her," Marie's voice is almost as soft as her touch.

I close my eyes. "I think you look like her more."

"I can see how chasing them could kill someone," Irma's sarcastic voice startles me. The back of my neck feels like a landing field for a swarm of stinging bees. Irma is standing right behind us. She walks to the dryer and removes her clothes. Her perfume lingers as she bustles past us and swiftly disappears. Ryan high tails it for his room.

Battered

"Can I have a picture of Mom?" I ask. "Ple-e-e-ase."

Marie ignores me, stands up and clutches the album to her chest.

"Where are you going?"

"To hide the photo album."

"From me?"

"No from Irma. Stay here and call me if you see her walk past this door."

That night I dream I'm back in Heart's Delight, standing by the basement door. Ryan is trying to take my cookie. I lean back to get away from him. The door flies open and I tumble down a steep flight of dark narrow steps. I bang my chest repeatedly. My arm twists underneath me. A skeleton picks me up. It's wearing Mom's black dress and high heel shoes.

I bolt upright in the bed and gasp. Marie drops her pen and folds a letter into an envelope. She whispers, "Go back to sleep."

While she writes on the envelope, I tell her about my dream.

She drops her pen and hops into bed beside me. "That actually happened . . . when you were two or three and Ryan was maybe five. The first time you fell, you and Ryan were fighting over a cookie." Marie stares at me, "How can you possibly remember that?"

"Marie are ghosts real? Was—is Mom a ghost?"

"I don't know. Probably so. After Mom died, Suzi lived with us, and at night, every night, we both heard her high heel shoes click across the kitchen floor." Marie rubs away my goosebumps. "If she is, she's not here to hurt you."

"I think Mom might be a real angel," I whisper. "She comes to me in my dreams and tells me stories. Sometimes she shows me stuff. You believe me, right?" The only response I get from Marie is a soft gentle snore.

It seems like I've only been sleeping a second when I wake up to someone pulling my toes.

"Get up," Dad whispers. "Make sure to wear something extra nice."

"Are we going to church?" Every Sunday, we would dress up nice to go to church but that grinded to a stop after Mom died.

Juanita Ray

I pull a dress over my head and rush upstairs. The boys are sitting on the couch lined up like bowling pins. This is eerily similar to how they looked when Irma arrived. Maybe she's leaving. Maybe my prayers finally worked.

We are introduced to a Miss Hughes. Miss Hughes barely glances our way. She sits next to Irma, comparing engagement rings. Irma's fake smile is accompanied by a fake voice, the one she uses for strangers. Dad says, "Miss Hughes is from the government."

Miss Hughes smiles and politely corrects him, "Children Services." She glances at me and says, "Well I guess that's it." She rises and shakes Dad's hand. They talk about jealous neighbors as he walks her toward the door.

Marie stammers, "Wait, aren't you going to ask us anything? How about Juanita? Aren't you supposed to take her away somewhere safe for a private talk?"

Miss Hughes pivots around, "No, no and no." Her voice is flat, "My job is to keep the family together, not tear them apart. I see nothing out of sorts here." She turns to Irma, "I'm glad you found such a nice man after having such a horrible husband. Oh, and congratulations on your engagement. I just love your home."

I stare at the closed door and whisper to Marie, "So much for praying, looks like she's staying."

My brothers, dash past us. Marie jumps up from the chair. "How could you lie like that? Everything isn't okay. Everything is horrible here."

A black storm cloud hovers in Irma's eyes. I know she's talking to Marie but she's looking at me. "If it's that bad once school is out, I suggest you leave."

"Irma she's only seventeen. Where would she go? How would she survive?"

"That's her problem not mine."

"But Irma—"

"Ned either I go or she goes. Make your choice." She struts toward the bedroom door pauses, turns, smiles and says, "And Ned I do hope you enjoy sleeping on the couch."

A Sink Full of Ashes

Two weeks ago, I turned eight. My birthday present, to myself, is a bracelet I'm making from gum wrappers, I found in my brother's dusty trash can. It's the end of August and Marie has been gone since June. Dad said things would get better, with less of us around, but they've gotten worse. Irma acts like the devil. She hates all of us. She even seems to hate Dad at times. And for some reason, she hates Mom more than anyone. A while back, Marie asked Irma why she hated Mom so much. Her answer was, 'She had all of you. That's why.'

My brothers vanished a week after Marie did. How could four boys disappear for four months, without a trace? I spent half the summer doing things I thought wouldn't set Irma off. I spent the other half doing nothing at all. Apparently, I can't even do that right. Now that summer is over, I have accepted one undeniable truth—everything I do is wrong. Every morning I promise God if he sends Marie back I'll read the Bible and never get her in trouble again. Every night I prayed for Irma to drop dead.

Juanita Ray

I'm trying on my bracelet, when I hear a bird singing. It's coming from the basement. I stay in my room until I hear the sound of Irma's footsteps click across the upstairs kitchen floor then I tiptoe toward the bird sounds. They lead me to Adam's room. I blink twice. A kid in a plaid coat, is sitting on Adam's bed whistling at some bird cards. He looks up.

"Ryan?" I poke him. He pokes me back. I sit on the floor too stunned to say anything. I finally come to my senses, yank on his foot and ask, "Where were you all summer?"

"Barachois Park, living in a tent. Hey, guess what! I can imitate over a dozen birds."

"Where's everybody else?"

"Helping Dad put away the camping supplies."

"Camping supplies?"

"Yeah. I told you we lived in a tent."

"A tent? Who looked after you?"

"Nobody."

"Who fed you?"

"They brought us food every weekend and if we got low, we'd fish. Sometimes we'd go swimming and catch electric eels and fry them up."

"You ate eels? Yuk!"

"I saw Eleanor Edwards and she asked about you."

"Where?"

"At the park. She said Irma told her a bunch of mean things and then told her not to come back."

"What did you say back? You didn't tell her the truth about what's going on, did you?"

"What if I did?"

"Irma said she would murder me if I told anyone."

"Yeah, but I'm not you now, am I?"

"I'll get blamed if anyone else from the government comes snooping around."

"Don't worry, I didn't tell her Irma beats the snot out of you and treats you like a prisoner."

Battered

"Thanks," I can't believe Ryan is actually being considerate. "Where did you say I was? I bet Eleanor hates me by now."

"Well, Eleanor said that Irma said you didn't like her anymore."

I groan.

"When she said Irma told her never to come back again, I said that was because there was no need for her to come back anyway, because you were adopted and Dad sent you back to your real parents," Ryan laughs.

"That's not funny!"

"She'll know it was a joke when she sees you in school in a few weeks. So, when did Dad close up the kitchen opening?"

"What kitchen opening?"

"The one to the dining room and living room, stupid. He put up two big sliding vinyl doors, and padlocked the handles together to bar us out. All the food cupboards have locks too. So do the fridge and both freezers." Ryan puts his tanned arm next to mine and smirks. "Oh, and don't bother dressing up for Halloween next month. You can go as a ghost."

"Is Irma letting you guys go trick—"

I dash for my room. I sit on the edge of my bed and wait as Irma's footsteps stomp my way. Little electric shocks are shooting through my chest. I can't breathe right.

She twists my arm. "How many times have I told you not to sit on the bed? And what's that piece of trash on your wrist?" She rips off my bracelet and dangles it. "What is this? Who gave you this? You snuck out of the yard, didn't you?" Sla-a-a-ap.

"Nobody gave it to me. I made it for my birthday."

Thud.

"Don't you lie to me you little bitch, you're too stupid to make something like this." My teeth pierce my lip. I try not to cry. If I do she'll hit me again. Not crying gets harder when her two fists rip my bracelet to shreds. "Get outside until I tell you to come back in. And don't you dare think about leaving the yard. As a matter of fact, stay out back and don't try to come in until I call you. Understand?" She pulls my ear toward the door.

Juanita Ray

It's a cold day and the wind is blowing from the north. I rub my sleeveless arms, but the goosebumps stay. I march around the tree trying to stay warm, while Ryan climbs to the highest branch and practices his bird calls. An hour later, Ryan climbs down and disappears around the side of the house.

By nightfall I'm freezing. When I look for Ryan to see if he'll share his coat, I can't find him. At nine o'clock that night, Ryan yells, "She unlocked the door and we're allowed back in."

Irma is hovering above Ryan. "Well it's bedtime and you two missed your dinner so get to bed. And next time I call, don't be so disobedient, or you'll get more than a missed meal." She glares at both of us. "Go. Get out of my sight."

"But—"

Her glare moves from me to Ryan's face. "Don't but me young man." She lifts her hand and swings it toward his head, I duck and run down the stairs as fast as I can.

Ryan yelps and runs behind me. In the basement, I whisper to Ryan. "Did she call us for dinner?"

"No. I even knocked but she turned the TV up louder."

"You knocked? Are you crazy? If she answered it she would have beaten the crap out of you. You know how hard she hits. She's gotten worse since you've been gone. Way worse."

"Yeah, but a beating is better than starving to death. Besides I think she beats you a little harder because you're a girl and you look like Marie and Mom. The good news is school starts in two weeks. She'll have to slow down soon or teachers will notice your bruises and people will come back asking more questions."

"Well if they do, they won't do anything anyway. They never do."

"Maybe next time you shouldn't be so scared and you should say something. I don't know why you won't."

"For the same reason you don't. I'm scared of what she'll do."

"I'm not scared of her, I'm just not that stupid. Besides, I seriously think she'll stop once school—" Ryan disappears.

Battered

I scoot under the bed. The stairs are creaking and groaning. I slide closer to the middle, hold my breath and run my fingers across my swollen lip.

I smell her first, then I see her shoes.

I scramble from under the bed and heave myself at her.

"Marie! Where were you?" I bury my head into her chest and sob. "I'm so glad your back. I missed you so, *so* very much. I prayed for God to send you back and he did. God finally heard me!"

"Good lord you're nothing but skin and bones. Let me look at you."

I snuggle deeper into her chest. I don't want her to see my face. I'm afraid of what she might do.

"Juanita, stand up straight." She pries me from her. Her lips narrow. She wets them with her tongue. "Tell me the truth, Juanita. How did your face get like this?"

"It's okay. She didn't do it," I lie. "I fell down the steps."

"You're not fibbing, right?"

I look straight into her eyes and say, "Right."

Marie sighs and says, "What is it with you and stairs?" She disappears but returns within a minute with a slab of ice. She cracks it into two pieces. Small shards of snow splatter over the edge of the dresser. She pulls a sock from the drawer, fills it with ice, bangs it on the floor several times, then holds it against my lips.

"Ouch!" I push her hand away and ask, "Where were you all this time? I was so lonely."

"I was at Grandma's."

"What grandma? Where?"

"Dad's mom. She lives in our old house. Dad rents it to her."

"Where did you get that ice?"

"I broke into the freezer with a hairpin, but that's our little secret, okay? Stop crying . . . it's going to get better. I'm back, and school's starting so there's no need to feel lonely anymore."

Maybe she was right. Maybe things would change during the school year.

But she was wrong . . . Ryan was wrong too.

89

Juanita Ray

School didn't make one thing better. Eleanor Edwards acted like she hated me, I got snickered at for what I wore and they called me cheap for making them homemade Valentine cards. By spring, the only friend I had left in the world was Marie and most times she had her head crammed in a book, hiding from Irma. Now that spring break's coming up, I won't be the laughing stock of the class anymore, but I'll be stuck with Irma day and night.

I stand on my bed and pull my sleeves toward my wrist. Last year all my clothes were too big. Now they're all too small. My pants are above my socks and my sleeves won't reach my wrists.

I bounce on my bed until I can see the sky. It's mostly blue. Today looks like a good day to be locked outside. I wait for Irma's footsteps but I hear nothing. Just the sound of water running and my stomach gurgling. I straighten up the bed sheets and wait for eleven o'clock to happen. I can tell by how much my stomach hurts, it's only minutes away.

"Get up here."

I know by her voice, it's a trap. Each step I take sends pricks down my neck.

"Clean this sink." She slaps me across the temple. "I want it spotless."

I try to hide my shock. Marie's empty photo album sits beside the box of matches. I rinse the ashes down the sink wishing they were Irma's.

She points toward the table. "Eat up and get out of my sight."

I stare at the wet slimy paste, take a small spoonful and gag. The milk tastes sour. She must have made the cereal yesterday.

Somehow, I manage to empty most of the bowl, but I can't seem to finish the last of it. I know better than to push the bowl away.

Her shadow looms above me. I gulp one more teaspoon of the sludge. Soft slimy fists beat on my tonsils. I gag again.

Sla-a-ap. "Eat it!"

I try to swallow my vomit, gag some more and swallow again. Seconds seem like hours. Every time I try to eat, I get the heaves. Tears flood down my face.

"Now, lick the bowl."

Battered

After thirty minutes, of eating the same cereal twice, I hear Dad's car door slam. Irma is yelling too loud to hear the door open. I stare at the leftover vomit in my bowl. Then I look up.

Change jingles in his pockets.

Irma freezes.

"What's going on?"

"That little pig gulped her cereal and choked on it until she had the heaves. She's too lazy and stupid to chew her food."

Dad's blurry face frowns at me. He glances at the clock. "How long have you been at this table? When did—"

"Ask me not her. I'm the one watching the clock. Oh . . . I see. You think she's the one telling the truth and I'm the liar."

"Irma, calm down, I didn't call anyone a liar."

Her fingers dig into my skull. She presses my face into the bowl, and squishes it back and forth. My nose is crushed. The edge of the bowl digs into my bottom lip.

"Lord jumpin' sufferin' Moses. There's no need to take it out on her. You need to settle down." He hands me a paper towel. His hand disappears into his pocket. Coins clink against each other. He pulls out two quarters and says, "Here, or did Irma give you money?"

Money? For what? Do I get paid for getting slapped? Irma's eyes are pinned to me. I'm too afraid to answer.

"Did you give her any money?" Dad snaps at Irma.

"Of course not, you idiot." Irma folds her arms and glares at him.

"I don't suppose you've changed your mind?" Dad's voice sounds tense. Coins jingle faster.

Irma glares at him. "Over my dead body."

"Just thought I'd ask in ca—"

Irma cocks her head to one side. "Shut up Ned. Do I look retarded to you?"

"Juanita, go get ready for the park."

I don't move. What is going on? Has he forgotten, unless it's for school, I haven't been allowed to leave the yard for the past two years? He flicks my ear and says, "Hurry up. Go get ready."

I stare at the two quarters sitting next to my bowl. Irma snorts, and stalks away. He slips another one in my hand. I gape at them. He closes my fingers around the coins and squeezes my hand three times.

I am about to slip the quarters into my sock when Irma reappears.

Dad jerks his head at my fist. "Put them in your wallet."

"What wallet?"

"The pink wallet I bought for your birthday last year."

"I can't." I glance nervously at Irma.

"She's too young to have a wallet. I sent it to my niece for her birthday. And if you know what's good for you Ned Rose, I suggest you stop giving me that look."

"Does she have a lightweight jacket?"

"Ned, she doesn't need a jacket. It must be ninety degrees outside."

"She can't stay in the sun for five hours without protection."

"Sure, she can. She manages to survive nine hours out back every weekend but if you're that worried, we can always leave her locked in her room."

"Irma. We had an agreement. We either keep the whole agreement or we don't."

Irma slants her eyes and huffs off.

He taps my shoulder, winks at me and points to the stairs. "Go get ready. And walk—don't run."

Is this a joke or for real? I grip my fist around the coins. I want to jump for joy. I can't believe Dad is finally standing up to Irma. I'm allowed outside the yard! I can go to the park! I've got money. I never get money. Thank you God! Near the cellar, a hand grips my arm and yanks me inside the dark room. Quarters fly from my hand. Marie's arms crush my ribs.

"Let me go." I panic and squirm out of her hold. I crawl across the floor. "Help me find my quarters. I need them. I'm allowed to go to the park." I scramble around on my knees, feeling for the coins but all I find are spider webs.

"Juanita stop, get up, I need to talk to you," Marie sounds as desperate, as I feel. "It's very important."

"So is this. I need them for the park. Everyone's waiting for me," I whine, "I don't want them to leave without me." I grope around in the dark. "Please help me before they change their minds." Marie kneels beside me. Her voice trembles, "Here are two quarters. Now give me a hug."

I give her a quick hug. She sniffles, "A real hug."

"I'll give you a big hug when I get back."

"JUANITA GET UP HERE. I'LL BE IN THE CAR."

Marie cringes and clings to me. I push her away.

"Leave me alone. I want to go. I'll never get this chance again."

"Wait, I need to talk to you for just one second."

"No. I can't. We can talk when I get back." I break free of her arms, dash into the bedroom and grab my jacket from the chair. It tips over. I don't stop to pick it up. Marie can. It's her fault I'm late.

I race past the cellar. Marie calls me again. Her voice breaks into a sob. I ignore her and run upstairs. I'll make it up to her when I get back home. I sprint through the kitchen and skid to a stop. Irma is blocking the door. She snatches the jacket from my hands and whips it at my head. "You don't need it. Your father has lost his mind. And just so you know this is a one-time exception. It won't be happening again. After today no leaving the yard, not even if you're dying. And at the park keep your mouth shut and stay to yourself. Understand me?" She steps aside but as I pass, she slaps the back of my head.

While the boys swim, I sit on the blanket and watch everybody having fun. I don't know anyone and if I did, I wouldn't dare join them because I know the moment I did, Dad would drive up and Irma would catch me red handed.

The sound of Dad's horn is the worse sound I hear all day but at least Irma isn't with him. I yell for Adam but he doesn't hear me.

"If you want, I can go get Drake and the others for you." A red headed girl, sitting on the next towel blows a giant pink bubble until it flattens over her nose. She peels it off and stuffs it in her mouth.

I cover my lips and look down. "How do you know Drake?"

"Er—well, he's in my friend's class and she has a crush on him."

While she talks about how cute Drake is, my eyes drift across the blanket of bodies stretched across a rainbow of towels. I'm tired of being barred out back or in my basement room. I'm sick of being friendless. I hate it that my life isn't normal anymore and it will suck if I don't get to come here ever again.

I try to picture this place in the winter. I console myself with how empty this place will be and wonder what do people do in the winter? Are they smiling then or are they cold and miserable like me?

"Hello, anybody in there?"

"Pardon?"

"I asked you where you live? You live with Drake, right?"

I nod, drag the blanket toward the car, and trip over it twice. The car doors are ajar and Dad is standing beside the open trunk. A bump from Drake sends me and the blanket against Dad's hip.

Dad crunches up the blanket, dirt and all, stuffs it in the trunk, slams the lid and in a hoarse voice says, "Get in the car."

"Oh I love your hair," Adam flutters his eyes at Drake, blows an imaginary bubble, curls his tongue around his nose and giggles.

"It was a red head, right? With hair as red as Drake's face."

"Almost as red as your shoulders. They look like raw meat."

Dad twists around in his seat and groans. "Why didn't you wear your jacket over your shoulders?"

"Irma took it."

He grits his teeth, slams his hand on the horn and leaves it there until the rest of the boys pile into the backseat. I'm not sure if he's mad at them, me, or Irma, but he's mad as heck at someone. He says nothing for the entire drive. The boys ask him questions but he remains lost in thought, until we get home. He slams the car door, and stomps up the steps. We trail close behind.

Irma is standing in the entry with her hands on her hips. "What took you so damn long?"

Dad points at the door to the basement. "All of you. NOW."

Halfway down the steps we hear, "What does it take to make you happy? I thought you'd be different, once we got rid of Marie. But you'll never be satisfied, will you? Who's next on your list?"

We stare at each other in shock

"They got rid of—" Someone covers my mouth.

"Ssshhh. Be quiet so we can hear where she is."

We huddle just past the bottom step and eavesdrop. My stomach feels like a car hit it. I glance at the cellar and burst into tears. And for once I don't care when I hear footsteps stomping toward the door above us. Everybody but me disappears.

"Get in your room, take off your top. Let me see the rest of your shoulders."

The corners of my mouth are touching my jaw bone. My whole body feels stiff. I push him away.

"Dad. Why? Why did you do it?"

He pins me down, picks at my shirt and examines my burn.

"Ouch. I'm stuck to my shirt."

"Don't move or try to get it off. I'll be back in a minute."

I pull out Marie's top drawer. It's empty. Nothing left in any of them other than some odd socks. My tonsils are stuck to the back of my throat. I lick my salty lips. I hate myself but I hate Dad more.

I don't say a word when he walks back in but my eyes won't stop yelling, 'I HATE YOU.' I hate me too for not listening to her.

Dad's sigh is broken and long, and my only thought is, I hope he chokes on it. He pauses, glances up at the ceiling, lowers his head and says, "She would have left next year anyway."

He puts the kettle on the dresser, shoves the drawers back in place and frowns at me. He pulls a pair of yellow rubber gloves from his left pocket.

He shakes the rubber glove above his opened palm and two tiny white pills tumble out.

"Here chew these." I curl up my lips and hold my hand under my chin. "No. Don't spit them out. It's aspirin. They'll help with the pain." My chest hurts so bad I decide to swallow them.

He undrapes the towel from his neck, folds it four times and says, "Bite it when you can't handle the pain."

Hot kettle water gurgles into the bowl. Steam swirls from the sponge as Dad wrings it out.

I shriek.

"Bite the towel as hard as you can."

By nightfall, my stinging shoulders are hot smoldering coals and before dawn, I open my eyes and find him changing my bandages. I drift back to sleep only to wake up moments later in unbearable pain.

I struggle to take off my top. The shoulders feel hard, like dried glue, not soft like the rest of my pajamas.

"No. Don't do that. You'll lose too many layers of skin."

I cringe the moment hot water flows from the kettle. Steam swirls upwards. "No-o-o-o-o Dad, it's going to hurt. It's too hot."

"No it's not. It only feels hot because you're burned so bad."

"But it's steaming. Look at it rising from your gloves."

"That's because the bowl is cold. I added ice cubes to cool it faster. That's why it's steaming. Now, lie on your stomach. The water has to be boiled but it isn't as hot as it seems."

"But you're wearing heavy gloves. You can't feel the HOTTT." He presses the sponge against my shoulders. I bite hard into the towel. An hour later my pajamas soak free and the bandages fall off. He smears ointment over my shoulders and tapes fresh gauze on them. "All done. Here have two more aspirins."

"Wait, don't go. Is Marie at Grandma's again? Is she coming back?" He turns around his eyes are watering worse than mine. "Yes," Dad lowers his voice, "but she won't be coming back."

"How come?"

"She needed a break."

"So a break means she'll be back, right?"

"Stop asking so many questions. Before you get into trouble."

"But—"

"No buts. Stay in bed until I get back. I have to go take the boys back to Barachois Park."

—•—•—•—

Once winter comes, no matter how bad the weather is I'm locked outside until after dark. I learn to fear weekends, dread storms and hate the bitter cold Christmas holidays. Each day, after school, I count my footsteps, stop, turn and make another row. At school I never go outside unless I'm forced to. During recesses and lunch hours, I hang out at the library and that's where I am when the principal's voice booms across the PA. It startles me out of my trance.

"Due to incoming severe inclement weather and a low windchill factor, school will be closing at noon. The temperature will hit subzero levels, not fit for animals, so be sure to keep any pets inside. The storm threatens to bring another three feet of snow which will cause another snow day close tomorrow."

In science we learned about windchill factors and how they made the temperature plummet even lower, but what I didn't have to learn from a book was what weather like that does to people. After every bad storm they always find some dead bodies, and so far, I haven't been one of them but this has been the fifth storm this month and each one seems to be worse than the last.

I find my brothers waiting for me at the school entrance. Halfway home, the weather turns nastier. Gusts of snow slap me in the face. My brothers and I hold hands to form a chain and for each two steps we take the wind blows us back one. The telephone wires looming above us are loaded with icicles, and the snow banks we walk on are so high, that two of my brothers can knock the icicles down with their book bags. By the time we reach the

97

house, all of us have white ice beads on our eyebrows and our hair is matted and frozen. We trudge up the driveway, through waist high snow.

The door is locked. Adam knocks for a good five minutes but the only response is the curtain moving. We take turns ringing the doorbell until everyone is too numb to move. The TV blares louder. Bruce spits at the door. "She heard us. Hear that? She turned the TV up to drown us out. I should bust the door down."

Drake nods toward the back, "Listen. Is that Pal?"

The howling wind smothers the sound but it seems like Pal is barking from somewhere inside the garage. Ryan and I huddle against the wall, while the older boys use their feet to clear the snow away from the side garage door.

"The shovel is buried around here somewhere," Adam's voice sounds muffled. He shoves his chin deeper into the neck of his jacket and tries to move the snow away with his bare hands. Drake shoves him aside, and fights to keep control of the garbage lid while he scrapes the snow away. Adam uses his elbows to rock the door back and forth until it opens enough to squeeze through. Cold and wet we take turns heating up our hands, on Pal's belly, while he licks our fingers back to life.

Dad's glove appears at the edge of the door and yanks it open. "Are you guys crazy? What are you doing out here? You're lucky you didn't perish."

Drake jerks his head toward the house. His mouth hardly moves. "Go ask her that question. She's the one who barred us all out and wouldn't let us in."

"She must not have known you were out here."

Bruce holds up his hands and flaunts his raw knuckles. "Well I guess she's must be deaf as a doornail."

"Supper's ready. Eat slow. It'll help warm you up."

We pile around the table. On top of my plate is a scoop of white creamy mush. Everybody else has sliced potatoes and cheese.

My supper looks like white glue with onions. It has no cheese and is mostly the oozing stuff scraped from the sides of the pan. My numb hands prickle with pins and needles. The fork escapes my grasp and clunks on my plate. Irma gives me a warning look. I chew the paste for a full minute squirting the onions between my teeth.

I reach for my milk but my fingers slip and the glass topples. White bubbles burst across the tablecloth.

Irma jumps up and grabs me by the roots of my hair. She screams, "You did that on purpose so you wouldn't have to eat it. Now you can drink it."

"She's not an animal Irma."

"Now you get nothing. I hope you starve to death."

I am half dangling above the top step. She lets me go. I topple down the stairs landing on my butt. The door above me slams shut. I sit on the bottom step and rub my throbbing hands against my aching skull. Strands of hair fall from my skull. I wait for an argument to start, for Dad to say something, for the door to open, but nothing happens.

I head to the bathroom and run the water until it's hot. As my hands come back to life, I realize the water isn't hot at all, it's only lukewarm, so I twist the hot tap higher. I keep my hands under the tap and wait for the buzzing to go away. In the bathroom mirror a stranger catches my eye. That stranger is me. How did I change so much? When did I change? My eyes are dull almost as dull as Irma's and I've forgotten how to smile. I don't even look like me anymore. I look like a skeleton with thin pasty pale skin.

I check my bedroom dresser mirror, hoping to find a different version of me. I look worse. Under my eyes the dark circles seem darker in this mirror, and one has a yellowish tint from the last time Irma slugged me. I stare at myself and wonder what I'll look like when I'm eighteen, if I live that long. I have at least another nine years of this life left—maybe six if they get rid of me early—like Marie.

I shiver in my blanket, hugging Marie's pillow. If Marie were here, she'd tell me to pray. With folded hands, I pray for God to take Irma away for good, and bring Marie and my mother back. I repeat the prayer every night, but the only thing that changes is Irma.

Day after day, week after week and month after month, Irma transitions into the worst monster imaginable. And despite all the snickering, school becomes my only refuge.

Juanita Ray

Every day my brothers and I trudge toward our prison camp, and bit by bit we lose a piece of who we are. The only time spent together, is walking home from school. Usually, as soon as we get near the house, my brothers stop clowning around and grow quiet. Today Adam breaks the silence. "I wonder who owns that car?"

The white car, parked in front of our lawn, blends in with the snowbank. As we pass by, the front window rolls down, and a plump woman with a pinched face asks, "Are you the Smith children?" Her eyes scan each of us from top to bottom. Her eyes stop and rest on me. I shift from foot to foot.

Bruce shakes his head. "Nope. Wrong house. We're the Roses."

Her lips curl into a faint smile. "Good I was hoping you were. I'm Mrs. Miles. I'm from Social Services."

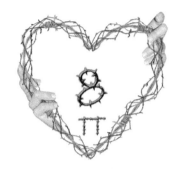

My Missing Sibling

It's a bleak, icy cold day with a furious wind. Nasty flurries swirl in circles and splatter across the five-foot-high snow drifts until they cover half of the upstairs windows. The lower two and three foot drifts are further away from the house but that's where the sleet hits the hardest.

My feet feel like two dead heavy rocks and I've lost all feeling in them and my hands. Exhausted, I fall face first into the snow waiting to smother to death. My jacket rises up into the air. Adam yells, "Keep moving."

"I can't," I gasp. "I can't feel my hands or my feet."

Adam carries me behind a tree, sits down, and settles me onto his lap. He bangs my frozen mitts against each other and says, "You clap and I'll sing."

"I can't feel my hands Adam. It's like someone changed them to wood."

"Then clap your elbows. I need a drummer." While he sings, he bangs my boots together. "First there is a mountain, then there is no mountain then there is, Oh Juanita, Oh Juanita I call your name."

For the first time ever, I feel jealous God took Mom and not me.

"Stop crying or your eyes will turn into ice cubes."

A laugh sneaks in between my sobs.

"I promise you we are going to get out of this mess."

"How?"

"I don't know. But by god, we will. You just have to get through a few more days. Before you know it, the holidays will be over and you'll be back to school and spring will be here."

I never thought I'd hate spring. I tried to hide my excitement when Irma said to stay out front. Now I'm horrified. Everyone passing by looks at me, the freak.

I count the water drops falling from the melting icicles. But icicles aren't the only thing dripping. My back is sopping wet. My hands are so sweaty, wool from my mittens is sticking to my fingers. Each time I get the urge to remove them, I hear Irma's voice in my head. 'Let's see who's underdressed now. I dare the neighbors to call social services and say you're outside freezing. And don't you dare take off that coat or those mittens if you know what's good for you.'

I shade my eyes and look up at the sun. Soon it will shift to the back yard and I'll be able to find a shady spot near the corner.

I move out of view of most windows and fumble to unbutton my coat, but while wearing my mittens, that's impossible. By the third button, I can barely breathe. Sweat drips from the sides of my face and the tip of my nose. I tug on the scarf but stop when I hear a sharp rapping from the window. It slides open.

Irma snarls, "Button up that coat."

The window slams shut.

I march up and down the driveway counting my steps. So far, I have walked up and down it thirteen times. Salty sweat trickles into my mouth while I count. I'm too hot and dizzy to play this game.

Two worn shoes walk toward me. The feet in the shoes belong to Claudette Miles. "A tad warm, are we?"

Battered

I'm too nauseated and woozy to talk. Her fingers press against my throat. "Who tied this so tight?" Her plump fingers pry the scarf from my neck. "It's a wonder you can breathe."

"Please Mrs. Miles—" The curtains move. My back stiffens.

"Child you can call me Claudette and for God's sake don't look so petrified. I don't bite and I don't . . ." Her eyes follow mine. "I get it. I take it I'm what terrifies you?"

Sharon, is standing at the end of the driveway, wearing a sleeveless cotton dress, like the ones I used to get for Easter. Mrs. Miles beckons her over.

The salt is stinging my eyes. I squint at Sharon. She frowns and taps my winter boots with the toe of her sandals. "Aren't you hot?"

"Of course she's hot. You could probably fry on egg on her. Stand next to Juanita. Closer." Claudette takes a camera out of her pocket and shoots a couple of pictures. A couple wearing T-Shirts wait while their dog poops on our lawn. She takes a picture of them and says, "We wouldn't want people to think Sharon was underdressed for the weather, now would we."

She pulls off my mitts and stuffs them in my coat pockets. Dad's car pulls up as Mrs. Miles hangs my coat across her arm.

His face is beet red. I'm not sure if he's mad at me or Irma but after Mrs. Miles leaves all hell breaks loose.

I lie on the floor and print I won't tell anyone, line after line, until my fingers cramp. I run them under hot water twice, and by the time I'm finished, I'm starved. I grab the three pages run up the steps and stop. I should wait until she calls. Before I can turn back, her shadow looms in the doorway.

"If you're coming for dinner, forget it, you're too late."

She reaches for the papers, and twists my wrist. "Don't you ever forget what you wrote. If anyone asks you anything you tell them nothing. Not one word. Do you understand me? What happens in this house, stays in this house, understand?"

I wince and nod.

She yanks my arm past her forcing me to hit the wall. "Now get your ugly self out of my kitchen."

Juanita Ray

I dash for my room but stop dead in my tracks. The rocking chair is rocking back and forth on its own, again. I tiptoe toward it. It's been doing that for months. Maybe it's Mom's ghost. I jump in it hoping to land on her lap. I close my eyes and wonder what she smells like.

"Juanita."

I slide out of the chair and land on my butt.

"Juanita."

Adam is standing over me.

"It's you, isn't it?"

"Me what?"

"It's you making the chair rock."

"Would I do that?" he laughs. His smile fades. He bites his bottom lip. "How many meals besides supper did you miss today?"

"None."

"What did you have for breakfast and lunch?"

"The same. Soggy cereal at eleven o'clock."

He pulls four small cookies from a paper wrapper and hands them to me. "It's not much but it's all I could take without getting caught."

"Where are these from?"

Adam winks and says, "I'll never tell."

I nibble on the cookies while Adam rocks in the chair. His eyes are solemn. The shine is missing. The Adam I knew was always laughing. He spent most of his time playing jokes and plotting the next one before the last prank was over. This new Adam is nervous, worries about everything and has dark circles under his eyes. Dark circles like mine.

Dad's voice makes us both jump. "Everyone. Up here on the double." Panic washes over me. My shoes feel like heavy bricks as I trudge toward the kitchen. "Get in here and sit down." Dad pulls the table out from the kitchen wall. "Do any of you have an inkling to Marie's whereabouts? Juanita, did she tell you anything?"

"No-o-o-o."

"None of you have any idea where she is?"

"You said she went to Grandma's," I say. My voice has a nervous squeak to it.

Dad drums the table with his fingers. "Well, she didn't."

"So where do you suppose she is?" Adam's voice is strained.

"If I knew that I wouldn't be asking you guys, now would I?"

"Maybe you should call Grandma," Adam says.

"I don't need to. Your grandma just called and said Marie hasn't been around since two summers ago."

Irma's heels click across the kitchen floor. She leans against the sink and scowls. "Ned, maybe the old bat's gone senile."

"I doubt it. She called you by name"

"Me? By name? What did she say about me, word for word?"

"She said, 'other than seeing Marie two years ago, I have not seen hide nor hair of any of the kids since Irma came.'"

"Oh really? What else did that old bitch say?"

"That's was it. So, calm down."

"Raise her rent. See how she likes it when she can't afford that. Better still, sell the damn house. We don't need it. Move her into an old age home. A cheap one."

"Irma this isn't the time. Please."

Dad unfolds his arms, shoves both hands deep inside his pockets and jingles a bunch of change until Irma yells, "Stop that. It drives me nuts."

Adam leans back on his chair and stares straight at Dad. For a split second, hate flashes across his eyes. "Then why did you guys tell us she was at Grandma's?"

Coins fly across the room and bounce mercilessly against the wall. Dad's fist pounds down on the table with a deafening bang. Adam's chair hits the floor. A few coins roll to my feet and spin to a stop.

"It's where she was supposed to go when we put her on the train. Where the hell else could she possibly go with twenty bucks to her name?"

Goodbye Gallant Street

The cellar is dark and threatening. I draw a deep breath and take one step inside. It has no light or window, because it was built to store vegetables and fruits, but like everything else in the basement, it never got finished. The black tarpaper on the walls makes it the spookiest and darkest room downstairs. Every time I pass it, I hold my breath and run, except for today.

Adam said the reason it feels colder than the rest of the basement is because a bunch of ghosts live in there. It always feels eerie to pass it, especially since this is the last place, I saw Marie. The memory of our last encounter weighs heavily on my mind. She tried to tell me something but selfish me didn't stop to listen. Maybe she knew where she was going. She could have had a plan for us. If only I had stayed. If only I could reverse time. If only Irma had not come. If only Irma had died and not Mom. If only I wasn't born. But all my only thoughts, are nothing but lonely wishes.

In the middle of my toxic thoughts, I see something shine from the corner of the cellar floor. It flickers when I move. I shift my body left and it disappears. I shift my body right and it flickers. I turn to leave and find all of my brothers directly in front of me. By Adam's reaction, I know he sees it too. Unafraid he gets on all fours and ventures into the darkness.

"Don't Adam. I have a bad, weird feeling."

Ryan shakes his head in slow motion and gives me the, there will never be any hope for you look, then he and the others go into their bedroom, while Adam continues to crawl around inside the cellar.

"It's pitch-black in here. Move so some light shines in. Wait! Do you hear that? I swear there's a wind in here. There it is again."

A faint scratching sound comes from the far corner. "Adam what's that noise? Are you okay?"

"H-h-h-help," Adam's voice is barely audible. It sounds as if he's being attacked. I move closer and peer deeper inside. A scuffling noise, a thump and a yelp, then nothing. I try taking another step but I can't move. My body won't bulge. I'm frozen.

"Grrr-rrr-rrrrr!"

I jump out of my skin, cover my mouth and run to my room. Adam laughs hysterically, races past me, and flops on my bed.

"Go away!" I push him out of my room. "I want a door! A door that I can lock. A door like the one at the top of the stairs. A door to keep you out."

"Trust me you don't want a door. Right now, you can move around in the basement because you don't have one. You can run out and nobody can bar you in. A door is not your friend . . . never a friend."

Adam leans against my doorframe. He has a quarter in each eye socket. "I found these on the cellar floor. Do you know why people bury corpses with coins covering their eyes?"

"What kind of coins?"

"Two quarters. It's how you pay the ferryman."

"For what?"

"When people die, you have to put a quarter in each eye to pay the ferryman for transportation to afterlife."

I tell him how I dropped them that day and how Marie was trying to let me know what was happening to her. "Maybe if I had listened, we would know where she is now."

He hands me both quarters.

"I don't want them. You can keep them."

He isn't laughing anymore. We don't talk. We just sit and stare at the quarters. Five minutes later, without a word, Adam leaves. I press Marie's pillow against my face and rock myself to sleep.

"Aren't you supposed to be packing?"

I can tell by her voice I'm already in trouble.

She hits me on the back of my head and says, "Turn around and look at me when I talk to you." She grabs my hair and twists my head to face her. A sharp pain travels from my neck to my shoulder. "Get off the bed." She yanks me to her right.

The wall stops my fall.

"Why do you have seven piles of clothes?" She rips the top sheet from my bed. My seven days, scatter and fall to the ground. She rips the case from my pillow and reaches for the second pillow. I hold my breath. Do something. Stop her before she gets the locket.

"IRMA," Dad bellows from upstairs. "We need more boxes."

She digs her claws in to my scalp, shoves me across the bed, and says, "I'll be right back," and runs upstairs.

I sit on the floor and think about Marie. If we move how will she ever find us? Moving reminds me of death. The last time we moved, after Mom died, the car trunk was filled with sleeping bags and bedding. Each of us had a bag of clothes sitting on our laps. Dad wanted nothing to do with any of Mom's things, while Marie wanted nothing but Mom's things and until Irma moved in, that was Dad and Marie's only argument. When Marie refused to leave without Mom's belongings, Dad left her on the doorstep, sitting beside two garbage bags, wearing Mom's favorite hat. He drove to the edge town before he swerved the car around to go back and get her but

Battered

Marie and the garbage bags had vanished back inside. When Dad trudged back to the car, carrying a bag in each hand he was wearing a bucket on his head and Marie was smiling. He made the boys cram their pillowcase of valuables between their feet, handed them the garbage bags and tossed me the 'barf bucket'.

Nobody wanted to move, especially Marie. She kept telling Dad it was a big mistake and she was right.

"Knock-knock. You okay?"

"Adam do you remember moving here? How sick I got? What if I get that sick again?"

"I got you covered. I reminded Dad to buy you some anti-nausea pills. He plans to give you one every four hours."

I pick up my clothes and throw them on the bed. "Moving here was the biggest mistake Dad ever made."

"No that's not true. Dad's biggest mistake was Irma."

"So much for Claudette Miles fixing things," I mutter.

"She may have fixed things better than you think. It might be why we're moving out. Dad and Irma have been arguing nonstop."

"They always argue."

"Yes, but this time they could be splitting up. I think Irma's in big trouble and won't be moving with us."

That night my only prayer is to thank God for getting Irma in trouble and for him to leave her behind.

Evicted

Adam's loud yell resonates through every room in the house. We pile down the hall to find him lathered in soapsuds. "Which one of you did this?" "Don't just stand there. Quick. Somebody help me." He takes a deep breath, disappears inside the foamy cloud and dives back out, gasping for air. Jiggling bubbles glisten and burst above his head. He sucks in more air until his cheeks are full and dives back in. Three dives later he gives up.

Drake grabs the vacuum from the hall, puts the hose in the exhaust end and blows Adam clean. He turns off the vacuum and asks, "What would happen if we sucked it up? It's mostly air right?"

Adam coughs and sputters. "I only put in half a cup. One of you had to add more."

"Is this the same wash I started? The one with my sheets?" I ask.

"How much did you use? Half the box?"

"Did not Drake." I flick some suds at him. "It's Adams fault. He's the one who added more."

Battered

Drake tilts his head sideways, jiggles his finger in his ear, wipes his finger on his shirt, and says, "Let's just hope they get stuck in traffic. If Irma gets back before we clean this up, we may as well dig our graves this very minute."

"Hang on I have an idea. If we can stay dry, we can act like it just happened." Adam rushes upstairs and within seconds, he's back with a few large dark garbage bags. He keeps one and hands the rest to the boys. Adam rips a slit in the bottom and two on each edge. He slips it over his head. Bruce helps him by guiding his arms through the holes in the sides.

Adam says, "Drake to go outside with the vacuum and Bruce put on a garbage bag and give me a hand."

"No way." Bruce grabs the hose from Drake. "I'm not going in there—in that. Besides, vacuuming is still my job."

"Fine. Ryan you go help Bruce. Get an extension cord and plug it in the side of the house. Bruce, when I open the window, make sure you throw in as much hose as you can."

"Wait!" Drake takes the hose off the exhaust and attaches it to the suction opening. He extends it several feet by adding an extension hose. Then he hands the vacuum to Bruce. After Bruce and Ryan leave for the back yard, Adam laughs so hard he looks like he's having some sort of seizure. "Drake you don't suppose they'll get electrocuted, do you?"

Drake howls. "What if the vacuum cleaner blows up?"

They howl some more, take a deep breath and paddle their way through the bubbles.

My job is to watch for Dad. The boys are barely finished when the car pulls in the driveway. He jumps out and directs a huge truck to park in on the lawn. If nobody knows we're moving, they must be blind and deaf. The truck is the size of two school buses, the words, moving company, are painted across it in bright red letters and its brakes sound like fog horns. I close the curtain and go outside. The boat is crammed full of boxes, sleeping bags and suitcases, partially covered by a gray tarp, that's tied tight with bright yellow ropes.

Juanita Ray

"Adam you come with me. Let's do one last check and make sure every room is empty."

"Cripers. I did all the bedding earlier but I forget to switch the load from the washer to the dryer."

"Let the movers worry about it, while I check the garage, you bring Juanita back in and make sure she pees before we leave and why do you smell like a wet dog?"

"Dad where's Pal" I run after him. "We forgot Pal!"

Adam pulls me back and holds me against the house. "Be quiet. It's too late. Pal's gone."

"Gone where?"

Adam's voice breaks, "Just gone." His eyes edge to the corner of the fence.

"No-o-o-o." Sounds of anguish tear from my throat. Adam muffles them with his hand. "Pull yourself together. Hitting the house won't bring him back."

"Adam, I hate them. I hope someone shoots both her and him. I really do. I hate them both so-so much." I pry myself from Adam's grip. "And I hate you too, for not stopping it."

"I didn't know until it was too late."

"But why? Why do it?" I wipe my snotty nose on my sleeve.

"Probably because of the move. Maybe there was no room. Maybe he was sick. I don't know why. Dad makes no sense anymore. I just know we have to leave. Come on we have to go now."

Adam drags me to the car and pulls me into the back seat.

Irma has an ugly scowl on her face. "This new place better be as nice as you say it is, Ned."

Dad laughs and teases her about being too spoiled.

I wish he was never born. I wish Mom married someone else and then had us. I wish my dog was in the front seat instead of that witch.

I close my eyes and pray, dear God, please let me get car sick and vomit right over the two of them.

Battered

Each time I swallow, the lump in my throat grows bigger. Did Pal whimper like Dork did, when he died? How many times did Dad have to shoot this dog?

I cup my hands around Adam's ear and say, "Dad's a murderer."

Drake whispers something to Bruce and chuckles.

Irma twists around. "Stop whispering."

For half an hour Irma complains about every person we ever knew or liked. She says mean things about Uncle Joe and Aunt Patty. She rants about the nerve of 'mutt-faced' Claudette Miles, until her tongue gives out and everything is deadly quiet.

"I hope we have a car crash and everyone dies! I hate everyone!"

I glance around to see who said it. Irma reaches back and slaps at the space in front of my face. My brother's eyes pop out of their heads. Their mouths hang open.

It's then I realize it's me. I'm the one who said it.

Irma retries to hit me but misses again. "Go ahead and kill me too. Then you can bury me in the back yard with Pal."

Ryan yells, "You said you were giving him to Uncle Joe, you're a liar! I hate you too!"

Irma can't reach far enough into the back seat to get us. "Ned, stop the car this minute and do something, or I'll jump back there myself and strangle both of them."

The car jerks to a stop. Irma's door flings open. I hope she throws me out of the car so I can go back and live with Uncle Joe. I shut my eyes and brace myself for whatever's coming.

"Let go!"

My eyes flick open. Dad face is six inches from hers. "I'll let you go alright. Go out that door and you walk. I've got nine hundred miles to drive and I'm already sick of listening to you. Close the door and shut up or get the hell out of my car."

I close my eyes and desperately pray, God let her leave, let her leave, please make her leave. If you do, I promise to be a nun or a priest, anything you want. Irma closes the door, grunts and says, "Trust me, you will regret this one for the rest of your life."

The entire trip is filled with the sound of tires beating against uneven pavement and the occasional bridge swooshing by. The trees blur as we speed past them. Even the rain doesn't slow Dad down.

I reach to hold Adam's hand, but it's as limp as a dead fish. I seem to be the only one awake. I close my eyes and listen to the swishes and flapping of the wipers until they lull me to sleep.

Then the nightmare starts. I dream I'm on a deserted shore. I take off my shoes, wade through some shallow water, and climb up a tall craggy rock that has a flat top. A huge wave hits and ebbs around the rock until it reaches near the top. The water seeps up the shore until the shoreline is unreachable. My shoes drift past me. Cold water swirls above my ankles. The sound of splattering gets louder until it reaches my neck. Then I wake up.

I'm lying on a hard cold floor. Thuds and thumps come from the hall. Everyone is grunting and out of breath. The noise continues for at least an hour. Every footstep sounds like thunder clapping in the distance. Every sound echoes from wall to wall.

"Keep it down." The voice sounds muffled and is accompanied by a knocking sound. Irma bangs her fist on the wall. Someone bangs back. Irma bangs harder, and the battle begins.

Five minutes later, the doorbell rings.

"It's our landlord. She could be looking to pick up the rent."

"You didn't pay her yet?" Irma asks.

"I mailed her a check but she hasn't cashed it yet."

"You rented this over the phone, didn't you?"

"Mr. Rose. I know you're in there. I'm not deaf."

After exchanging a few words, a thin neck supporting a mop of yellow curls stretches past the door frame and glances left and right.

"Doesn't look like you had a chance to destroy it, so here."

She rips a check in half, passes it to him and walks away.

Dad frowns at Irma. "Looks like we've been evicted."

"She can't do that. We rented the place a month ago."

"Had she cashed the check, you'd be right." He drops the pieces of the check onto the counter. "Apparently her daughter, who lives next door, told her we sounded like a bunch of wild animals."

"That's ridiculous. Go change her mind."

"There's no point. She's convinced we'll destroy the place."

Irma runs to the door and yells, "Everything sounds loud when you move into an empty house at four in the morning. Now we're making noise you eavesdropping, no good for nothing bitch."

A strange smile lurks on her lips as she watches the boys trample out with the last of the boxes. The smile is still there when we drive away.

Dad's relaxed smile widens into a grin. "I can't believe you left a mess behind. And here I thought you had OCD."

"Shut up Ned. I just like my house to be clean and stay clean. I couldn't care less what happens to hers."

We pass some barracks, and just before the road ends, a small lonely house appears to our left. The sound of crunching gravel announces our arrival. Fine wisps of dust hover around our ankles as we hop out of the car and circle the trailer. Dad drops the chain from the hitch and leaves us standing in a cloud of dust.

Adam coughs, gags, bats at the air, and gropes for the doorknob. I trudge behind him kicking at the dust fumes. The worn hallway has two openings and three doors. To the left is a small living room no bigger than my old bedroom. The kitchen is the same size and has a short counter and a chipped porcelain sink. The first door past the kitchen is a tiny bathroom with one sink and a shower stall. The small window above the toilet rumbles as a plane flies overhead.

Adam's eyebrows arch upwards. "Is this a bedroom or a walk-in closet?"

"I don't get it. Did you see Irma smile? This place is smaller than the house she moved from."

"Oh I guarantee you she's not smiling about living here. Let's go outside and help unpack the trailer."

"But the boxes are too heavy for me and I want to see the rest of the place."

"If you want to see the rest of the place it's this way—outside." He prods me toward the door. "Go see if there's a shed out back."

Outside is a whole lot of nothing. Not a single neighbor within sight. Just a long dirt road leading to high voltage warning sign and a wire fence that hums hello from across the road. The hum falls silent under the roar of another low flying plane.

"There's no shed, so where do they plan to put everything?"

"In storage," Bruce wipes streaks of dirty sweat across his brow. "They left to rent a unit and meet the movers. They're supposed to be—" A plane circles overhead. I unplug my ears once it lands.

"Get used to it." He points toward the wire fence. "That's an air base."

When Dad worked at the base in Stephenville, we never lived this close to the barracks, and now I get why.

Drake mutters. "I'm done. The rest of these boxes are your share. I bet we'll be here less than a week and we'll be moving all over again."

Bruce grunts, "Why?" and passes him another box.

"Because it's no better than the house Irma lived in before us."

Ryan picks up a dusty blade of grass and chews on it, and asks, "Where's everybody going to sleep?"

Adam points at a tent in the hull of the boat.

"Funny. Ha-ha-ha." I wrinkle my noise at them. After they erect the tent and unroll sleeping bags, I realize it wasn't a joke. A gasp slips from between my lips. "What about the winter?"

"Then the tent's all yours," Adam says. "By then us boys'll be in the new house."

Ryan pokes his head from above a box. "What new house."

"The one Dad expects us to build over the summer."

By November the tent is stored away, we're sleeping on the floor instead of the ground and the house won't be finished until next summer.

The sound of the wind, sweeping blankets of snow against the window, lulls me into a deep sleep. I wake up with a jolt of pain in my ribs. Irma's foot slams against the sleeping bag again. This time she gets me in the stomach. She holds up a small bottle of milk. "Why didn't you drink this?" she shrieks. I'm stuttering so bad I can't answer her. She hauls me outside and pushes me into a snow bank.

I panic. I can't breathe. My limbs won't move. I can't yell.

She screams at Dad's car. "If you think I am looking after your damn kids while you go bowling without me, you're out of your mind. You can take this hateful thing with you or better still, let her lie here and freeze."

The taillights flicker. The car hurtles backwards toward me. My voice still won't work. The back fender hits the snow bank near me. His tires spin. He rocks the car back and forth. I open my mouth. My vocal cords shrivel up. The faster I gasp the less air I get.

A cackling noise sounds from my throat. I close my eyes, flood my lungs with air, and push out a blood-curdling scream.

The car engine is still running when he scoops me up. My teeth chatter uncontrollably. With one arm, he whips off his coat and wraps it around me. He rattles the doorknob, bangs the door, wraps two arms around me, takes two steps backwards, shivers and kicks the door until it cracks and splinters. It seems like forever before someone opens it.

"Quick, go pour her a hot bath." Dad's voice sounds as cold as ice. He lifts my face up. "You okay?"

I stutter incoherently as Irma charges at me, like an angry bull.

The Man with the Rope Belt

From the bathroom, I can hear Adam's high pitched voice echoing through the open beams. "Juanita, oh Juanita, come out wherever you are.". I find him on his hands and knees with his head tucked under my bed.

"Adam why do you guys get bigger windows than me? Why is mine so small and so high up?"

"Because this room is at the front side of the house where the ground is higher. You're lucky you even got one. Dad wasn't going to put one there but I talked him into it."

"What are the white spots on the walls?"

"Spackle. There's tape underneath to cover the nail holes and the seams. Feel how smooth I mudded the gyprock."

"Gyprock?"

"Gyprock is that gray wallboard. Some people call it drywall. The spackle gets sanded and causes that white dust." He brushes my arm. "The stuff you're covered in. What did you do, rub up against every seam you could find?"

"No. For your information, I walked through open beams, so I don't know where this came from."

"It's probably in the air. We swept this place twice and all it did was rise up and settle back down quicker than you could prop up the broom. Too bad the windows don't open."

"How come the windows don't open?"

"I don't know but I'm surprised Irma didn't make Dad put bars down here."

"Do you think Irma might act nicer now that she's got the house she always wanted." The room turns darker as a shadow crosses my window. Dad's boot appears in front of the glass and taps on it. He yells something in a muffled voice.

"Oh, I almost forgot. Dad sent me to get you. He wants you to help us."

"Do what?"

"You'll see."

I spend the rest of the day crawling through a barbed wire fence in the forest beside our house gathering branches while the boys cut down some saplings. The branches are taller than I am, so I drag them through the trail and toss them one by one over the barbed wire fence.

Adam pries the barbed wire apart to let me through. "Never mind picking twigs out of the wire, help me get these, over to the side of the house." He grunts and groans under the load. I pick up a branch and do the same. "Really? That must be busting your back, or is that the twig groaning?"

Up ahead Dad swings the mallet above his head and pounds a spear into the ground. The two long lines of skinny tree trunks look like giant pencils. He crisscrosses them to build a framework. I sit on the top step and watch a giant walkway on stilts grow until it reaches the far end of the yard. It looks like an elevated wooden driveway. Dad leans against the boat admiring his handiwork.

The door digs into my back. "Next time move," Irma growls. My elbows are stinging and my knees are burning. Before I can get up off the ground,

119

Irma steps over me and tosses empty white buckets into the boat. She kisses Dad and says, "I'm ready whenever you are."

Dad lifts two fingers under his tongue. A loud shrill whistle gets everyone's attention. "Let's get rolling. Everybody in the car. Adam, you and Juanita can ride in the boat."

Adam hops in and pulls me up.

The boat swings left and right but straightens out once we get past a giant sign for a flower shop. I point to it. "I don't see any flower shop. Where is it?"

"It's a bunch of greenhouses, up at the far end of that lane."

A bucket rolls against my foot. "Why do we have all these barf buckets."

Adam ignores me and smiles while he waves at anyone who'll look at him. "Juanita, wave down to the lovely peasants." Adam takes the oars and waves them in the air. "See how fast I can row. We must be going sixty or more." The boat jerks and the oar barely misses a passing car. "He jerks the oar to the right. Fast, aren't I?"

Dad blows his horn and puts his fist out the window.

"That's sign language for stop," Adam grins, "I know more sign language but Dad's watching, so I can't show you right now."

I open my mouth to laugh and inhale the unmistakable smell of the ocean. Dad slows to a stop. While Adam passes down the fishnets and buckets. I try to spot a wharf. Nothing not even one single fishing pole, yet the whole place smells like fish guts.

Dad and Irma yell at each other but I can't make out what they're saying because giant thunderous waves roll over the beach and drown every other sound out. The same roaring wave opens its jaw and spits thousands of foam bubbles across the shoreline. Then the foam turns into white fish bellies that skip and flip across the pebble-filled beach.

"Let's get this show on the road!" Dad yells. My brothers race into the water and scoop up a bucket of fish. "Go watch your brothers and do whatever they do."

I take off my shoes and wade into the cold water, and mimic my brothers. In seconds I have a bucket of gaping fish.

Battered

I am mesmerized by thousands of white bellies and black backs, shimmering in the sun. I set mine free to join them.

"What are you doing?" Adam taps me on the head. "Hello. Anybody home?"

"Is this where Jesus turned three fish into thousands?"

"No. This is where it takes a thousand fish to make three worth eating."

Drake wades over, hands me his bucket and takes my empty one. "Take it to the boat." He waves away the seagulls but they keep circling and swooping, to scoop the skinny little fish, into their overstuffed beaks. "We've got some fierce competition," Drake yells, as another flock of seagulls, skid across the beach, gobbling their fill. Another roaring wave refills the buffet. "Don't touch those," Dad yells. "Scoop them up fresh from the surf."

It takes twenty minutes to fill the boat and twice as long to get home. Along the way fish flop against my knees and flip out of the boat. A few hit the windshield of a bus. "Why were there so many fish there? What's that place called?"

A slow smooth smile lights up Adam's face. "God's country."

The passing bus flattens a few fish and reveals a sign on the far right. "It's not God's Country. That says Middle Cove. You're a big fat liar."

"God's Country is all of Newfoundland. Ask anybody."

"But you said it was called the rock."

"It's like us. It has three names," he laughs.

The fish roll to the end of the boat, as Dad swerves the trailer up into the driveway.

"Do we have to eat all of these for the rest of our lives?"

"If it was up to Irma, yes, but lucky for us, Dad plans to bury most of them in the ground for fertilizer."

My thoughts flip from the twitching fish to Pal. "That's not fair to catch fish just to bury them. Dad's as bad as Irma."

Irma stalks around the trailer. I stiffen, hold my breath and wait to get slapped in the head. "Get those fish back in the buckets."

Slimy fish slip between my fingers. I can't seem to get a hold of them. Adam winks at me and uses the bucket and his boot to get them in.

"They stink like crazy."

"You think this is bad?" Adam smirks. "Wait 'til next week."

Two days later, the stench coming from our back yard is putrid.

The reek of rotting capelin is overpowering, so unbearable Irma insists Dad take her out for dinner. As they leave, Dad points at the flake and orders us to turn every fish over so the sun can dry the other side. "Before tonight, I want every one of them turned."

As soon as the car leaves, my brothers fight over who steadies the ladder and who has to turn the capelin. While they head into the garage to get the ladders, I run up the lane past the sign, and find the greenhouses at the far end. Rows of plastic buildings stretch as far as I can see. I promise myself to only stay fifteen minutes and not a second longer. I peak inside a doorway and suck in my breath. Rows and rows of plants cover every inch of every bench. For every plant on the ground, there's one hanging above. I saunter through the plastic rooms and touch every plant I can reach. Drips of water splatter on my arm, lady bugs flutter from plant to plant and the scent of flowers mingles with the earthy smell of fresh clay.

I bend to smell a rose. My nose tickles and the loudest sneeze I ever made, attracts an old man, waving a pair of cutters.

"I don't see any parents with you so scat!"

I run as fast as I can toward the house but stop dead when I see Dad's car in the driveway. I run back up the lane toward the old man. I'd rather face him than Irma. Surprisingly I don't have to. He's vanished.

An open meadow of wild flowers to my left, leads to a thin patch of trees that ends at the edge of a short dirt road with only two houses on it. I cross the main street, and dart into the woods, and head through the trees toward the capelin smell. I duck behind the flake, hold my nose and wait the longest time before venturing toward the door. The car is gone and I can hear the boys laughing.

They're sitting around the table joking loudly. Everyone hushes and turns when I close the door.

Ryan bites into a chicken leg. "Where were you?"

"Outside. Out back."

"No, you weren't—you're lying. I know that because I'm the one Dad sent outside to look for you."

"Well you obviously didn't look hard enough," Adam glares at Ryan. "And stop talking with your mouth full."

"Yes Irma."

"I'll Irma you. If she were here, she'd shove that chicken bone down your throat."

I glance toward the living room then back at Adam.

"Don't worry, they won't be back until late. Dad dropped off some chicken and left me in charge. Lucky for you Irma waited in the car." He nods to a plate. "I made sure to save you some."

I nibble on my chicken savoring every single bite. After the others scatter, I help Adam clean up.

"What's wrong?"

"I miss helping Marie clean up. I still worry if she's okay."

"Me too." A grimace clouds Adams face. "How about," he raises his brows "you and I play ping-pong."

I learn how to serve by tossing the ball straight up in the air, but I can't seem to hit it right. Frustrated I pull back and swing as hard as I can. The ball ricochets behind the large piece of wood that covers the plastic covered opening to the back yard.

"Young lady you just forfeited the game. Now go fetch the ball."

"Don't care. And, I'm not a dog." Wiggling through the gap between the wood and the wall I climb five steps and point at the opaque plastic. "What's the point of this plastic? Is Dad building a small greenhouse?"

"It's until he makes a door."

"Why can't he just buy one." A gust of wind billows against the plastic.

"He did, but it didn't fit. But that's greenhouse grade. Nice and thick."

My eyes scan every crevice. "The balls not anywhere."

Adam pulls the boards toward him. "Come down out of there, before you get hurt."

123

"Let me help," I say. I reach for the wood panel and grunt.

"Get out of the way. If these boards fall on your head, they could kill you."

"Can you teach me all about ping-pong?"

"Maybe next time they're gone," he says with a grin.

"But—but that could be a year or two away."

"I don't think so. This morning I caught Dad loading Irma's suitcases in his trunk." He raises his eyebrows, like pieces of proof.

"Maybe he's finally getting rid of her," I say with a doubtful smile.

"Dad doesn't have enough guts to do—Hear that? Sounds like they're back. I'll go see if it's them. Wait in your room."

In two minutes, he's back.

"It's them alright and Dad wants you outside."

My throat tightens.

"Don't worry. He only wants us to help with the fish."

Bruce and Ryan have clothes pins hanging from their noses. One is flipping capelin while the other tosses the rotten ones in a bucket. Dad appears to be supervising. He hands me the pail. "Bring these to Drake. He's over by the driveway making a flowerbed."

I squeeze my nose and wrap my other hand around the handle.

"Don't drop them. Use two hands."

I find Drake leaning on a shovel. I hand him the pail. His smirk widens. He points at his chest shakes his head, points at me and nods. "That's your job. Mine's digging. Toss two in each hole."

"No way."

"Would you rather have Bruce's job and crawl all over the capelin, picking out dead ones? Smells way better over this way." I pick one up by its crusty tail but it breaks away from my fingers and topples into the hole. Drake dumps the entire bucket in and fills in the hole with soil.

"What are we doing? Having a funeral for the dead capelin?"

Adam drops a pallet of plants at Drakes feet. He makes the sign of a cross on his chest. "May their souls rest in peace."

Drake laughs. "Dad's making Irma a flower bed."

Battered

Adam whispers in my ear, "Hang in there. Tomorrow will be a better day." He grins and walks away.

Drake moves a foot away, swings the pickaxe high above his head and slams it against the ground. The pickaxe bounces up and pierces his forehead. Blood gushes down his face. I run inside and yell, "Drake's bleeding to death. He split his skull wide open."

Two eggs splatter to the floor.

Irma leaves the fridge door open and runs outside. Drake has his shirt pressed against his forehead. "It's just a scratch. Nothing ice won't fix."

Irma glares at me. I back away from the open door until I bang into the fridge. Her out clenched hand hovers above my head. She grips me by the neck. I lose my balance and reach for the fridge shelf. A carton of eggs crashes to the floor. She shuts the door and slams my head against it

"See the trouble you cause?" She slams my head into the fridge door again. "Are you deaf? Answer me. Do you see the trouble you caused? I SAID ANSWER ME."

Bloods rolls down the fridge and drips to the floor.

"ANSWER ME."

"Yes," I cry, "I see and I'm sorry."

She drags me by the hair and shoves me downstairs. "Get the hell out of my site. If you think for one minute you are going to ruin my week, you've got another thing coming."

I crawl under my bed and sob. I can taste blood in the back of my throat. It reminds me of the first day I saw her. The day of my sixth birthday. I would trade every present I ever got back then, if God would just take her. The concrete feels cold against my back. Slowly my room turns different shades of gray until everything is pitch-black and every noise in the house fades to quiet. I slide out from under the bed, crawl between the cold sheets and shiver myself to sleep.

The next morning, I wake up to sun rays shining in my room. I creep out of bed, sneak to the bathroom and use one of my socks to wash the crusty brown blood from my face. I clean the sink, wring out the sock and stuff it under Marie's old dresser to dry.

Juanita Ray

I hear Dad's car drives past my window. Usually he leaves at eight but I can tell by the beams in my window that it's ten o'clock. I know in one hour, Irma will call me for a bowl of soggy cereal, my one daily meal.

"Juanita. Oh, Juanita I call your name. Come get your breakfast. Hurry up or I'll eat it." Excited I dash upstairs and find Adam singing to the radio and flipping eggs. "How would you like yours? Scrambled or fried?"

"I don't know." I feel the bump on my forehead and stare at the fridge door. "I don't think I like eggs. Where's everyone?"

He tosses some toast onto the counter. "Hand me that butter. Never mind, you're too short. I'll get it. The trick to tasty toast is to butter it while it's hot." He passes me the plate. "What else do you want on it?"

"This is all for me?"

"Yes, all two slices." He laughs. He lines several jars of spreads in front of me and says, "Take your pick, little lady."

"Can I pick two?"

"Pick as many as you like."

"Which ones would you pick Adam?"

He taps the jar of cheese spread and the peanut butter.

"Where are Dad and Irma?"

"I killed Irma and Dad in their sleep, Bruce dumped their bodies in the back seat and Drake is driving them to the dump."

Bruce pulls out a chair and sits beside me. "Tell the truth Adam. Where are they."

"I don't know and I don't care. They went somewhere on vacation."

Ryan dips his finger into the peanut butter jar. "I know something you don't. I know where they we-ent. Going to the chapel and they're gonna get mar-ar-ar-ried."

"Shut up Ryan. You sing like a donkey."

Bruce taps Ryan on the head. "Hello-o-o. Dad's not stupid."

"I bet I'm right, because for the past three months Irma's been collecting bridal magazines, and when I picked up the mail there was something from the court in there."

"From the court?" Adam twists toward Ryan. "Like what?"

Battered

Ryan shrugs. "I heard Dad talking about divorce pap—" The door opens. Everyone breathes a sigh of relief. Drake grins and puts three bags of groceries on the counter.

"How did you carry all that up the hill? Did anyone drive you?"

"Nope. I drove."

Adam peers out the door. "Drove what?"

"The wheelbarrow. So, who really knows where they went?"

"Who cares," Bruce takes a bite of my toast. "Let's just celebrate the fact they're gone." He spits out the toast. "Tastes like crap. Cheese under Peanut Butter and Jam? Are you going to eat that?"

"No, she's going to lick it like a dog."

"Shut up Ryan nobody asked you."

Adam's mouth twists into a sly smile, "Maybe they'll have a car crash and Irma will end up in a coma drooling for the rest of her life."

"Yeah then she can live in the basement," I say, and take a bite of my toast. "Yuk. Bruce is right. It does taste like crap."

Adam dumps it in the trash. "I'll make you more. The cheese spread is better by itself." He chews his lip, checks the toast and pops it back down. "Only the good die young. They'll return when we least expect it, to catch us off guard, so keep the place clean."

"Adam can I go across the road to look at the flowers?"

"No."

The third time I ask, I get a yes. But he wants me to wait until tomorrow to make sure they don't return for something they forgot. I pester him while we wash the dishes. He finally caves in.

"Don't go anywhere yet. Wait here."

"For what."

"Give me a minute."

My heart is thumping out of my chest. I'm so excited I can hardly breathe. I follow him outside. "Please Adam. Can I go now? Why do I have to wait?"

His eyes dart toward the flower garden. He rips a plant out of the ground, stomps on it, and throws it to one side.

Juanita Ray

"If you are caught outside the yard, or if you see their car in the driveway, bring me back something to stick in this hole. I don't care if you have to steal it from someone's yard. I'll pretend an animal dug this one up and I'll say I sent you over to the greenhouses to buy a new one."

"But you said they're gone for at least a week."

"I know but wouldn't put it past them to park down the road just to spy on us. Got it?"

"Yes. I got it. You sent me to get a plant."

He tucks a five-dollar bill into my pocket. "I want this money back. Don't spend it unless you see Dad's car. If you end up having to buy a plant, buy one like this." He flips it over with his boot. "It's something purple."

I bolt across the road and run up the lane. I can't believe I'm out of the yard again. I yell at the sky, "Thank you. I'm free!"

I have one foot inside the place when the grouchy owner of Hollikan Nurseries drives me away.

I walk behind the wooden building and instead of turning left I take the lane to my right. Toward the end is an unbelievable inviting sight. A bunch of people are wandering in and out of tons of plastic tents.

The hacking cough behind me, belongs to the old grouch. I run to my left and hide in a grove of trees. When the muttering old man disappears, I follow a path that seems to lead to nowhere but a small grove of short trees. Then I spot a little shed with a weathered door. A tiny voice inside my head says stop. I take two gulps of fresh summer air and pry open the door. There's nothing inside but some new green plastic pots and a big dog bed. In that moment I decide I am never returning home. It doesn't matter if or when they come back because I won't be there when they do.

I mosey around checking out the grounds of my new home. The nearby yard is more interesting than any I've imagined. It's like a dump for broken pots and dead flowers. Tons of dark used plastic pots are scattered everywhere. I stack them in a tall pile but they keep toppling over.

I realize the dirt trapped inside is the problem. I find a stick and scrape them clean. I rearrange them by size and sort them in stacks. The door of a small cottage creaks. Mr. Hollikan stalks out the opening. I sprint over a grave of broken pots. but he bellows at me to stop. His voice is so loud it makes my ears ring. I freeze in my tracks.

"Turn around."

I twist to look. He is standing with the door wide open, propping it ajar with his army boot.

"You may as well come in here where I can see what you're up to." His bony fingers motion for me to enter. His icy blue eyes look foggy and the right part of his mouth droops downward.

He kicks the worn toe of his brown boot against the door. A clump of dirt falls away. A twisted water hose hangs over his bent shoulder.

He looks weird and a little mean. His gray frizzy hair is sticking straight out in spiky clumps as though someone tried to electrocute him.

He ushers me through a large wide greenhouse and leads the way out the door and down a narrow tunnel. I follow the piece of rope that holds up his pants, to a door at the end of the path. We walk through a second tunnel of plastic walls. Several doors lead to more green houses. We enter the last one on the left. It is full of small poinsettia bushes.

"Want to see what happens late September?"

Even though it's July, I nod.

His dirty fingernail flips off the light switch. All I can see are the whites of his bulging eyeballs, glimmering in the dark, like bright ping-pong balls.

"This is what they need, fourteen hours every day. Kept in the dark, without a speck of light. Poinsettias can't bloom any other way. That's how God planned it. It's how he plans everything." He flicks a switch and the room floods with light. "There's always darkness before the light."

A faint smile crosses his lips. He digs his hands into his pocket and rustles around for a few seconds and says, "Hold out your hand." Two quarters fall into my palm. Just like they did, the last day I saw Marie.

"I don't want them."

"Oh yes you do, and come back tomorrow for two more."

Bald Ugly Me

The fat on the back of the driver's arm jiggles as she changes gears. The bus swerves to the right, does a U-turn, faces our house and leaves a cloud of dust swirling around the faded Hollikan Nurseries sign.

The driver has a biker scarf tied around her frizzy short stub of hair, held together by a yellow elastic band. Her two-inch ponytail pokes out from above her collar. It reminds me of the matted stray that hangs around the school grounds, the one that doesn't like blueberry sandwiches, or sour milk, any more than I do.

The bus jerks to a stop at the last red light before my school. This is my favorite street. The window feels cool against my nose. I hold my breath so the window won't steam up.

Skinny tall houses are joined together in a long row. Each one is painted a different color from the other but they all have black peaked roofs. The streets are old with patches of grass peeking through the cracks. The cobblestone sidewalks are flooded with flocks of pigeons but the pigeons don't move. They expect people to walk around them. The streets belong to them. I wish I was a pigeon. Free to go wherever I pleased. The pigeons always walk away from each other and each does their own thing. They remind me of my brothers.

At school, I keep quiet and to stay to myself. I don't bother to try to make friends. There's no point. They expect to be invited over or called on the phone. And nobody likes to hang around with somebody that wears old fashioned, second hand clothes, that are two sizes too big. I know today will be the same as every other day. I'll get stared at, laughed at, and finally I'll get ignored.

At recess, I notice a strange creature watching my every move. She walks straight and rigid as though her back was a plastic mold. She has the longest hair I've ever seen. Usually I don't look back when people stare at me but something about her is distinctly familiar. If it were anyone else, I would have glanced away, but for some strange reason, while she scrutinizes me, I can't take my eyes off her. I'm waiting for her to tilt her head forward but she never does. Maybe she broke her neck and it's stuck like that.

Every day, every week, no matter what part of the school I am in, the tilted head girl, loiters nearby. Does she have her nose up in the air to breath better or is she trying to make her hair appear longer, which means she's just as insecure as I am. At recess, like me, she sits alone and during class, she joins everyone else, as they stare a hole in the back of my neck.

At noon, I lean against my locker and read the supply-list for the home economics class. Learning to cook and sew sounds like fun, like everything else I can't do. I twist the list into a tight roll. Dad isn't poor, so I don't qualify for the free supplies like some other kids and the school expects me to buy this stuff. I feel a knot in my stomach. I'm not allowed to ask for food, or a new outfit, so there's no way I'm asking for sewing materials. Maybe if I say someone stole my book bag and my list, I won't get detention again.

"I wouldn't ever want to be that piece of paper. Sorry. Didn't mean to make you jump." The girl with the rigid back holds out her hand for me to shake. "I'm Cynthia." She says something about the list but her words go

131

in one ear and out the other. She pokes me and says, "You're not even listening, are you?"

"I'm sorry, what?"

"Pardon, ladies say pardon not what."

I blink. "Do you have a relative named Irma?"

"Who's Irma?"

"Never mind. Nobody."

"What happened to your arm?"

I pull my sleeve lower. "I fell."

She scoffs, and looks downward. "When I fall, I bruise my knees not my—What are you staring at?"

"Your head. It bends."

"Of course, it does. How else would I study? Where do you hang out for lunch? You're never in the lunchroom."

"The library."

"Well at least it's not the gym. The real snobs stay in the gym until lunch is half over, then they make a grand entrance. I like to go there before anyone to get a good seat and watch the show. Join me?"

"No thanks."

"Suit yourself."

Two minutes later, I change my mind, grab the nearest empty table and unpack my lunch. The bread has a soggy blue indentation from the milk bottle. The sopping wet heavy sandwich flops from my fingers and splatters onto the table. I hide it with the bag and unscrew the lid from the mustard jar. It smells weird but I take a sip anyway. I start to spit the sour milk back in the bottle, lift my head and find the only person looking at me is Cynthia. Today I'm her show. She smiles and waves.

I scoop the contents of my lunch, into the worn wrinkled paper bag and walk out with my eyes peeled on the exit sign above the door. When I reach the corner, I break into a run, smack into a boy who is walking backwards, drop my leaky paper bag, swoop it up, run to the bathroom and spit my mouthful of goop into the sink. I wash the sour taste from my stained tongue and spend the rest of the afternoon trying to hide my blue lips.

Battered

By the time I board the bus, they're still blue.

"Hi, move over, I'm Samantha. Daniel is cute, isn't he?" She pulls out two bottles of nail polish, shakes them vigorously, paints the nails on her left hand orange, and blows them dry.

She slaps her right hand across my knee and hands me the black nail polish. "Can you do my right hand?"

I feel ashamed to tell her I don't know how to apply nail polish. Maybe I should have watched Marie more. She was good at it but back when I was six and I didn't care about nail polish.

"I can't. The bus is too shaky."

"I'm going to be half witch and half pumpkin for Halloween. What are you going as?"

I answer her with a question. "Who's Daniel?"

"You know, the guy you banged into earlier, when you were leaving the lunchroom. That's what all the girls do. Drop something so you can touch his hand when he picks it up."

"I didn't do it on purpose."

"What happened when he picked it up?"

"He didn't." I didn't tell her I was halfway down the hall before he had a chance to bend over to help.

"That's weird. You're the kind of girl he goes for. Pale skin, high cheek bones, and chocolate eyes. I'm surprised he hasn't hit on you before."

Someone hit on me?

For the rest of the ride home I can't forget what she said. I watch her blow on her nails and wonder what it would be like to have a boyfriend. As the bus pulls up to my house the cold truth reclaims my imagination. I'm not allowed to have a friend, much less a boyfriend.

Irma is waiting on the porch. Her eyes are bloodshot and she's mad as hell. "Don't just stand there staring at me, you ugly little bitch, get in this house—now."

I take my book bag off and hang it on the porch hook.

Irma holds out her hand. "Your lunch bag. For tomorrow."

A vision of the crumpled, blue-stained paper bag, flashes across my eyes. If I tell her I tossed it, I'm dead.

"What lunch bag?" my voice squeaks.

The vision is replaced by the palm of her hand.

Slap. Sla-ap! It bounces from my cheek to my nose.

"Don't act stupid with me. The paper bag."

"Pardon?"

She reaches up and yanks the belt off the hook.

"Don't pretend you can't—" WHACK "—hear me you little bitch!" She strikes again. I lurch backwards. The belt grazes my chest and sears my left shoulder. As I lift my good arm to cover my shoulder, she demands to know how I tore my blouse.

Like an idiot, I say, "Pardon?" My brain is stuck on rewind, searching for missing lunch bag excuses.

"Don't pardon me. I know you're not deaf." The crack of the belt hits my waist near my shirt seam. "How did you tear that?"

She's panting heavy like a rabid dog. I rack my brains for an answer. I need to say something about the blouse before she murders me. I try the truth. I look down at my blouse and say, "I didn't know it was torn." She towers over me with the belt raised. Look her in the eye and say that again. I try, but all I see is hatred and the shiny part of the buckle aimed at me. I put my hands up to try and stop the buckle. Blood splatters on my blouse and my right arm is throbbing. A pulsating pain travels down my wrist and up my elbow. Something makes her madder.

"STOP—crack—LYING—crack—TO—crack—ME!" She slashes me repeatedly. The belt buckle hits my face. The blow to my eye sends sharp excruciating pains lodging deep inside my socket. It feels like shards of glass are stabbing my eyelid. She continues to beat me until I crunch up in a ball, in a bed of warm piss. My brain goes dead. It knows there's no right answer.

Finally, she throws the belt at me and snarls, "Don't move an inch," walks away and paces back and forth across the kitchen floor. Then the stalking stops. I try to listen to where she is.

Battered

The floor boards creaks. She's about four feet away. Quick sharp pangs of fear stab through me. I open my eyes but it hurts to move them. Everything looks blurry. I blink my eyes to clear my vision. One eyelid feels like sandpaper scraping against my eyeball. With my one good eye, I stare at the door and try to will it to open. If it does, I'll run through it. In my mind I practice reaching it. I envision me taking steps through it, but I'm in so much pain even twitching hurts. I know if I try and fail, she'll kill me. My ribs feel broken. The porch door seems like it's a million miles away. I stare at the blurry door, while my brain twists the knob a thousand times, but it remains shut until Dad arrives.

I half sit up, crouched in a corner with my back against the wall. His shoes stop near my feet. My heart screams, 'Can't you see me?' but I keep my mouth shut. I try not to wince when he presses the palm of his hand against my forehead and pushes his thumb against the bone below my eyebrow and shoves it up toward my forehead, forcing my eye to open wider. It won't co-operate. It feels like his fingers are steel toe boots doing push-ups on my skull and it's giving me a headache. A wince escapes.

"She's not dead," Irma snarls and swoops past the opening leading to the living room. The slam of their bedroom door gives me a small sense of security. It means she's finished with me. I'm safe until the next time. Dad brushes off the knees of his pants and walks away without saying a single word.

I struggle to get downstairs to my room. Everything hurts when I crawl under my bed. My hands hurt when I pull at the bedsprings. They bong back into place. Despite the pain I pull again and again. With each pull Marie's Bible bangs against the mattress. I'm mad at God. He's a rotten father. He's as heartless, as Dad. Why didn't he protect Marie? And why would he swap Mom for Irma? I pull the springs as hard as I can. "Why? Why? Why? I hate you." The Bible gyrates. I gasp and feel instant remorse.

"Please God, I'm sorry. I didn't mean that. I'm sorry I called you a rotten father. I know you're busy helping people with bigger problems than me but I need your help. I'm just a kid and she's—"

Juanita Ray

"Juanita who the hell are you talking to?" I slither from under my bed and gaze at my blurry brother.

"Jesus Christ!" Adam lurches toward me. "I swear I'm going to frigging kill her." He paces, hits the wall with his fist, and paces again. He slams his fist into the wall a second time and leaves.

"Please God, don't let him go upstairs."

"Are you still talking to yourself? How many aspirins do you see?"

"Two white ones." I don't tell him about the gray ones.

"Good." He hands me a sock. "Wet this and wash your face. It's an odd one. I'll trash it later. Can you walk to the laundry tub?"

"She didn't get my legs."

My mouth can't quite reach the tap because pressing against the tub hurts my ribs. I pull away.

"What's wrong?"

"They're stuck in my throat."

"Drink more water but it's okay to chew them up."

"I can't reach the tap."

"Use the sock. Wet it and wring it in your mouth."

"It looks dirty" I hang the sock over the edge of the tub, hold my hands under the tap, and cup the water to my mouth. Most of it dribbles down between my shaking fingers.

"White socks always look dirty when they're clean. Go lie in bed. The aspirins will help you sleep."

He takes off his watch and sets it with the aspirins under my pillow. "If you're awake at ten o'clock take one more."

"Why not two, like I did just now?"

"Because aspirin can make your stomach bleed."

"What should I do if my stomach bleeds?"

"It won't. But if it did, you'd stop taking them. I've got to go to work. I'll be home around midnight and I'll bring you a treat." He forces a smile. "What would you like?"

"Nothing . . . Adam if she ever kills—if I die will you make sure they don't bury me in the back yard? I want to be buried by Mom."

Battered

Adam snarls, "If anyone gets buried in that back yard, it will be that monster, not you. And don't let me ever hear you say something like that again."

It takes two weeks for most of my bruises to fade. At first my face looked like a blueberry patch. Now the dirty yellow blotches are hardly noticeable. Both of my eyes match again. When my teacher and Cynthia asked what happened, I told them exactly what I was instructed to say. My brothers were practicing golf out back and accidentally hit me.

I lean against the bathroom wall. Everybody else here at school is wearing pretty clothes and fixing their hair or their makeup. Everybody except me. One girl puckers up her lips, catches my eyes in the mirror, pivots on her heel and says, "Bruce said to say hi to you."

I squint at her. "How do you know Bruce?"

She motions me over and lowers her voice. "From last year. He was in my class and from this year, because he's sleeping in our shed." She leans closer, cups her hand over my ear and whispers, "And I know all about your nasty little secrets."

Before I can recover and say one word, another girl loops an arm through hers and sweeps her away.

For the rest of the day, and the entire bus ride home, my nerves are frayed and I'm lost in a daze. Does she gossip? Is Bruce really gone? I try to recall when I last saw him. Lately, I haven't seen much of anyone. I don't always get to sit at the dinner table, and most days, if I get to eat, it's at a tiny tray table, facing the wall. Usually it's no dinner and I'm barred in the basement or the back yard. Either way, I'm always alone—alienated from others.

When I enter the house, Irma immediately grabs my knapsack to retrieve the paper bag and bottle. Horrified, I hold my breath as she reaches in the wrinkled paper bag. How did I forget to trash the sandwich?

"Blueberry sandwiches not good enough for you?" She dumps it from the crinkled paper bag and slams her fist on it. Drops of purple slime ooze from the wax paper. "Consider this your dinner. Sit down and eat it now and don't leave one single crumb."

Crumb? It's a saturated blue slab. I keep my face down and try to hide behind my hair. The muck plops and falls between my fingers and splatters on the table. It reminds me of the time we made homemade French toast at school, when I left the bread in the egg mixture for five minutes.

Irma slams a spoon on the table. "DON'T PLAY WITH IT, EAT IT."

I scoop up a spoonful of the gooey blue mixture and slide it between my teeth. I take a second smaller spoonful without swallowing the first one and lower my head a little more.

She lurches out of her chair. It topples over and crashes on its side. Silverware clatters. The drawer slams shut.

I close my eyes and brace myself for whatever it is she's going to hit me with.

Buzzzzz. Buzzzzz-zzz.

Cold steel vibrates against my left temple. I keep my eyes on the chair leg and grit my teeth. I know better than to move an inch. Clumps of hair fall to the floor. The blades rip across my right temple twice, before she snarls, "Now let's see you hide behind that mop."

Hair is up my nose, in my eyes and sticking to my tongue. She places a bowl on my head and snips above my right eyebrow

"Tada! I'm home!"

The bowl clatters to the floor. Irma pushes me away. Dad's mouth opens and closes several times.

"Now look what you made me do? Get downstairs," she says through gritted teeth. Her eyes bulge at me. "Are you deaf? I said get downstairs. NOW."

I run straight for the bathroom.

My quivering lip is uncontrollable. Horrification, anger, humiliation and shock fight for first place. Tears roll down my cheeks. I tilt my head sideways. Above each ear I have a jagged three-inch bald patch.

I recoil from the ugly girl in the mirror. Her eyes are blinking so fast I can't see what color they are. Her chin quivers and her bottom lip trembles. I try not to blink back, because every time she blinks her lids rain tears.

Battered

I want her to disappear. I smear soap across the mirror and run to my room and crawl under my bed.

I want to stay under here forever but I don't. I take a deep breath, lean against the dresser and revisit the ugly girl in the mirror.

I gather hair from the top of my head and try to cover my sides. It won't stay in place—won't cover the bald spots not even if I hold the ends in my mouth. I try wrapping the ends crossways toward my forehead, like a scarf, but my hair won't reach. I take off my sock and use it like a hairband but it's too short. I make pigtails and wrap the elastic around my ear lobes. I look retarded but not as bald. I don't know which is uglier the new haircut or the new hairdo. I hate the skinny, pale, ugly girl facing me. I turn my back to her and slump against the dresser drawers.

I don't get why God made me. I wish I were dead.

I don't remember how I got from my bedroom to the bathroom, but I'm here searching for razorblades. I rummage through the drawers like a mad man . . . and then I find the metal case of aspirins.

I eat them all, one by one.

Stolen Underwear

It's dark outside. My room is the color of tar. Is it just after dusk or is it close to dawn? My stomach twists and spasms. I get momentary relief followed by more spasms and cramps. I roll over on my side. Something is scraping my arm. I touch my temple. My heart races. Please God let this be a bad dream, let me be dead.

The blackness around me changes to charcoal. In this moment, I dread the dawn. I dread the idea of going to school. The more I think about it the worse my stomach feels. My right side feels like someone stabbed it. I roll on my back and wait for the pain to go away. It gets worse with each breath. My guts twist into pretzels and rip apart. It feels like I'm dying. Maybe the aspirins are working. I turn over on my back and wait for the grim reaper. I wait for an hour but he doesn't want anything to do with bald ugly me either.

I climb out of bed and stumble over my scattered clothes. I pace in unsteady circles around my room, trying to ease the pain. I count the circles.

Battered

I'm at fifty-six circles when something warm, almost hot, drips from between my legs.

I check to see what it is. Did I accidentally pee? I dip my hand into my pants and hold it up toward my window.

It's blood!

I take off my white underwear. I don't need to hold them up to the window to see the solid red stains. I panic. I'm scared about the blood. How do I hide this from Irma? What do I do with my underwear? I stuff them between my legs and press hard like they taught us in first aid. I waddle toward the laundry tub and find an old roll of paper towels sitting on a crossbeam above the laundry tub.

My fingertips are within inches of reaching it. I must have grown some in the past six years yet I feel as short as I was back when I tried to unlock the chain at the top of the door, to let Irma's boys escape her clutches. Back then I wasn't beaten as much. She had them to take everything out on. Maybe I should have let them stay trapped in the room. Maybe they would have gotten a share of my beatings.

Back then I wore pretty dresses. If I had them now, I'd never tear the frills off—well maybe today, I would.

My elbow brushes something cold. I grab the swaying hanger and hit the paper towel rolls. They topple into the laundry tub. The first few paper towels are a crusty beige color and have paint splattered on them. I tear off a clean square, fold it and roll it into a cigar and push it inside of me.

Irma's footsteps stomp above me. I panic. The roll of paper towels is covered in bloody fingerprints. If she beats me for nothing, what will she do to me if she has a good reason? I take the paper towels, and stuff them and my underwear up under my bedroom dresser, in the far corner opposite my quarters, and dive into bed.

Once her footsteps fade toward Dad's room, I sneak back to the tub and wash my hands. Another cramp sends me to my knees.

If Marie were here, she'd know what to do. I miss Marie so much. I try to remember what she looked like but I can't. I try harder until finally I see her as plain as day complaining about the sock ghost living in our washer.

Juanita Ray

I bolt upright. That's it! I have Marie's old dresser. I have our old sock drawer! I rummage through it and I find several odd socks. I choose the smallest one, pull the paper towels from under my dresser and stuff them in the sock. Later I'll ask Adam for tape but for now I put on one extra pair of panties to help keep the sock from falling out of place.

With every step I take, the sides of the sock rub and burn the insides of my legs. Maybe it's because I'm pressing my legs together so the sock won't drop.

I practice walking with my legs apart. It's impossible. I put on a third pair of underwear and it works. I can walk normal and the sock doesn't move.

By Sunday night, the sock wreaks. I open my drawer and look for clean underwear. I only have two pairs. I stuff the dirty sock under my dresser but after one hour I can't stand the smell. I find a pair of scissors, cut the dirty sock in pieces, and flush the pieces down the toilet. It takes forever for the tank to stop hissing and fill up so I can flush again. After three flushes, I'm finished. I wash my hands three times and crawl back into bed waiting for the day to pass by, for the bleeding to stop but it doesn't. Adam said aspirin makes your stomach bleed, but he didn't say for how long.

—·—·—·—·—

By Monday morning, my stomach still cramps. I'm not sure if it's because I'm still bleeding or because I'm at the mirror trying to fix my hair.

I give up, take two deep breaths and enter the kitchen. Irma is nowhere in sight. Dad's eyes glance past my left eye than past my right. His chest heaves. "Eat."

"My stomach hurts. Can I skip eating?"

His eyes drift back to my haircut. He mumbles something.

"Pardon?" I gaze past him and imagine all the snickers that I'm about to encounter at school.

Astonishment washes across his face. "You really didn't hear me, did you? Wait here."

He grabs a phonebook and sprints to his bedroom.

Battered

Her voice is raised. "There is nothing whatsoever wrong with her hearing, Ned. I'll prove it to you. Pass me my house robe."

I don't wait. I quietly close the front door and run down the driveway to the bus stop. Please, please hurry up. Just as I'm thinking about running over to Mr. Hollikan's, the bus shows up. I scramble inside, knowing I'll pay dearly for this tonight, but I pay for something or the other every night, so why not earn it?

I press my nose against the window to hide my hair cut. A few blocks away, down the hill, I spot the StayMart. The giant sign invites me in—in to steal underwear. But by the time I fight the people getting on the bus and reach the door, it closes in my face. The bus driver twists, pushes some newspapers to the floor and pats the seat behind her. She pushes her knapsack closer toward the window and taps the seat again.

I shuffle into it, pick up a newspaper from the floor, and bury my head behind it until she taps the paper and asks, "You asleep? Or are you planning to hang out with me all day."

"Can I borrow this section? I'll bring it back."

"You can keep it."

I poke my fingers through 'Dear Abby' and peek through the holes until I reach my locker. I sit down and take off the extra pair of socks I'm wearing. I step inside and take the extra underwear out of my knapsack, remove the sheets of paper towels from between the pages of my math book, and stuff them in the far corner of my locker. I keep my head poked inside, fiddling at nothing, until after the bell rings. I know I can't bring a newspaper to class—the gym—I almost forgot I'm expected at the gym.

I tilt a book against my face so I can see over the binding but the cover hides my temples. At least I hope it does. I drag myself to the gymnasium, open the door and gasp. The room is filled with chairs and kids. A few feet away, Daniel Noseworthy is sitting beside Cynthia. She jumps up, runs over and says, "Isn't this great," she chirps, "You guys get to practice in front of real people, and I get to see who has stage fright. And why are you hiding behind a math book?"

I back away from the door, turn and run. She yells, "It's normal to have stage fright at first. Come back." I dart into my empty homeroom, sit at my desk and bury my head in my arms and cry.

"Why are you not in the gym with the rest of the student body?"

I put on a brave face and slowly glance up at my teacher. "I'm not in the play anymore."

"You still need to be at the gym for—what happened to your hair?"

"My baby sister."

"Your baby sister?"

I nod. I plan to say nothing, instead, I say, "While I slept."

Another raised eyebrow from the teacher.

I look her straight in the eyes and say something truthful. "She did it fast. It's uglier than ugly isn't it?"

She strokes her scalp, above her ears. "You didn't do this?"

"No, why would I?" My throat tightens. My nose burns.

"A baby couldn't . . . how old is she?"

"I don't know."

"You don't know how old she is?"

I shake my head and bite at a hangnail.

"It will be okay. Hair grows faster than you think and there will always be another play. Tell me, who made that decision? Your music teacher?"

"No. The whole class was sitting there and I . . . and I—I look like this, so I ran."

The teacher pulls a tissue from her sleeve. "It's clean. Dry your eyes then blow your nose." She points to the trash bin beside her desk. "Grab your books and meet me in the principal's office."

I cram books into my knapsack and trot down a partially empty hall. One student points at me and bursts out laughing. A few feet away a cluster of students turn and snicker.

I, pause at the door to the principal's office, close my eyes and pray, please don't call the house.

The principal tilts his glasses toward his nose and hands me a note. "For your parents."

"You mean my Dad?"

"Of course." His voice is softer. "Your father works by day?"

"Yes sir."

"Who will look after you?"

"My older brother Adam. He goes to college—but we have a housekeeper. Can you please call him?"

"The housekeeper is a he?"

"No. I meant call Adam, not the housekeeper. He's the boss of me." I hold my breath and suck my lips between my teeth.

His knobby fingers curl around a pen. "Your phone number is?"

Adam made me memorize his college number in case of an emergency. I hold my breath while he calls it. "Hello I'd like to speak to Adam Rose please." His eyebrows knit together. "Yes, I would consider this urgent." His frown widens. He leans back away from his desk, pulls out a drawer, rummages through various files and signs documents while he waits.

While he interrogates my brother, I try not to fidget.

He holds the phone toward me, "Your brother would like to talk to you."

"Juanita, just say yes, or no, to my questions. Can you hear me?"

"Barely."

"Can they?"

"No."

"Can you find somewhere to go until you can catch the bus home?"

"Yes." I bite the inside of my lip. The real answer is no.

"Tell them I told you to wait at the bus stop until I pick you up and give the principal back the phone."

"Okay."

They talk for another few minutes. He hangs up and says, "How long has your brother been a student at the Trades School?"

"This is his first year."

"And how old is your sister?"

"What sister—I mean which sister? I have an older one too."

Another teacher comes huffing into the office dragging some boy by the scruff of his collar. The principal shakes his head and rises to his feet. "What have we here and why am I not surprised to see you again, Master Reynolds?"

From a glance, I can see his window, has a clear view of the playground but not the bus area.

My teacher follows me down the hall.

The click-clack of heels, gets louder until she reaches me. "Read two chapters ahead in literature and finish the current chapter in math."

My stomach twists into a knot. I lurch forward, double over and wince as the cramp tears across my left side. My knapsack topples to the floor.

She kneels beside me. "What is it?"

"My stomach hurts so bad I can hardly bre—ugh-ugh-urgggh!" Another cramp buckles me in half. She picks up my knapsack, holds my hand and says, "Come with me. Nerves can do that sometimes but maybe we should take a quick trip to the nurse's station to make sure everything is okay." She rests her hands on my shoulders, and twists me in the opposite direction. My palms sweat. "Don't you have to get back to class?"

"No. I'm sure Mrs. Hathaway is doing just fine."

Mrs. Hathaway? I thought she was single. Who would marry someone as mean as Mrs. Hathaway? Her ruler has rapped me on the knuckles more than once.

"Well what do we have here?"

"She has a complaint of stomach cramps."

The nurse checks my pulse, feels my forehead, takes my temperature, and says, "She's running a slight fever. It's probably her cycle. I'll take it from here."

My teacher hands me my knapsack. "Don't look so worried. She treats this sort of thing all the time."

The nurse points to a day bed. "Lie down."

After I answer several questions, she asks, "Do you have any spotting?"

"Spotting?"

"Bleeding, do you have any bleeding?"

I'm afraid to say anything. I can't tell her about the aspirins. I open my mouth and close it twice.

Battered

"Well?"

"What kind of bleeding?"

She nods toward my private area.

I can feel my face flush.

"I take it by your face the answer is yes. Has anyone told you about the birds and the bees yet?"

"Pardon?"

She smiles and puts a tape in the video player. "Watch this."

It looks like a cartoon, for the first few minutes, until I see this cat is not your normal kitten. When the cartoon is over, I stare at the black screen more depressed than ever. There's no way I can ask Irma for sanitary napkins. How am I going to keep from running out of socks every month? For the next while, my haircut doesn't seem as important as my new problems.

The nurse returns with a little pink purse. She opens up the package of pads and a package of tampons, removes one from each and says, "You may find you prefer one over the other."

"What if I prefer neither?"

"We all do," she laughs.

She demonstrates how to use them on the dummy. She hands me a couple of tampons. "I think I prefer these." With all the face slaps I get, these would come in handy for my nosebleeds.

She jerks her head toward the dummy. "Your turn."

My face feels like a furnace.

"Go on."

I whisper, "Sorry," to the plastic dummy and plug her vagina with the wooly white cigar. I peel the glossy paper from the pad and stick the pad against the crotch of her panties. It's too crooked, so I rip the pad away and try again. After three tries I get it right.

"You seem better with tampons, but which do you prefer?"

I shrug.

"Tell you what, I'll give you samples of both because this is one of the most important decisions a girl your age has to make."

147

Juanita Ray

She hands me the pink purse. "It's yours to keep. There's a bathroom right there, where you can freshen up."

It takes a while for me to feel clean. By the time I do, the small tin garbage can, overflows with paper towels. I cover the soiled paper with clean white napkins and close the bathroom door.

Another cramp rifles across my stomach.

The nurse points to the bed and suggests I lie down for a while. I'm still moaning and groaning when it's time to leave and catch the bus.

My feet scurry outside toward the parking lot and hop up the bus steps. The bus is packed so I set in the seat behind the driver, next to her duffel bag. The driver adjusts her mirror to and from my face. I slump against the window and fret over my underwear shortage. As the bus pulls up to the stop near my house, my main concern is sneaking the purse past Irma.

I'm surprised to see Dad's car idling in the driveway. In case Irma's in the car, I slink past the driver's side. Dad's window rolls open. "Get in."

I climb in back, behind Irma, and don't dare speak. This could be good or bad but either way the odds are I'm undoubtedly in some sort of trouble.

After a silent twenty-minute car ride, Dad parks in front of a large brick building that looks like some sort of institution.

Inside, I sit in a chair between Dad and Irma. She picks up a magazine and with every page turn, she glances up and showers every person in the lobby with a fake smile. Her perfume lingers in my nostrils and smothers my lungs.

"Juanita Rose?"

"Go with the nurse sweetheart." I glance around the room to see who Irma is talking to. She pinches my arm and says, "Go on darling. She won't hurt you."

I cringe and look down at the floor.

The nurse calls my name again.

"Go with the nurse." Dad nudges and points at her. He smiles and says, "My daughter seems to have hearing problems."

"We'll see," Irma's says in a crisp voice.

The nurse slaps a thermometer under my tongue.

Battered

"It's a tad high. How long have you had this fever?"

I pretend not to hear her.

"How long have you felt hot?"

I ignore her and pick at the scab on my wrist.

"The doctor will be right in," she yells.

"What's he going to do?"

"Check your ears of course. You were bought in for a hearing test."

"What!"

She raises her voice, "YOU ARE HERE TO GET YOUR EARS CHECKED." She writes something in my file and hangs it on the door rack. The file swings outside and the door clicks shut.

Straight in front of me is an eye chart, like the one we have in school. I can read every single letter. On a tray are different sized metal bell shaped domes and one small hammer. The domes are all in a row. I wonder which end he will start with.

I glance back at the eye chart and see the letters start out large and get smaller. There is one dome on the tray for each line on the chart. My guess is he'll start with the louder ones, so I'll have to make sure I'm deaf before he reaches the second last row of domes.

The door opens. An Asian doctor says something, chuckles, pulls on my earlobe and sticks a black tool in my ear. He skims over my chart and puts a plug in my right ear. He hits the first dome and gives me a quick nod. I nod back.

On the fourth last dome my hearing suffers a significant loss. He looks concerned and taps it with a little more force.

My response stays the same. He tries one more dome but I act as though it's silent.

He writes something in the chart and instructs the nurse to follow him. She returns with a needle, orders me to bend over the gurney, tugs my pants down five inches, and jabs the needle in the cheek of my butt. The sting of it makes my eyes water.

"You'll need one of these, every Friday, for the next six weeks."

"Am I done? Is he finished with me?"

"Yes, and your father said he'd meet you at the car."

I find him leaning against the car door. Irma's eyes flash like lightning. Her mouth is twisted and her arms are clenched against her chest. She glares at me, slams the passenger door shut and says, "She faked it. I know she did."

"Irma nobody can fake a fever. It's the first sign of an infection."

"How could she get an ear infection when she doesn't swim?"

"Maybe it had something to do with the other week. Maybe when you hit her with the belt buckle it—"

"Shut up Ned. I know for a fact she faked this whole thing. And you," she twists around to look at me, "you faking little bitch, if you think for one minute, you've gotten away with anything, you have another thing coming, I grant you that."

"Irma. The doctor said her ear canal was red and infected."

"How do you know what he said? He could hardly speak English. There's no way you understood one word he uttered."

"That may be so but if you didn't hear what the nurse said maybe we should bring you back and get your ears checked too."

I sink back against the back seat and close my eyes. I'm surprised he didn't say I had an infected nose. After Irma hacked my hair off it took me forever to clean up. If he had to spend two hours digging small bits of hair out of his ear, he'd have a red one too.

"Knock it off, Ned!"

They continue to argue and for once I'm not the center of attention. She doesn't even bother checking my knapsack. My feet can't get downstairs quick enough. I find Adam loading the washing machine. "Wait don't turn it on yet, I have to get a shower first." Before he can answer, I dash into the bathroom and lock the door.

The bathroom towel rack is empty. So is the hamper.

I trudge back to my room, pull my pink purse from under my pillow and click the lid open and shut.

Click. Click. Click-click.

Battered

What would have happened if I died last night? Do angels scoop you up right away or is there a waiting period? Would Dad have cried? Would I have ended up in heaven or in hell? Did God see me steal from the locker room last week?

Click. Click. Click.

Does it count like stealing? It's not like I spent it on candy. The cancer collection jar was almost empty. Nobody cares about donating to cancer when they still have everybody alive in their family. "I promise I won't do it again, God. I don't want to go to hell when I die, because that's where Irma will be and I don't deserve to be stuck with her forever."

The door creaks. "Who is it?" I ask.

"It's the bad boogeyman, here to destroy your life."

Click.

"You're three years too late."

"I thought you said you were getting a shower?"

"Can't. There's no towels."

"That's what's in the washer, waiting to be washed. Want me to take one out?"

"Naw. It's okay."

Adam frowns. "Where were you? I was a little worried."

"I was at the hearing doctor. Dad thinks I'm going deaf. So does the doctor. You know . . . maybe Dad has feelings after all. He looked anxious and worried, like you do now."

"The only thing the old man was worried about was how much the doctor's bill might cost."

"Why? He has money. We're not poor right?"

He tugs at my oversized shirt. "This looks like it belonged to an eighty-year-old. The point is you look poor and you shouldn't. There's no need for her to buy you used clothes from the Salvation Army. She's made him so tight he squeaks. Heaven forbid he spend a nickel on one of us. She'd have a fit."

"I wish we were poor. If we were poor Irma wouldn't be here would she? She wouldn't have bothered with Dad."

Adam stares at my temples. "Probably not. How can a person be so frigging cruel? I don't get what Dad sees in her . . . I just don't get it at all. I guess you got made fun of at school?"

"Adam what can I do with this?" I dangle the handle of my pink purse on my index finger. It rocks back and forth. He darts his eyes and bobs his head left and right.

In a low monotone voice, he says, "Yes. I am now hypnotized. What? Oh no, not me. I have never told a lie. Yes. Yes. I am deaf as a doornail." He buckles over laughing, "Deaf. Juanita, that's a good one. I never would have thought of that in a hundred years."

"Adam please I'm serious."

"Yes and so am I. I'll tell you who is deaf in this family. The old man! Anytime I try to tell him the effect that Irma is having on you, it goes in one ear and comes out the other."

"I don't care about that. I care about this."

"Fine, I see, you have turned into a little woman and the school nurse told you about the birds and the bees?"

"How do you know?"

"Everybody over thirteen knows about those pink purses, one way or the other."

"I need to hide this . . . you know . . . for next month."

"Okay, fine. Follow me." He leads me under the steps, reaches behind the trunk and retrieves a skinny flashlight. He wraps his lips around it and unlocks the trunk. He grunts, pries the lid open, hands me the flashlight and says, "Give me the purse."

He presses the purse against his ear. "Do you hear that?"

"What?"

He puts the purse against my ear. "Listen. Can't you hear that?" His eyes turn dark and serious. "Don't tell me you can't hear those bees buzzing around in there? Oh, that's right . . . I forgot, you're half deaf." He chuckles all the way back to my room.

"We have to figure out where you can go for the next week. Where did you go after your principal called me?"

"The nurses' station. Until bus time."

"Do you think you could stay there for two more weeks?"

I cross my arms and tilt my head.

He wipes the smirk off his face, "What about that old fart, over at the greenhouses? Or did you wear out your welcome?"

I bend down, reach under my dresser and retrieve the quarters. "He gave me these and I told you before, he said I could come back any time. Remember?"

"If Irma finds this money, you'll have to say you stole it. You can't tell her the truth or she'll murder you for leaving the property and kick me out for not telling on you."

"She'll kill me if I say that."

"You need a better hiding place. If this dresser gets moved the slightest inch, they'll fall out."

"Well I don't want them locked in your trunk, so where?"

"Why not?"

"I need to buy more underwear and what if I get the chance and your trunk is locked? What place is better than under my dresser? A place the boys won't look?"

"Keep them in your knapsack."

"I can't. They might jingle. Irma might hear them. Besides she always checks my knapsack."

"For what?"

"She reuses the paper bag."

"Why? She already has a shitload of them. Enough to make a papier-mâché mansion."

"There must be somewhere safe I can keep my quarters."

"I'll think about it at work and I'll see you when I get home. Stay out of trouble okay?" He pats my head.

"I will."

"Don't forget to do your homework."

In bed, I manage to read an entire chapter of literature and solve two math puzzles, but gunshots and Indians yelping from the blaring TV upstairs, forces me to stop. I close my math book, tuck it under my pillow, and glance up toward my window. I didn't realize how late it was. My eyes must have adjusted to reading in the dark. I watch the shadows dance on my wall until I see one shaped like Adam. He creeps into my room, teeth first, grinning from ear to ear.

"Scoot over."

I move away from the edge of the bed and sit up.

He's bursting with excitement. "I spent all night trying to figure out how to fix this and guess what?" His grin grows wider. He passes me a roll of masking tape and raises his eyebrows up and down and says, "Problem solved." I'm not sure what I was expecting but it wasn't this. "Tape your quarters to the inside cover of your math book if you need to bring them with you, that way they won't jingle in your back pack. Or if you want to hide them in your dresser, do this."

He pulls a small drawer from the middle of the dresser and places it upside down on the bed. He pulls a sugar pop and a Twinkie from his pocket and tapes each one to the outside back of the drawer. Then he takes a longer strip and tapes the roll of tape beside the Twinkie. He says, "They make these things so there's half a foot or more between the drawers and the back board." He pulls the drawer in and out. "You see Juanita, it shuts perfect and that candy pop is an inch thick. You could tape a rat in there and it would still shut!" he laughs, delighted with himself.

"What if it doesn't hold?"

"We used duct tape, back at trade school, to hold up broken bumpers. If hell broke loose this stuff could hold it together." His voice turns serious. His eyes drift upwards. "If she catches you with money say I gave you quarters for—" he looks around the room, "—for a . . . how did you get the other money?"

"I got the dollar for helping Dad when he was locking Irma's boys in. I got the ten dollars for Christmas the year Irma came. Dad took it away but he gave it back to me at that restaurant."

"And you've kept it all these years? Man, he's changed so much since then, it's unbelievable. He was never like this before she came. We always had money and not once did we have to hide it. You know something? I think Irma has something she's holding over Dad's head. She has to. And it's got to be something really good."

He glances around and lowers his voice. "You know, if you're caught with that money, the old man won't bail you out. He'll never admit to Irma that he gave that ten dollars back to you. He'll call you a liar if it means saving his own skin." For a minute he looks deep in thought and stares past me. "Just tell her I gave you everything she finds. Say it was for your birthdays."

I grin. I doubt Adam even knows when my birthday is.

"You said Dad was different but I don't remember Dad being a whole lot different. I just remember he was never home much."

"He wasn't home often but when he was, he was a great Dad. At times I get a glimpse of the old him, but not too often though. Hardly at all. Now get some sleep. I don't know about you but I can hardly keep my eyes open."

I don't have the same problem. I can't keep my eyes shut. Before dawn I get dressed, make my bed and lie on top of it until I hear some footsteps upstairs. I smooth the wrinkles from the blanket and wait at the foot of the stairs.

The door swings open. Dad starts down the steps, sees me, turns around and leaves the door ajar.

I close it behind me, and stand by the table.

"Drink plenty of water with it."

I swallow the pill and drink until my stomach hurts.

Dad pours two cups of coffee. "Irma, hurry up or we'll be late." He shoves the bowl of cereal closer to me. It looks crispy and fresh. "Hurry up and eat. Irma is late for her doctor's appointment and I need to lock the door."

I hand him back my bowl of cereal, tell him I'm not hungry, grab my knapsack, and head for the door.

"Wait."

I pretend not to hear but he chases after me. "You forgot your lunch bag."

"Thanks."

"Looks like your bus—coming over the hill. Hurry or you'll miss it." He leans in the car and honks the horn.

"That's not my bus. It's the—"

He glances at his watch and honks again.

Three kids, I've never seen before, are waiting at the bus stop. I stand behind them until Dad's car passes out of sight.

The minute it disappears the bus arrives and slows to a stop. I crane my neck to make sure Dad's car goes over the next hill. It does. The driver's horn startles me. "Girl I don't have all day. Lord knows I wish I did."

"I just came to say my Dad is driving me to school, and will be for the next couple of weeks."

"Oh is that so?"

"He's on vacation from work. After that I'll be taking the bus again."

I trudge back to the house and wait on the steps until the bus is long gone. I pull my hood over my rotten haircut and walk to StayMart.

I spend the entire day in the toy section. Twice I'm asked where my mother is and the second time I say, "I'll go get her. She's taking way too long."

I weave in and out of aisles until I hit the underwear section. Blocking the aisle is an old woman leaning on a shopping cart.

"Excuse me do you know if they charge tax on the underwear?"

"Honey the government taxes everything. They even taxed the teeth in my mouth." She glances around, picks up a package and slides it down the front of her pants. "They're nothing but a bunch of thieves," she complains, and rolls her cart further down the aisle.

I pick up a package of panties, slip them down inside the front of my slacks, and follow her out the door.

"Excuse me," I yell after the woman. "What time is it?"

She grumbles, "You following me?"

I shake my head and wait for her to tell me the time.

Battered

"Will you stop following me if I tell you the time?"

I nod.

She pulls a box out of her pocket and opens it to reveal a man's watch. It still has a price tag hanging from it. She shakes it and says, "This says four o'clock." She pulls out a second watch and says, "And this one says five o'clock. They're both stopped. But I told you the time, so scat."

I sprint out of the parking lot and run across the road. Tires screech behind me. I stop dead in my tracks.

A Pregnant Monster

The stench of rubber fills my nostrils. The driver shouts, "Are you crazy or what? I almost killed you!" His face is only inches from mine. "What the hell is wrong with you?" He turns and paces back and forth in front of his fender. Driver's blow their horns and pass by. He ignores them and mutters, "I can't believe how close I came. What the hell were you doing in the middle of the damn road?" he growls, and slaps the bonnet of his car.

My lips feel dry. "I was trying to cross it."

"Get in for Christ's sake," he raises his eyes up to the sky and back to me, "let me give you a lift before someone else kills you."

I don't hesitate. I hop into the car and think, What's the worst that could happen? Murder me and put me out of my misery? He shuts the passenger door and walks around the front of the car shaking his head.

He releases the handbrake, "Where do you live?"

"Up there, at the top of the hill on the right."

His head jerks toward me. "Are you for real?" A dumbfounded look flitters across his face. "Kid, why cross the road when you live on the right?

Why would . . .?" His eyes leave mine, rest on my scalp and climb up and down my temples. "You do know you're lucky to be alive?"

"I guess so."

His eyes linger on mine. "You don't seem so sure about that."

"Yes. I am. I just got a fright."

"You and me both."

My eyes are peeled on the bus up ahead of us.

"Must be someone pretty special on that bus."

I nod. "I was trying to catch it."

"That so? Well let's see what old Pearl can do to change your destiny." He passes a couple of cars and within minutes, we are behind the parked bus. It's unloading at my stop. He pats the dash, "Good job Pearl. Good job." He leans his left arm on the steering wheel and puts the other on my shoulder. "Stay safe."

"Thank you so-o-o-o-o much sir." I jump out of the car and walk toward the house. I don't look back. Pebbles crunch behind me as his car pulls away. I lean my chin on my chest and pray, "Please don't honk your horn in front of my house," and he doesn't.

Dad's car is not in the driveway and the door is locked. I sit on the concrete slab at the back of the house and read a literature chapter dedicated to Edgar Allen Poe. I lean back to relax against the makeshift basement door. My body stretches the plastic backwards and it loosens at the side. I try to pry at the corner of the exterior frame to tighten the plastic but instead it slackens. Maybe nobody will ever notice it. I move toward the front of the house to sit on the sidewalk. When I turn the corner, Irma is facing me.

"That little bitch has been eavesdropping."

Dad turns toward me.

Irma wiggles her index finger at me and says, "Get over here."

"Pardon?"

Dad says, "I doubt she heard a word. Not with her hearing."

He climbs the steps, shakes his keys and selects one.

Irma snarls at me and raises her arm to hit me. Adam appears out of nowhere and grabs her wrist. "Hit her and it'll be the last time you hit anyone. I've had enough of you."

Irma freezes. "Ned. *Ned.* Do you see *this*? Are you going to let him get away with *that*? Ned! DO SOMETHING!"

Dad waits a full ten seconds before he says, "Do something about what Irma."

"He had me grabbed by the wrist."

Dad's face is stern. "Get inside here all of you."

"No. Not until you promise me Irma won't touch her."

"Irma has no reason to touch her."

"She never does, but that never stops her."

"I guarantee you Irma won't touch anyone."

Irma spits at Adam, "You will pay for this, I guarantee it." She glares at Dad, "And so will you!" She pushes Adam and stomps past him, into the house.

"I call pushing touching. Come on Juanita let's go." Adam grabs my hand and heads down the driveway.

"Stop, you don't need to go anywhere. We can settle this inside. There's no need to leave."

"Settle this? How? By being gutless? You're nothing but a puppet. You can't even stand up for your own kids." Dad's jaw drops. Spit flies from Adams mouth. "If Mom was alive she'd have you arrested for impersonation and send the police out looking for the real Ned Rose."

"Adam settle down. I made a promise and I intend to keep it. Irma won't touch a hair on her head."

Adam scoffs. He pulls down my hood. "Really? I know you're not blind. She's the laughing stock at school because of what Irma did to her hair. She's a friggin' monster and she's got you wrapped around her finger. You're letting her get away with bloody murder."

The curtains move. The hair rises on the back of my neck. If we go inside, I know I'm as good as dead. I tug on Adam's sleeve and whisper, "Please, I don't want to go in ever again. What if it's a trap?"

Battered

Irma raps on the window.

We leave Dad to his fate. Their voices are loud enough to hear from the end of the driveway. Adam shrugs. "With any luck, one of the neighbors might call the police and get them both arrested." His hand tightens around mine. "Lucky for you I got paid last night."

"Oh no! I forgot my knapsack. It's in the back yard."

"Hurry. Go and get it while they're busy arguing. Run as fast as you can. I'll wait right here." He picks up a big rock from the garden and moves to the corner of the house where he can see the front steps. "If anyone tries to hurt you, I'll split their head wide open."

My feet won't run fast enough. I grab my knapsack, swirl around, and two books fly out. I, scoop the books into the bag and bolt toward the side of the house, and skid into Adam.

"Who were you talking to?"

Adam laughs nervously, "I don't know. I think I'm picking up some of your bad habits. Maybe it runs in the family. Who knows?" He slings my knapsack over his shoulder. "I'll carry it. Let's go."

"Where?"

"I don't know. I'll figure it out while we walk. Maybe we can visit the greenhouses. You went there, today right?"

"No. Actually I didn't. I stole from StayMart today."

"StayMart? Stole what?"

I pull at the package of underwear. The plastic is stuck to my skin. I peel it loose. "Slow down, I need to put these in my knapsack."

"Underwear? You stole underwear?" Adam stops and kneels in front of me. "Juanita you can't do things like that. That's what she's waiting for. She wants you to be the bad one, that way she's off the hook. Don't give her an excuse to get rid of you."

"She doesn't need an excuse, so it doesn't matter."

"It does matter. Why underwear. Are you out?"

"Not anymore."

"Listen . . . I'm trying to save money, but I can afford to buy you some underwear, so next time ask. It's stuff like this that riles me up. I'm going to fix this, I promise."

"How?"

"By moving out. I plan to take you with me."

"When? How long from now?"

"As soon as I can afford it. Right now, I'm saving every cent I can, but I'm paying board so money's tight. But at least I get to stay and keep an eye on you. Lately, I've been working on Dad." His jaw tightens. "You know she got rid of Bruce."

"Why did she do that?"

"She's getting rid of all of us, one by one. She's halfway there, three left to go."

"You mean four left to go."

"No three. Yesterday Drake left. He couldn't take it anymore. Said being homeless wouldn't be any different than being here. And Ryan, well he's out of here as soon as he's old enough for the military."

"Where did they go?"

"I don't have a clue where either of them went."

"I think I know where Bruce is."

"You do? Where?"

"A while ago Samantha told me Bruce was living in their shed."

"Who's Samantha?"

"She goes to my school and she lives at the end of the road—the road by that airport, at the end of the road where we lived."

"When did she tell you that?"

"Remember that time Irma hit me in the eye with the belt buckle? It was somewhere around then. Maybe it was about a week later . . . I can't remember. Did Bruce run away or get kicked out?"

"Kicked out. He's underage but she doesn't care about the law. She belongs in jail. I mean, my gawd, how is Bruce even going to find food to eat? From garbage cans? A doubt they gave him a dime." He kicks the dirt, pivots and shakes his finger at our house. "See that? That's what really pisses me off. He can order two truckloads of topsoil and let it just wash away in the rain."

"What's it for?"

"The lawn. Those two loads are new since the rain. But lo and behold he can't afford a tutor for Bruce or decent clothes for you."

"I think it's Irma's doing—not his."

"It's his doing. He's letting her do this. And that house—he painted a brand-new house twice because her highness preferred a different shade of blue. Yet he'll let you dress like an orphan, and only God knows who owned them before you did. I swear he wasn't like this before she came. You were probably too young to remember but he spoiled us rotten." His mouth turns downward. "He used to make forts, hug on us, bring us home stuff—we were spoiled rotten. He was a totally different man back then."

"You mean when Mom was alive?"

"No. He was like that right up to the time Irma came. You remember how the laundry room was more like a playroom, filled with toys and food—we were always stuffed—always had more food than we could eat. It makes absolutely no sense at all. We're his own flesh and blood."

"Do you think we'll ever see Bruce and Drake or will they be gone forever, like Marie?"

His voice softens. "Not at this house we won't. Not while she's here. What worries me is Bruce left with a pillowcase of clothes and I think Drake left empty handed. Winter's around the corner . . ." He glances upwards.

"Maybe they're camping at Barachois Park."

"Juanita, Barachois Park is 800 miles from here."

"How will they keep from freezing to death?"

"Exactly. They won't survive out there alone. You hardly manage in the back yard. The only thing that kept you alive was knowing you could get inside at night for a warm up. It pisses me off that he's not doing a bloody thing to stop her, and she needs to be stopped."

"If that buckle ever hits me in the temple and kills me, will you promise you'll tell the police on her and get her put in jail?"

"No. Most certainly not, because she'll already be dead." He pats my head. "Let's go fatten you up. What kind of candy do you like best?"

"Any kind." I stretch my fingers around his wrist. "You're not so fat yourself. Adam, how long can a person live without eating?"

"I don't know. Water is more important than food and there's enough of that around here. They could go anywhere on this island and find plenty of it. And where there's water, there's fish."

"I bet Drake and Bruce can survive better than you. At least they can fish and hunt."

Adam shoves my shoulder, "Young lady, I should just leave you to fend for yourself. I'll have you know, I can shoot a deer, between the eyes from half a mile away and I have caught more than my fair share of salmon." He blows on his knuckles and rubs his shoulder.

"Being cruel to animals is nothing to be proud of." I point to the road to our right. "Guess what? You can get to the greenhouses from there."

"Good, let's go."

"I wish I was born an animal."

"No, you don't."

"I don't?"

"No, most certainly not. People kick animals."

"Like Irma kicks me—but most people don't kick anyone, and they pet animals and feed them."

"Tell me about the purple flower. Show me where you found it."

We walk and talk. I show him the secret route through the field to Mr. Hollikan's greenhouses, the pots I stacked and the shed I found. It's oddly quiet and there's no sign of life anywhere.

"Maybe the old fart died." Adam walks around the side of the greenhouse. There is a sign on the one facing the lane that is across from our house. "He's been closed for a week. He's back tomorrow." He feels the side of the greenhouse, "Maybe we could live in one of these, it's warm enough," he sounds serious. "Let's go."

"Where?"

Battered

"Let's go back through that meadow and spy on the house. The old man and Irma are probably looking through every window in the place. I should have brought my bird binoculars."

"I don't want to go back. I'm afraid. Let's go find Samantha's house and look for Bruce instead."

His fingers tighten around mine. "Don't be scared. I'll protect you. If I have to, I'll use your knapsack, as a weapon."

"What about me?"

Adam chuckles. "Oh, you can use the panties."

We spy until Adam feels it's safe to slip cross the road and walk up the driveway.

I hesitate at the front steps and pull back on Adam's sleeve. The knot in my stomach is doing head stands. Adam's hand twisting around the knob reminds me of the time Irma twisted hers around my neck. My throat tightens. The door flies open.

Dad does nothing but jingle coins in his pocket. His face is solemn. He looks tired, old and defeated. He motions us in.

"Wait here. If I don't poke my head back out the door in five seconds, you run over to that old man's place break in and call 911."

Adam is talking to me but he keeps his eyes pinned on Dad.

"She's locked herself in our room. Go ahead. Look around if you don't believe me. Knowing her, she won't be out for a week."

Dad stands stolidly against the wall. Adam pries my fingers from his sleeve and slips past him. I back away a few steps, watching, waiting, ready to run. My ears tingle. My heart is beating faster than ever. Dad twists and watches something inside the house. Footsteps get closer. My heart sounds like a war drum.

Adam's face is more relaxed but he isn't smiling. He reaches for my hand and squeezes it tight. "Come on Juanita, it'll be okay. Dad was telling the truth."

"One thing I'm not, is a liar."

I hesitate and whisper, "You lied to Marie. You made her promises you didn't keep. That's lying."

165

Juanita Ray

Adam tugs me toward him. The further we get inside the house the less brave I feel. By the time we walk through the kitchen the coward in me takes full control.

"I'm in a bunch of trouble, aren't I?" I whisper.

"I promise you it'll be okay."

Each step takes forever.

My shoes feel like heavy rubber tires.

The room spins into a funnel of darkness and takes me with it.

Slap. Sla—ap.

Adam's head zooms in and out.

"Wake up. I need you to wake up."

Someone is looming over me. The darkness returns . . .

My hand feels heavy and hurts. There's a tube taped to it.

"You scared me." Adam heaves his chest and covers his mouth.

"Am I in trouble?"

"No. Actually it's a good thing."

"What happened to me?"

"Dehydration, malnutrition and you're a bit anemic. Nothing to worry about. The doctor promised you're okay. You'll be fine."

We leave with a bottle of dark brown medicine and some clear pain pills. After we get in the car, Dad makes me take a capful. The crud smells like old boots.

The drive home is silent. Deadly silent.

Dad parks in the driveway, clears his throat, coughs twice and says, "Soon things will change."

"When? Before or after Juanita is dead?"

"Stop talking nonsense. You heard what the doctor said."

"It only takes one good blow to the temple to kill someone and you know Irma has come really close, more than once. My gawd, are you blind? Can't you see what she's doing to this family?"

Dad's tone is ice-cold. "You're out of line and you're wrong."

"You're right. I am wrong," Adam admits.

Dad smiles.

Battered

"I'm wrong in referring to us as a family. She destroyed that years ago. We're just a bunch of strangers living under the same roof."

Dad's eyes burn into Adam's.

Adam doesn't flinch. He looks straight at Dad and says, "What I don't get is why you don't do something about it. What's she got on you?"

"Nothing. She's having mood swings."

Disbelief blankets Adam's face. "So, you're admitting she's sick. You know she will never get better."

"No. The doctor thinks the mood swings will stop, after Irma has the baby. But he also said they could worsen over the next few months."

The Scissor Chase

I spend the next few days, over at Mr. Hollikan's. Everybody at home, except Adam, thinks I'm at school, and it's a good thing I'm not, because if I was, everyone would think I had head lice. The stubble that is growing out of the sides of my scalp is itching like crazy. Mr. Hollikan flips an empty five-gallon bucket upside down and motions for me to sit beside him.

"So, which one of those losers beat you, him or her?"

"Nobody." I squeeze my fists together, not because his question upsets me, but because the stubble growing on my scalp is itching like crazy. He points to it and asks, "What did you do to deserve this?"

"Nothing."

He points to

"You must be doing something wrong?"

I try to think. It's hard to remember. I've blocked a lot out. Sometimes it's over milk . . . and onions . . . they just won't stay down my throat. I shrug and keep my thoughts to myself.

Battered

His old eyes look sad. He pats my head, "It's okay, forget I asked. Let's talk about tomorrow. Tomorrow we plant seedlings."

"I can't. I can't come back for a while. I have to go back to school."

"If you don't come back who's going to help me fertilize the plants? So they'll grow fast and hardy?"

"Could plant food make my hair grow faster? If I put some on the shaved parts?"

He slumps forward and makes some weird guttural choking sounds. I shake his arm, "Are you okay?"

"No, I'm about to die laughing, but what a way to go." He wipes the tears from his eyes.

"It's not funny."

His smile fades. "I know but you are mighty cute and I'm going to miss you like nothin' else." He bends forward and reaches for something on the ground. It's a rusty screw. He scrapes the dirt from underneath his nails. "You know I could make a call. Get you out of there . . . if you weren't being treated right."

Flickers of panic spark across my chest. "I'm okay so please, please, please don't."

He raises an eyebrow and sighs, "If you think it's best."

For a while we sit, and gaze at the air in front of us.

He half-smiles at me, "You and I are more alike than you think, and we both got some pretty ugly scars underneath our skin, now don't we. The only difference is yours are younger than mine." He wipes the screw on his pants and pops a toothpick in his mouth.

"Could Irma die in child birth?" I try to conceal my hope.

He bites down hard on the toothpick. It snaps in half. "That all depends. Is this her first kid?"

"No, she had two boys. They don't live with us because Irma was mean to them, so they're with their Dad."

He sits up straighter. "I see. And how do you know she was mean to 'em?" He leans back and scrutinizes my face. "And who's this Irma?"

"She's the housekeeper, but I think Dad might have married her, back when you first met me. They went away for two weeks."

"Well I hate to be the bearer of bad news but chances of her dying in child birth are next to none. That never happens today. At least, not after having some kids. Don't fret, you'll grow up all too soon and you'll be bringing your own kids here to visit me. So, if you have to be a stranger for a while, don't be a stranger forever. Next time I see you, I'll have a nice surprise waiting for you."

"Like what?"

He snickers, "Ha. It wouldn't be a surprise if I told you, now would it?"

I walk backwards and say, "I'll be back but I don't know when."

The sun is winking at me from the wrong spot. I can tell I'm late and it seems past the time my bus gets home. I rush through the clearing toward home and fall face first, down the slope. I stretched out my hands to save myself and roll down to the bottom. My wrist has a nasty gash. At first, I see white spots but no blood. That's when I notice the broken beer bottle.

I press hard on my wrist and wait behind a bush until the bus comes. It passes by without stopping at all. I race toward the house, past the car and up the steps. Dad's nose is pressed against the kitchen window.

The door swings open. "Where have you been? I know it's not school," Dad yells.

Irma glares at Dad, "What's the point of asking her anything now, you idiot? Now she knows we know she wasn't at school."

"Irma, calm down."

"No, you did it on purpose." Blood vessels are popping out of her head. Her stomach looks like it's going to burst. She slaps me across the head. "Stop staring at the baby." I stumble, fall on my wrist and wince. Her foot lifts back and flies toward my face. I protect my head with my arms.

Dad yells, "Stop Irma. Calm down before you hurt yourself and the baby."

She kicks me twice before her foot lands square on my wrist. Then she grunts, slams a final kick to my stomach and retreats into the living room.

Battered

Dad steps over me and walks into the kitchen. He returns with a wet cloth and wipes blood from my face.

"Where the hell are you bleeding from? It's not your nose. Your face doesn't have a scratch on it."

I hold out my wrist.

"Holy dyin' sufferin' Moses."

He presses the skin together. "Hold it like that."

He cuts some V shapes in a couple of bandages and closes up my wound.

All weekend Irma stays in her room. Sometimes it's quiet, but most times the upstairs sounds like a battle field

I tiptoe upstairs, making sure to skip the step that creaks. Crank my neck to find the empty kitchen. The table is bare. There is no paper lunch bag, no soggy cereal and no signs of life.

I sneak outside, leaving the door one inch ajar and run as fast as I can down the road. Not a single soul is at the bus stop. Something isn't right. Did I lose track of days? Is it only Sunday?

A dog dashes across the road but stops in the middle. The owner drags it to the curb. I sprint toward her before she reaches the other side.

"Excuse me, excuse me," I pant. "What day is it?"

She looks at me with a half-smile, "Monday."

"Is today a holiday?"

"No. I don't think so," her smile widens. "Why?"

"I think I missed my school bus."

"It's too early for a school bus. It's close to seven—Hmmm. I bet you forgot the time went back last night. Remember spring ahead, fall back?" She leads the dog down the sidewalk to a bush.

I turn toward the house and fumble with the idea of returning. If Irma is up, she's going to accuse me of being out all night and kill me. A dozen needles dance across my chest. I turn to ask the woman the exact time and find myself face to face with Pearl. A head sticks out the window. "Old habits are hard to break. I knew it was you before I saw your face. Need another lift? Or do you want to wait for the next car to hit you?"

"I thought I missed my bus, but I didn't."

171

He laughs, "This is either fate or a curse."

"The woman said the time went back. Is it near seven?"

The stranger looks at the clock on the dash of his car. "I'll be damned. Pearl we can't have that, can we?" He leans ahead and changes the clock back an hour. "Looks like I have an hour to drive you all of twenty-five feet."

I slink down into the seat. "Please can you go to the next stop instead of here?"

"In trouble, are we?"

"No, but I will be if you don't." My words surprise me. I say the only thing I can think of. "For riding with a stranger."

His head twitches ever so slightly. He glances at the side mirror, pulls out onto the road and asks. "Where's the next stop?"

"The store around the bend."

"By the way I'm Mark Matthews, and you are?"

I lift my head and look backwards toward the house. My hood slips off. I sit up straight and try to act normal but that's impossible when he's driving with his head turned sideways. He slows to a stop at the store.

"Can we stop somewhere different?"

"Sure. Where's the next stop?"

My mind is blank and my filter fails. "I don't know. I don't have that part figured out yet."

Mr. Matthews pulls over, rests his elbow on the steering wheel, cups his jaw, and eyeballs my bandaged wrist. Then his eyes graze my temples. "Then we have a big problem. If you don't know where the next stop is how's Pearl supposed to get you there? Isn't that right, Pearl?" His hand strokes the dash. "How about you tell Pearl the name of your school."

"Bishop Abraham."

"Huh. That's my daughter's school. Do you know Karen Matthews?"

I shake my head.

"How about Samantha Matthews?"

"The only Samantha I know has long braids and wears orange and black nail polish."

"That sounds like my girl," he says with a proud smile. "Considering the time, I think we have two options."

I wait, while he taps his wedding ring against the steering wheel. "You can get out and walk back to whatever stop you want or you can ride with me to my house and take the bus with my girls."

"Okay."

"Okay to which one."

"The bus with your girls." The ride to his house is shorter than I expected. Up ahead, he turns left on a dirt road and then makes a sharp right. Just past several airport signs, he pulls into a house on the left, located at the bottom of the road we lived on years ago. "I lived up at the end of that road a while back."

"Really?" Mr. Matthews raises his arm against the back seat and twists to look at me. "That's surprising. I know someone else that lived up there. Wait here. Don't go anywhere. I'll be back with the girls and give you guys a lift to school."

A minute later, the door flies open and Samantha jumps in beside me. "Ouch!" She feels the lump on my forehead. "What happened to you?"

I shrug and ask, "Where's your shed?"

She frowns. "Sorry, he's gone."

Mark slides into the front seat. His other daughter sits beside him. I don't recognize her at all. "Who's gone?" she asks.

Samantha cocks her head toward my wrist, ignores her sister's question, and asks me again, "Well what happened."

"I fell in a field."

"Sure, you did."

She unzips her purse, flips it upside down and shakes it above her lap. "My birthday was yesterday. Want to see my new makeup?" Lipsticks and polishes of unimaginable colors, different than a rainbow, spill over her lap.

"You're allowed to wear makeup?" I whisper.

"Only me, not Karen, until next year," she says in a taunting tone. Her sister twists around, fires her a dirty look and turns the radio up another notch.

"You're still supposed to wish me a happy birthday, even if it was yesterday, because it's the polite thing to do."

"I'm sorry. Happy Birthday, Samantha. How old are you?"

"Thirteen. How old are you?"

"I'll be thirteen this summer."

"What do you want for your birthday."

"Nothing anyone can buy. Besides we don't celebrate birthdays." The truth is if I had a cake with candles, I'd wish to be somebody else's kid. Anybody else as a parent would do just fine.

Mr. Matthews turns the radio down. "Are you a Jehovah Witness?"

"What's that?"

"What religion are you?"

"Anglican but we don't practice it since Mom died."

"You lost your Mom?"

"No. She died."

"The girls lost their Mom too. Well we're here. Have a fun day." He winks at Samantha and says, "Don't kiss too many boys today."

She blushes, "Dad, knock it off."

I thank her father for the ride and shuffle over to get out on Samantha's side. "Maybe you guys can be friends. Maybe you can teach my daughters a few manners."

Karen says nothing when she struts past us.

"Don't mind her, she's just jealous because she's barely twelve. Let's try out some of my new makeup."

Every morning, for an entire week, we meet in the bathroom before school. Every day she gives me a beauty tip and makes me up. Friday's beauty tip number five is wear the same dress length as everyone else. She rolls up my skirt band. "Nobody wears skirts that long. There, now you look much better."

"But my waist looks fat," I say.

"Boys don't look at your waist. And you're so skinny you don't even have one. Besides, boys like to look at your legs." I stare at the stranger in the mirror. "You look beautiful. Even your hair looks sort of cute. I did a good job, of hiding the bald spot with mascara, didn't I?" Samantha murmurs, while she brushes some on her fluttering eyelashes.

"I love it. I wish I was allowed to wear makeup. How does it come off?"

"Don't worry it washes off easy. She'll never know." She cups my ear and whispers, "I told you before, I know all about Irma."

"Is Bruce still at your place?"

"Only at night. Dad makes him go look for work every morning. He just goes for the day, not forever. He sleeps in a sleeping bag out there. He seems to like it."

She shoves the mascara brush into the holder and screws it tight. The mascara reminds me of Ryan's shoe polish.

"Dad said you can come live with us, if you ever want to, but there's one condition. Drake has to visit you! I have a mush crush on Drake, he is just so scrumptious."

I don't tell her Drake's missing too and it's obvious she doesn't know where he is either.

After school, I nearly miss the bus because I spend too much time trying to get the makeup off. My temples were easy to clean but my face feels hot because I scrubbed it three times, but it all came off, just like Samantha promised.

By the time I get home my face feels cooler.

I hang my knapsack up on the hook in the porch and hurry past the empty kitchen. I can't wait until Adam gets home so I can see the look on his face when I tell him Bruce is still living in Samantha Matthew's shed.

"Turn around and look at me," Irma's voice cracks like a whip.

I stop, turn and cower. One hand is behind her back the other is on her hip. A belt dangles between her legs.

She yanks a chair far away from the table and orders me to sit.

I hesitate.

"I said sit down." Her voice is loud and harsh. The outfit she is wearing looks like she stuffed three pillows inside of it. "What the hell is this?" She throws a blood-stained sock on my lap. It's the one from the day she beat my face into the fridge. I forgot I stuffed it under Marie's old dresser. She grabs my hair and pulls my head upwards, "And what the hell is on your face?"

She throws the belt on the table and moves toward the kitchen sink. The two-inch brown leather belt slithers from the table. The tarnished square buckle clanks to the floor. It looks worn and stained. Is it from blood, or the sweat of her hands?

She braces her two legs against the side of my chair, scrunches a white dishcloth across my face and scours my cheeks. My eyes sting with soap. Bubbles go up my nose. When I gasp for air they trail from my mouth and burst. She scrutinizes the cloth, stalks to the sink, returns with a scrubbing pad, and scrapes it back and forth across each searing cheek. They feel scorched.

"Beet juice! You put beet juice on your cheeks," Irma shrieks and shakes her finger at me. "You're the one stealing beets out of the beet jars."

Beets? She's out of her deranged mind. She's finally gone insane.

Her nostrils flare wide open. "Don't you dare move one inch." The kitchen drawer slams shut. She pounces toward me with the scissors in one hand and the shaver in another. Her black wild eyes are inches from my face. Is she planning to cut my cheeks off?

I push her away, launch out of the chair and bolt downstairs. Adam's door blurs past me. I know I can't hide in any of the rooms. I'll be trapped. My eyes dart all over the place. There's nowhere safe to go. I speed past my room and around the corner toward the ping-pong table. I run toward the boarded opening. A whipping sound cracks to my right. I pull at the corner of the board. I hear it crash, behind me, followed by a curse. I turn to see if it hit her. She's nowhere in sight. Maybe she went upstairs to call Dad. I twist back. She's up ahead, coming straight at me. I run around the table twice. She switches direction and glares at me with her two hands on the side edge of the table, panting for breath.

I'm panting harder.

I look behind her and scream, "Dad, stop her!" She turns around to look. I dash in the opposite direction. She screams and yells the foulest names at me. She's so close I can hear her heavy breathing, ticking like a time bomb.

Battered

I pass the wood pile again. I need to crawl under it and bust through that plastic door, but how?

Heavy panting sounds are getting closer.

I run past my brothers' room again. Up ahead a bunch of 2x4 studs lean to the left of my room. I slow down and topple some directly toward her.

"I'm going to kill you, when I get you, you little slut!" She's clutching her gut but she's not slowing down.

I run past the ping-pong table, drop to my knees, dive under the gap in the wood, scramble up the steps and claw at the loose plastic like a deranged lunatic. It won't rip. Her screams are directly below me. I tear at the plastic like a wild animal. I punch it frantically with my fists but all I get is a bloody wrist. Not even a dent. It's too thick.

She's cursing me out. The sound of scraping wood sounds like fingernails across a blackboard. She's slid the end panel a foot away from the wall. I turn and scream. Her head and shoulders lurch toward me. Then she gets stuck. Her stomach gets pinned between the wood and the concrete opening. She lurches forward. The panel shakes and shifts an inch more. Her arms stretch and grope toward me. She snarls another threat.

I clamp my jaws around the loose plastic and spit out the pieces. I use my wrists and arms to make the tear bigger.

Thud.

My back jolts forward. A second piece of wood cracks against my ankle. I claw and claw. More wood scrapes behind me. She's almost through.

Something sharp bludgeons the muscle of my left leg. I attack the plastic and yell, "God get me out. I need to get out!"

Like a savage animal, I hurl against it twice, hurtle through the opening and tumble to the ground.

My chin slides across the grass and skids to a stop. The fence— the woods—everything seems so far away. My lungs are burning like crazy and the ground is swirling.

RUN. GET UP AND RUN.

R-i-i—i-p.

Juanita Ray

Barbed wire tears through my shirt and scrapes across my back. Bushes and branches whip my face. My throat is on fire, fighting for air. I stagger toward the biggest tree and hide behind it.

I pant and wait . . .

A Failed Escape

I'm not sure how many tears it takes to wash away seven years of being a coward, but however many I cry, it doesn't help me feel any braver. I'm still terrified. Terrified of the monster.

The smell of trees mingled with dead foliage reminds me of Mr. Hollikan's place but going there is out of the question. It's too close to Irma. Dad should be on his way home by now. I know he'll come after me, because Irma won't let him rest until he drags me back home.

I lurk at the tree line, close to the field at the edge of the grove. The main road is only six feet away. Each time a car passes by, I duck and look. It's the perfect spot to see the cars coming from both directions. The problem is they all look like Dad's. What if Irma doesn't make him go after me? Where would be safe to go?

The sound of a horn yanks me from my thoughts. Fear flushes through me. I squat down and wait for traffic to slow.

It's getting gusty and chilly and I don't have a jacket. I cross my arms to shield my chest from the wind. The sun is sinking fast, but it's still shining on the other side of the road. Cars crisscross leaving me stuck here. Near dusk I spot a decent break in both sides of the traffic and break into a run.

The ground crackles when I reach the dirt shoulder. There is a massive field to my right, protected by a barbed wire fence. A faded red lettered sign threatens to prosecute trespassers.

Samantha's house is straight across from me beyond that field. I can't see it but I know it's there. It's the only place I can go. They helped Bruce, so maybe they'll help me.

Pebbles and dry brown silt tumble down the ditch and roll across my shoes. I slide to the bottom, dig into the dirt and catch my balance.

I scramble up the other side, grab hold of the chain link fence and climb up two feet. A gust of wind whips my hair over my eyes, and bends every tree and every bush. I climb higher. I'm a foot from the roll of barbed wire. An airplane roars like thunder above my head and the grass rolls like ocean surf. I can see forever but I don't see any houses. Not one.

I climb down to the sheltered ditch. Here I'm safe from the wind—invisible to cars. I walk along the bottom until a cool trickle of water seeps in my shoes and curls around my toes. I'm thirsty and all I can think about is wetting my throat. It's not light enough to see if it's clear or muddy. Maybe it's full of bugs, or animal pee.

It splatters against my legs with every step. Five minutes later I reach a putrid pool of still stench. It's shallow, so shallow that if Irma were buried in it, her belly would stick out above the slime.

I step backwards, lick my dry lips, and roll my tongue against the roof of my mouth. The taste of salty dust won't disappear. I wipe my tongue with my shirt and climb toward the road side. Halfway up I slide back down and land near the edge of the festering slime. I scramble on all fours, across the side of the ditch make it past the slime, to the top and stumble back down in the ditch again. The wet cracked ground turns to a stew of crunchy twigs and dead leaves and the only sign of water is my cold feet sloshing in my socks. My sneakers squeak with every step until the sound is overpowered by the hum of tires and the roar of engines.

Battered

The ditch takes a sharp veer to the right. A huge concrete culvert goes under the road forming a pitch-black tunnel. Fear smothers every breath I take. I try to convince myself, there are no monsters here, but I know Irma can't be the only one alive.

I take a deep swallow and slowly edge my way through the sloped murky tunnel and pray there is nothing inside. At the end I'm greeted by a large spider web and a shallow dry ditch. The ditch flattens into a path, and in the distance looms two vague shadows. Within minutes they turn into houses. I quicken my pace. Fear switches to excitement. Bruce. I get to stay with Bruce. I sprint toward Samantha's house.

The house seems larger in the moonlight. The driveway is twice as long as I remember it. I skid to an abrupt stop. Where did the shed go and what happened to the fence? I don't recognize the veranda. Does the color look that dark at night?

I retreat back to the side of the road. A car drives by and lights up the next house about quarter of a mile away. There are no lights on it either, but from the headlights I can see it has a fence and maybe a shorter driveway. Good I'm not lost.

I cross the yard to the shed. The door is ajar. I tiptoe through it excited to find— nothing.

It's empty. No Bruce. Just a smelly old empty shed. I open the door wider. How could Bruce fit in here and keep his legs straight? A crumpled sleeping bag is stuffed in the corner. I sit on it and stare out at the house. It doesn't look as friendly in the dark. I curl up in his sleeping bag and cry myself to sleep.

Deafening vibrations jerk me out of my dreams. The shed shakes. I cover my ears with my hands, and wait for the walls to crash down but they don't. Four more planes fly over and each one seems louder than the last. The noise diminishes. I uncover my ears and listen to the gentler sounds of morning emerge. A bird pecks at the grass in front of the shed door, chirps and hops out of sight. I poke my head out of the doorway, and watch it wrestle with a worm.

"Oh my god! I can't believe it! You ran away, didn't you?"

I turn and blink. Samantha looks like a glowing angel, in a burst of light. The sun is shining through her white dress.

I squint up at her. "Do you know what time it is?"

"Almost noon. When did you get here?"

"Last night."

"You slept out here all night?"

"Yeah. I think something bit my eye. It feels sore and swollen."

"Did you knock on the door?"

"No. The car was gone." The truth was it never occurred to me to knock on the door. Irma had brainwashed us not to knock.

Samantha points to a small garage behind the house. "At night, Dad parks Pearl in there."

"Where's Bruce?"

Samantha frowns. "He was gone when we got home from school yesterday. Dad said he got a job on an oil rig."

"What's an oil rig?"

"Dad said it's like a home on the ocean. They give you a giant allowance to live there."

"Does he get to come home?"

"To where? Bruce doesn't have a home anymore." Her face is kind, and her voice is soft but her words stab my heart.

"Well he does now, because he loves the ocean—that's his real home. It's his favorite place. He'll spend every free second he gets, fishing."

"Does anyone know where you are?"

"No. and I don't want anyone to know."

"What happened to you? You're full of blood and you stink."

I sniff myself.

"You look horrible and you do smell really, *really* bad. You need to come inside and get a bath."

"Am I allowed? Shouldn't you ask first?"

"I don't need to. Dad lets me have friends over all the time. And he seems to like you, so it'll be fine." She grabs my hand and leads me to her front door.

I shrink back. "Please go ask first."

She scoffs and pulls me inside. "Dad, look who I found sleeping in the shed."

Mr. Matthews doesn't turn around. He reaches into the cupboard and retrieves a mug. "Bruce my boy, I told you the ocean is tougher than it looks." He tips the pot of coffee toward his cup.

"It's not Bruce, but you're close! Guess again."

He glances over.

"Dad the coffee!"

Tar colored water splatters over the counter, spills down the lower cupboards and pools at his feet. Samantha releases my hand, grabs a roll of paper towels and unrolls it onto the puddle. "DAD put down the coffee!"

The dripping coffee pot, dangles midair. He drops it on the counter, steps though the puddle, kneels in front of me and grabs my shoulders. "Who did this to you?"

I focus on the wet footsteps, leading from the puddle to me, and mumble, "I'm alright."

"You don't look alright. You're about the furthest thing from alright I have ever seen." He lifts my wrist, and slowly unwinds the muddy gauze. He presses the ruptured wound further apart, forcing the dirty cut open.

"This should have had stitches. Let's deal with this first. Samantha, get the peroxide from the bathroom." His eyes travel up and down my body. He circles me twice before Samantha returns.

"Dad what's Peroxide?"

"It's in a brown bottle. It's the stuff you put on your ears when you had them pierced. And bring me the tape, gauze and scissors."

His eyes are inches from mine. They don't leave my face. He pulls a chair behind his backside and sits in front of me.

"What happened?"

"I-I-I got in trouble."

He asks, "Why?"

"I don't know."

Samantha returns with a plastic bin. She pulls out a long skinny plastic bag. "Here's the gauze."

"Unless you're planning to remove your nail polish we don't need this. Sweetheart, hand me the bin and go run her a bath, but first find her something clean to wear."

Mark lifts my face. "What did you do? Nuzzle a grinder?"

I recoil.

"Relax. No one here is going to hurt you. Hold out your wrist. It only stings for a minute."

I flutter my lashes trying to force the tears below my lids.

"Am I hurting you?"

"No." I whisper. Tears well up. His hand blurs. It bothers me that no one has ever asked me that before. The kinder he is the worse it hurts. What hurts the most is knowing this is how fathers are supposed to be.

"It's okay to cry." His hug feels smothering—uncomfortable. I want him not to care. I hate that I'm crying for nothing.

"Ready? It will only hurt for a second."

"That's a lie. It stings really bad. And I mean *really* bad. For more—"

"Samantha. Shush."

The peroxide scorches my wrist. I grit my teeth. It bubbles up and turns to a white frothy foam. In seconds the pain completely disappears. So does Samantha.

He pours some on my leg.

"Dad, the bath is ready."

"Good. Time to get you cleaned up. You smell like sewage."

He pauses and picks a bright colored garment off the bathroom doorknob, "You call this thing clothes? It's fall. What's with this?" He dangles the swimsuit in the air.

"It's warm out today! Besides, we have to help her bathe and she can't bathe with one hand and she can't bathe naked."

"Good point. I'll be back after you help her into this."

"I can do it myself. I'm used to it. I hurt my hand over a week ago."

Battered

Mark's mouth shapes into an O. He raises his eyebrows. "Then we shall wait outside together. Once you're ready get in the tub." He bows and pulls Samantha out the door. She kicks it shut with her foot.

Three minutes later Mr. Matthews raps on the door. "You haven't drowned in there have you?"

"No, but I'm in the tub now."

Samantha giggles at her father. He tickles her back. A pang of envy travels across my chest. My teeth bite into my top lip.

Samantha plops on the floor and holds my hand over the edge of the tub. "Dad, look at the color of the water."

Mr. Matthews pulls the plug, runs some water then refills the tub.

"Dad can you help hold her arm, while I wash her back? It's full of dried blood."

"That's okay. I can hold it up myself."

"There's a lot of dirt under those fingernails. Try to soak them but keep that bandage—" Mr. Matthews lurches for my wrist.

"I'm sorry. I keep forgetting."

"No problem. Samantha, make yourself useful. Go get the baking soda. I'll be back in less than a minute."

"BAKING soda?"

"For her back. It's good for minor cuts."

"Mom used to say it whitens sneakers and got rid of smells."

A faint smile crosses his lips. "We may need it for that too."

The water drips from the tap, two hundred and thirteen times before he gets back. The shovel drips across the floor. "Don't worry it's clean. I hosed it good." He holds the shovel upside down across the edge of the bath. "Rest your arm across the blade." He leans against the back of the toilet and yawns. "How did you get like this? How did that wound reopen?"

"I was trying to climb out of a ditch."

"What were you doing in a ditch?"

"Hiding from cars."

Samantha bursts into the bathroom. "We're out of baking soda."

"Who did this to you?"

185

I suck in my breath. "The trees."

"And ..."

"The fence."

"Let's talk about the scar on your leg. Can you tell that story?"

My wound looks fresh. "What scar?"

"That one on your inner right thigh, the one shaped like an eye."

That story is easy to tell because it happened so long ago. I should have known better than to ride a bike with no seat. "My friend Sharon, had a bike leaning against her fence. The seat was broken and all that was left were rusty wires, so I had to stand up to ride it. She gave me a push to help start me off. I couldn't find the brakes and crashed into the fence and the wires got me."

"Who fixed you up?"

I try to remember. "Somebody cut the bike from my leg and somebody drove me to the hospital. I don't think it was Dad. I think he was fishing. But I think he came to the hospital before they stitched it up. I had thirty-two stitches, some of them were inside. I think and for a while Adam carried me everywhere."

"So, Adam is . . .?"

"My brother. He's almost twenty."

"Now what happened ten minutes before you ran away."

I shrug.

"Okay. How about I ask you some questions about Adam? Would that be alright?"

I nod.

After I answer three questions about Adam, he asks if I have any aunts or uncles. I tell him about Aunt Patty.

". . . but she's fake. I don't know any real ones."

He swishes his hand in the water, and pushes on the hot water tap. He swirls the water toward the back of the tub, then shuts it off.

"How about friends. People you go to movies with, or visit for sleepovers?"

I watch the water roll around me. "I-I-I can't do that kind of stuff."

Battered

"Dad quit it! Can't you see you're upsetting her? Stop asking all these questions. It's not like we've known her forever. It's only been a week and she's sort of a loner. She doesn't have friends, and she doesn't trust anyone. Besides you didn't ask Bruce half as many questions as you're asking her."

"That's different, boys get kicked out all the time and Bruce wasn't beat up when he arrived here."

"What do you mean boys get kicked out all the time. Did you get kicked out when you were a kid? You did, didn't you Dad? That's why you helped Bruce, and you're helping her—isn't it?"

Confined

Samantha whispers, "That's not Dad's special knock." The creaking outside of the door reminds me of Irma. We each hold our breath until the footsteps leave the landing. Three of us peek through the blinds.

"Adam! Adam!" I rap on the glass. He twirls around, throws his arms up into the air and smiles with half of his face.

"It's my brother!"

Samantha opens the door. Adam runs inside and crushes my ribs against his chest. "You scared the living shit out of me."

I lose my brave face. Tears turn to sobs. Uncontrollable sobs.

After five minutes he pushes me away and scans my eyes.

"How bad did she get you this time? I know damn well it had to be pretty bad for you to run off without telling me. What happened to your face?"

I glance at Samantha. "Tree branches. Through the woods."

"What started it?"

"I missed the bus."

"You walked eight miles? It's three to get here."

"The hardest part was running around in the basement."

For the next hour, Adam rocks me against his chest.

"My eyelid feels tender."

Adam forces it open. "It looks like a sty." He turns to Samantha and asks, "I don't suppose you have a bike siting around, that I can borrow?"

Samantha says, "It's pink."

"Oh, that won't do," Adam laughs. "I prefer bright purple with pink polka dots but beggars can't be choosers."

I stop crying and burst out laughing,

"I hate to leave you, but if I don't get some drops for your eye, your lid will swell double that size, in no time flat."

"What if Dad followed you?"

"When I figured out where you were, I snuck out while he was showering. Nobody followed me."

"Are you sure?"

"Positive and if they find you it won't ever be because of me."

—·—·—·—·—

"You awake?" Samantha whispers.

"Yes." I shift to a more comfortable position.

"I can't sleep." Samantha rolls over on her side.

"Me neither," I say. "Do all girls have rooms this nice?"

"The ones I've been to are nicer. But those girls had moms."

"Why do you have a caseworker?"

"Oh," Samantha pauses a moment, checks to make sure Karen is sleeping, and says, "Dad got so depressed after Mom died, he started drinking. He got caught with a DUI and had to go to jail for a while and we had to go to a foster home."

"How did she die?" I grimace and pick at a woolly on the blanket.

"Her car crashed. One day she complained about the brakes, and the next day she was dead. Dad told her to go easy and he would fix them on his next day off, but that next day never came. She went through a red light and couldn't stop in time."

"How long ago?"

"Five years ago. Two years later we got put in a foster home. We got to come home last year but the caseworker still checks on us."

"Where did you live?"

"On a farm. Karen liked it better than I did. I . . ." her voice drifts off.

"Why? What was the foster home like?"

Samantha murmurs something that turns into a snore.

———————

I ignore the counselor, and think, what a great day, my worries are over. The guidance counselor pulls on his beard a few times. "It seems you've been missing a week."

"Missing? Me?"

"This is your only chance to tell me your side of the story."

I glare at the counselor.

He slaps my arm with a file folder and says, "I'm giving you a second chance . . . your story?"

"I don't have one." What point would there be to tell the truth?

"Fine, we'll just keep meeting like this until you have one."

He opens a drawer and pulls out a black book. It reminds me of Marie's little Bible. Is he going to make me swear on it? I remember the last time I swore on a Bible. I wonder if God saw my fingers crossed. It was the first year Irma came. I was finishing first grade, learning about shapes. It was almost near the time that the spankings turned to beatings and locking me out went from being weird to being normal.

It was the first day she never answered the doorbell. The more I rang it, the more it started to look like a miniature door with a door knob, so I drew a little square around the doorbell, a triangle for a roof and a little rectangle with smoke and before I knew it that door bell was the center of a huge village. I had to stand on the lower part of the railing and stretch on my tiptoes, to add some clouds.

Battered

Dad was furious. He made the boys repaint it and I got away with minimal punishment because Dad told Irma I wasn't that good at drawing. They blamed it on Ryan, even though he insisted he could draw much better than that.

The counselor taps my head with his pen and leans back in his chair, "Hello? Anyone home?"

I jerk upright in my chair as he says, "Don't forget I gave you every chance I could." He writes something in his book and slips it back into his drawer and hands me a pink slip to give to my teacher.

An hour later, at one o'clock, a loudspeaker message plays over the intercom, calling me to the guidance counselor's office.

My teacher frowns when I tell her there's a mistake.

"But my slip says two o'clock, tomorrow, not today."

"I'm sure there's a good reason he rescheduled."

I walk down the hall toward his door. It's ajar. I slide into the chair and watch him twiddle his thumbs around each other. He stops and rolls them in the reverse order.

I sit, sigh and pick my nails while I read the name plate on his desk.

"Should I call you Mr. Chadwick?"

"You can call me whatever you want as long as you tell me the truth about what is going on at your house." He flips a page back and forth. His red face looks like a balloon about to burst.

If I tell him the truth about where I am, he might make me go back home or he might help me, like Mr. Matthews did. I try but all I manage to do is open and close my mouth three times.

"You're twelve, correct?"

"I'll be thirteen this summer."

"So that makes you twelve? Correct?"

"Twelve and three months, but we don't celebrate birthdays."

"Jehovah Witness?"

It's the same question Mr. Hollikan asked. Maybe it's a sign. Maybe I should tell somebody. "No sir. I was born Anglian."

"Hmmm. Why don't you celebrate birthdays?"

Juanita Ray

I don't find that question as threatening as some others he's asked. Every year when my birthday comes, I think about all the girls that get to celebrate theirs, all the parties I never get asked to and wish I was them and not me. Now that I've seen what a normal family is like, I want one more than ever. I inhale an extra mouthful of air. Should I start with the first day at the fence, or the beet juice and buzzed hair cut? I fumble around for a place to start.

Mr. Chadwick looks at this watch and says, "This is your last chance."

I open my mouth but the words stay inside.

"Well, don't say I didn't try," his irritated voice chides. Before I can protest, he picks up the phone and says, "Send him in."

A shudder starts in my neck and plummets to my gut. I feel faint. My voice cracks. "Send who in?"

"Your father is here to pick you—"

"Wait. You can't send me back. I can't go."

The door opens and Dad steps inside. My chest caves in.

"No. Please. No. She beats me. You can't let him take me back to her. She's a monster. Please I'll tell you everything. Please don't do this."

"Juanita, thank God you're safe. I was so distraught over your disappearance. We were worried to death. We searched for you everywhere." I watch his mouth spit out one lie after the other.

—·—·—·—·—

I spend winter weekends walking in circles, retracing my steps, without smudging them. Every time it snows, I restart the game.

Today, my feet are too frozen to walk. The wind is ferocious. Snow crystals blast my face. My mittens are lifeless, frozen solid into two red chunks of heavy ice. I try to move my fingers but I can't feel them. The snowdrifts completely cover the opening where the plastic door once was. Today there is no game of retracing my steps. The only steps I make are trying to find a more protected corner to hide behind but the wind whips at me wherever I go and the drifts immediately cover any footprints I make.

Battered

I spot a higher drift and move toward it, hoping it will cut down on the cold. It doesn't. It's worse. Moving away from it, I sink up to my waist and have to lie on my back wiggling backwards to free myself from being stuck. I spend the next hour praying to die. Then I remember the Matthews.

What if . . .

The wind swirls furiously around finding me no matter where I choose to hide. I kick my boots against the frozen tree trunk. It doesn't warm them up. Instead, it sends dull pain vibrations across my ankles, deep into my legs.

I spend the next two hours marching up and down beside the barbwire fence. My gut is gurgling with the desire to run. The only thing that stops me is the cold. I have nowhere to go and I don't want to freeze to death curled up at the bottom of a tree two miles away.

The more the wind swirls the snow, the faster my mind whirls. What if I had run to Mr. Hollikan's instead of the Matthews? What if I never went back to school? What if I tried again?

The sky is my clock and finally it tells me I've almost made it. Soon the door will get unlocked. Soon the light will go on. And it does.

I go inside, thaw out and dread the next day, but it always comes.

Storms rage every day for the next two months. The odds that I'll be found dead in the snow, increase daily. Each day I survive, seems to entice nature to rebound with a stronger attempt to kill me, and today I've come closer than ever before.

I've lost all feelings in my hands and feet and my body is having spasms. My hands burn as I hold them under the faucet of the laundry tub. "You're scalding me. The water is too hot.".

"Juanita the water is cold, it's not even warm."

"It's too hot it's burning me. Honest."

"It's just the frost bite tricking your brain. How are your toes?"

"I can't feel them yet."

Adam slumps to the floor and stares at the ceiling beams. "Juanita, I swear to God, I just want to kill them. That's all I think about lately. Lucky for them I haven't figured out how just yet."

193

My fingers won't work right. I can't unbutton anything or grip my socks. Adam sees me struggling and helps peel them off. My toes look painted white. Adam lifts me up and runs water over them.

"I would love to see the police knock on the door and say, Adam, I am sorry, but Mr. and Mrs. Rose are both dead, from a car accident. I wouldn't even go to their funeral. No that's a lie. Yes, I would. I would go just to spit in their coffins."

Adam rubs my feet back to life.

"Mr. and Mrs. Rose? Are they married for real? Ryan was right, it was when they went away, wasn't it? Ouch! Adam, stop working my feet. It's making electrical jolts run through them."

"I've got to get your blood circulating and I don't know if they're married or not. She's been calling herself Mrs. Rose but I don't think she is yet, because if they were, she'd have photos of it hanging in the hall and on every other wall in the house. But you can bet she will be before that kid gets much older."

"Adam, are you deaf or what? Get up here and shovel the driveway so I can get my car off the road before the snowplow comes back."

"I'll talk to him while we shovel. Work your feet until they stop burning. Later, I'll try to smuggle you something to eat, okay?"

I rub my toes with the palms of my hands, until they tingle back to life. I hate the pins and needles, but not as much as the fiery heat that itches like crazy. I try to distract myself so I won't claw them off but my bare room has nothing in it worth looking at. The walls are bare and the only item on my dresser is a comb. Samantha's room had books, games and stuffed animals in it. Mine looks like a dungeon.

My closet is empty except for some pieces of gyprock. Most of my dresser drawers are empty too. According to Irma there's no point in buying me a bunch of clothes when the new school has uniforms.

I break a small piece of gyprock from the bigger piece that is leaning in the back of my closet. I peel away the paper from the gyprock to expose more chalk. I pull out my sock drawer and turn it upside down. I play tic-tac-toe on the bottom. To make the game interesting, I close my eyes and touch the drawer. I open them and the closest square is where I put the x. I do the same for the o's.

On game three, the stairs creak. I scoop my socks into the drawer, and return it to the dresser. The footsteps are directly behind me. Too heavy to be Irma's. I twist around. Dad is in front of me holding the belt.

"What did you do to make Irma so upset this time?"

"Nothing. Maybe she's mad at you. That's usually when she hits me the hardest. You guys should stop fighting."

"Well you must have done something. Bend over."

Instinctively, my hands cover my head. But the belt barely grazes my butt. It hardly hurts. Once or twice, he hits the dresser, instead of me.

Cries from a screaming baby fill the air.

"The baby's hungry, always hungry." Dad mutters. He slips his belt back through the loops and slowly walks away.

The baby cries more than either of her first two sons ever did. But according to my home economics teacher, that's what most babies do. Irma had the baby, last fall, a few days after I ran away. I think running after me put her into labor or else she squished it out when she tried to squeeze through that opening between the boards.

Every time I hear it cry, it reminds me of when she first came and locked her boys in the room.

For a second, I wonder who the baby looks like. It won't look like Marie, Adam, Ryan or me, because we all look like Mom. It won't look like Drake because he doesn't look like anyone. Maybe it looks like Bruce. Adam thinks Bruce looks like the Reids, but I think he looks a little like Dad.

If it looks like Irma, I will hate it forever. Dad promised things would change after she had it. She changed alright. She's got even worse.

I have no clue if it's a boy or a girl, but the truth is, it doesn't really matter what it is, because the monster made it.

A Bus to Nowhere

My room feels like a tomb, especially since the light bulb blew out last week. Gray dismal walls and dark shadows have become my best friends, but anything beats being outside freezing.

My dresser is bare, just like my life and I'm bored, bored, bored. I have invented and mastered so many games I'm running out of versions, so this winter I've set a limit on game playing. The only place I allow it is outdoors and the only time I allow it is on weekends and holidays, but after so many long winter days, the games are too monotonous and don't distract me from the cold.

I'm tired of spotting and counting icicles. I enjoyed knocking them down with snowballs, until I got a nasty beating for hitting Irma's bedroom window with one. Since then I count icicles only if they are dripping. It's too depressing otherwise.

Dripping icicles mean temperatures are above freezing, and it's warming up. My favorite game is counting the drips. That's one of the only games I have never mastered. That game doesn't last long because it's usually during late spring, which is right around the corner. I like spring. It's when everything dead comes alive. Spring means I survived the winter.

This spring, I'm looking forward to inventing a few new games. Overall, they should be less boring but there are a few favorites oldies, I plan to keep around. One is trying to count the new buds on the short bush out back. They never stop growing and I've yet to master that game. But the fall version, of when they die, is far less challenging and makes me wonder if I'll be next.

After the bush was leafless, I counted how many times the wind blew the branches and tried to predict what direction they would bend. I'm pretty good at predicting things, like Irma's moods, what day I might not get a beating, how many meals I'll have to skip, and I've become an expert at counting.

There isn't much around here I haven't tried to count. I've counted ants, spiders and I've even counted rocks. I think all this counting is why I hate math class so much. Right now, I'm counting how many days there are before the next full moon.

I spend most nights reading smuggled books by the light of the moon, the only problem is, I've read all the books twice.

There's no point in getting the Bible out from under my mattress because the print is too small. I can't read it is unless I stand under the window in a full moon, and right now, there is too much snow against my window. All I can see is frosted glass.

A scraping sound above me catches my ear. Adam whistle a tune and clears the snow from my window. He does it every night, in between shoveling the driveway and it usually takes him thirty minutes. Tonight, the upstairs is unusually quiet. My guess is Irma is busy feeding the baby and that means I have fifteen minutes to rummage through Adam's trunk, rearrange it in the same meticulous order and get back into my room.

The tarnished bronze lid weighs a ton. The last time I rifled a book from it was eight nights ago, and I almost got caught. I kneel in front of it, unlatch the rusty gold buckles, and hold my breath as the lid creaks louder than normal. Adam usually has everything lined up like a grid but the trunk appears rearranged. I feel the edge of a thin paperback. It's something new to me. I can't see the color or the name but I grab it and close the lid.

On nights like this, if I stand on the chair, I can usually read for at least an hour but the snow has already drifted over my window and blocked my window of opportunity. I tuck the book under my pillow and wait for Adam to clear the snow for a final time. Every night it snows, no matter how many times he clears my window, he always clears it a final time, once he finishes shoveling the driveway.

The grinding of the shovel halts. Adam taps my window. I stand on the chair while he grins and makes faces. Then he points upwards and moves aside. It's a full moon!

I hold the book up to the light and flip through the pages. It looks like the recipe books we had in home economics, except the pictures are birds and they all look related to each other. It's more boring than my room.

It takes me two minutes to switch out the book and the entire time, my stomach sounds like a drainage system.

I can't remember the last time we all ate dinner together. Whenever it was, has to be years ago. These days, when I do get dinner, it's usually on a little table in the corner of the room or facing the hall wall. It all depends on Irma's mood.

Adam's voice startles me, "Where are you?" He flicks the light switch several times. "What happened to your light?"

"Irma switched it with a burnt-out one from the laundry room. She said I didn't need it anyway."

He disappears and returns with a bulb, climbs onto my bed, unscrews the blackened bulb, and replaces it with the one in his hand. He screws it tight until it fills the room with light.

"Where did you get it?"

"From under the stairs," he chuckles.

"I thought it was burned out, too."

"No. I unscrewed it so she wouldn't be able to see inside my trunk."

The baby upstairs starts screaming again.

"That baby has got one helluva set of lungs."

"I'd cry to if I had to have her as a mother. Do you think Irma beats it?" I ask.

"Juanita you don't have to waste one minute worrying about that baby. It's spoiled rotten already and wants for nothing."

I spin my empty spool of thread on top of my dresser. "Adam do you have any little nails? About twice as long as my finger nails?"

"As a matter, of fact I do," he grins. "I made a little box for my watch parts and I only used half of them."

"You wouldn't need a parts box if you stopped taking watches apart and not putting them back together."

"There's no point in putting broken watches back together, unless you have spare parts."

"Can I have some?"

"What? Parts?"

"No nails."

"What do you need fixed?"

"Nothing, I want to build something with this." I hand him the thread spool.

He laughs, "What a new house for fleas?"

"I'm serious. I want to make something with it. Please."

Adam shakes his head, "You know you're really starting to worry me. You're acting stranger every day. Whenever I come into your room, you're talking to yourself and now you think you can build something out of an empty spool of thread?"

"I want the nails a certain way—and I never talk to myself."

"Oh, I see. We have an invisible friend, do we?" Adam chuckles. "Well tell me, have you named this friend of yours yet? I don't mind it one little bit if you want to introduce me."

"I talk to God."

Adam stops laughing. "You're joking right?"

I shake my head.

His smile disappears. "Well the next time God shows up for a conversation, come get me because there's a word or two I'd like to have with him, myself."

"Adam, do you have a hammer?"

"If I had a hammer, I'd hammer in the morning—Yes, and no you can't borrow it. But you can borrow this," he hands me a pen, "to mark the spots." He half chuckles under his breath, "And I can't wait to see this one."

I mark the spots on the spool.

"I'll nail them in my room. I'll be back when I'm finished."

"Wait, Adam, I need them to stick out about half an inch. Don't nail them all the way in, okay?"

In two minutes, I hear Adam's laugh before I see him.

"Here's your weapon." He licks his top lip, in a failed attempt to wipe the grin from his face and plops down on my bed.

"So, Juanita, tell me, what night are you planning to creep into Dad's bedroom and poke out Irma's eyes with this thing?"

I laugh, reach into my sock drawer and take out a small ball of red wool. "Remember that old mitt? The one with the big hole in it? I unraveled it. Watch this."

I loop it around the nails and after I reach the first loop, I make a second loop on top of the first one. I use a rusty old hair clip to lift the first loop off and over so only the second loop is showing. After a minute, a tube hangs from the hole in the spool. I stretch it down and say, "See?"

Adam watches, fascinated. "I don't know how you come up with some of the stuff, you come up with. Like that bracelet you made from my empty gum wrappers." He leans in close and runs his fingers along the soft red tube hanging from the bottom of the spool.

"What is this thing? A fancy strangling noose?"

"No, it's going to be a ribbon for my hair, for when I'm at school, or maybe a bracelet."

Adam's mouth twists to one side. "Or give it to someone with buck teeth to use as dental floss."

"Stop making fun of me. Don't you have to go to work or something?"

Battered

"It's a state of emergency. Dad couldn't make it down the road. His car got snowed in so we shoveled it out and just finished pushing it back in the driveway."

A faint memory of being excited about snow flashes through my mind. When I was small, before Irma came, we all went tobogganing. Back then snow could be fun, now it's petrifying.

"The whole city is shut down. The good news is, it's only supposed to last for a day or two, then it's supposed to get warmer. Warm enough that there'll be no more frostbite for you."

"When will it get warmer?"

"The weatherman said next week. This is supposed to be the last cold spell."

My mouth feels dry. Next week is too far away. I look at my wet mittens and socks on the baseboard heater. The more they drip, the dryer my mouth gets.

"Adam what if my mitts don't dry by tomorrow?"

Adam says, "Don't worry. You're safe. They wouldn't put a dog out in this one."

The next day I find out that Adam is wrong. He comes outside to keep me company and yells something above the howling wind.

"How come Ryan didn't get sent out?" My teeth chatter with each word.

"I don't know where the hell he disappears to, but he's around here somewhere—or maybe he went with Dad." He cuts a perfect snow rectangle, tilts the shovel, lifts it aside and cuts another.

"I thought you said the roads were blocked."

"They are. But Irma ran out of milk."

"The store is open in this storm?"

"Mr. Mercer never closes. He's tighter than the old man is."

His eyes dart around the yard then return to his pile of snow cubes. He meticulously makes a circle of blocks. He removes three, puts them on top of the first ones, and overlaps the edge a couple of inches. "I almost forgot about the door."

"Where did you learn this?" I ask.

Adam grins, "Back in grade four. Geography had a chapter on Eskimos."

We stand back and admire the white dome. Adam shovels snow up the sides and over the top, to camouflage the igloo to look like a snow bank. He wiggles inside. "Come in. Check it out!"

I crawl inside and listen to the wind howl The air is still. No flurries. No sprays of snow slapping against my face.

"See! Now you can crawl in here to get warm, just be careful not to lean too hard against the walls," Adam warns.

And that's what I do for the next two days.

It takes five days for the igloo to turn in to a small wet mound. And it takes five more for the road banks to shrink to half size.

Two weeks ago, before the storm, the snow banks were rock solid and covered the tops of telephone poles and the snowplows were covering the icy roads with salt. Now the shrunken banks are big white sink holes, speckled with brown dirt.

Every morning the snowplow beats down the banks and spreads the piles of snow over the road and every afternoon, I watch my bus splat the sludge, back up the banks.

Day after day the road widens and the heat from the traffic transforms the streets into rivers of salty slush that splatter everything and everyone on a daily basis.

In Newfoundland, clearing the banks, not flowers, is always the first sign of spring. Another sign of spring is our clothes. Our boots and pant bottoms have the same jagged white rings around the edges.

I've been at my new school almost eight months and although it hasn't been a year since I ran away, Irma decided to resume her role as my personal torturer and my wrist feels like she broke it.

Writing my detention lines is a torture in itself and every time my ribs touch the table, I squirm in pain. But the worst part is the fear building up in my chest. I'm literally having a panic attack.

"Do you need to go to the restroom?"

I shake my head and resume writing my lines.

I will not audition for any more plays because I am a quitter.

Battered

My music teacher blacklisted me from any future auditions and when she asked if I felt guilty, saying, 'No, because they have a spare lined up, eager to replace me,' was a huge mistake. Not because I have to write fifty lines but because detention means I miss the bus. The truth is I loved that lead role. But when the time came to rehearse after school hours, I had no choice but to quit.

I will not audition for any more plays because I am a quitter.

I will not audition for any more plays because I am a quitter.

Finally, the buzzer rings. I tear toward my locker and slam straight into a hand holding a small carton of chocolate milk.

Splat!

"Sorry," I yell and run faster.

"JERK!"

"How rude."

"Idiot."

"Ewwww, look at her shirt."

I fly past the mingled comments and unbutton my brown stained shirt. I'm guaranteed a beating if I walk inside the house with this ruined shirt and if I change it, I lose any chance of catching the bus and I'll get beaten for that. The worse beating, I ever got was over a shirt. She beat my face with the belt buckle, and almost blinded me. She could kill me over the shirt. Maybe the bus is late, and there's a chance I can still catch it. I have to take that chance.

My locker door is jammed. "Urrrrrrrrrgggggggggggggggg."

I yank the door open, rip off my shirt and rummage for a clean one. I know I have a spare in here somewhere. I smuggled it to school, last week after Irma beat me for ruining one during gym.

I stand on my knapsack, feel around the top shelf and pull out my last clean shirt. You are saving my life. First chance I get, I plan to wear two of everything to school to keep as spares. I slip my arms into the shirt sleeves, toss my knapsack over my shoulder and button up on the run.

A group of boys whistle at me. I flip them off, run past hoots and hollers and lurch into the parking lot just in time to watch the bus drive away.

"STOP. STO-OOO-OP." I run down the middle of the road. "PLEASE GOD NO. DON'T DO THIS TO ME AGAIN."

I stagger to a stop. My chest heaves. A horn blares from behind me. A woman yells, "Get off the road, idiot."

I sit on the side walk, hug my knees and cry my face off.

Horns blare up ahead and try to pass a car with hazard lights on. The crunch of metal, brings traffic to a deadlock. I jump up and chase my out of sight bus, praying for an accident, or at least a traffic jam that will make it stop too.

I run until I'm out of breath. When I get a second wind, I run again. The entire time my frantic mind flip-flops between panic, hope and doom.

Occasionally I consider throwing myself in front of a passing car. The more I think about it the better the idea sounds.

I rest for a few seconds, pant, regain my strength and think why not? I have absolutely nothing to lose. If I don't die, I might get to watch TV in a hospital, hopefully for a few months.

Just a few feet away I hear chaotic laughter. It sounds like I might sound if I laughed in this exact moment. It's coming from a bus stop booth.

I swerve to avoid a wheelchair and collapse on the bench. An adult with weird looking teeth smiles at me. His head twitches uncontrollably against his neck brace. I stare at him for a full five minutes before I realize he's mentally ill. An older person, with tired kind eyes, pushes the wheelchair back and forth, like a cradle.

"Getting hit by a car is never a good thing."

Still panting, I say, "Pardon?" How does she know I'm thinking about jumping in front of a car?

"My Samuel was hit by a drunk driver thirty years ago," she says. "I was selfish and asked God to save him for me and God answered my prayers."

I picture me in a wheelchair stuck at home with Irma forever. I never believed things could get any worse, but that image wins, hands down. I jump up, bolt down the road and pray for God to keep me safe. I think up hundreds of excuses to use for missing the bus but none of them are good enough to avoid a beating. Even a note from God wouldn't stop what I have waiting for me at home.

By the time I reach the house, I have already lived and relived my fate a thousand times. I grimace and take a deep breath . . .

"Get in this house," she growls between gritted teeth.

Breathe, Juanita, just breathe.

Irma slams me into a wall, shoulder first. I stumble and try to regain my balance. She has a broom handle raised above my head. I cringe. That's when I realize Dave Hogan was right. When she's on a rampage nothing's going to stop her

I hear the baby gag and scream. She gets in one good whack, the broom makes a splitting sound, I look up and she's aiming for my face. I cover my hands over my head and duck to the left.

Craaa-aaa-ckkkk.

She throws the broken handle at me and runs to the kitchen. A red welt rises on my right forearm. I lean forward to see where she is and what new weapon she has. I stare at the front door. Open so I can run through you! I hate it for staying shut. I hate all of this house. Why didn't I hide in my locker and after they locked up, sleep in the gymnasium?

Stupid, stupid, stupid.

The doorknob rattles. If it opens, I'm running.

Sunlight shines between Dad's pant legs. He blocks the entrance. And surveys the area.

"I didn't touch her," Irma lies as she sways the crying baby left and right. "She tripped and fell on the broom and broke it in half."

Dad lifts his eyebrows.

"The handle was already split so it wasn't entirely her fault."

I can't believe my ears. Did she just say something nice?

"What's going on?" he asks. His eyes rest on my forearm.

"She's been out screwing around. She just got in the door," Irma snaps. She jerks the baby up and down. "Ssshhh. Sssssssshhhh."

"I meant young Ned," he says. "What's going on with him?"

205

Juanita Ray

The baby screams louder. "He's being a brat. I think he's teething." Irma shoves him into Dad's arms. "Here you take him. He's been this way all damn day."

It's a boy. That's just great. I'll still be the youngest girl to pick on. His screams turn to hiccups. Dad cradles him over his shoulder and beats him on the back until a loud long burp escapes from between his drools. He blinks, gurgles, smiles at me and tosses his bottle.

"He keeps dropping his bottle. He knows how to hold it, but he's doing it on purpose, the little jerk," Irma swoops down, picks it up and tosses it in his playpen. "He's doing it just to annoy me."

White curdled slime dribbles down Dad's shoulder. Dad lays the baby in the playpen, props the bottle up on a blanket and sticks it in his mouth. "I'll give you a hand as soon as I change. I've got spit-up all over me."

The baby chews on the nipple and cries some more. I watch the boy scream bloody murder and throw his bottle out of his playpen again. "Don't just sit there, make yourself useful." Dad nods at the bottle. "Help feed him while I go change."

I hesitate. This is where Irma is supposed to say something nasty and kick me downstairs.

Dad turns and says, "His bottle is under that chair."

I'm nervous. What if he chokes or gags? Is that what she's waiting for? Is that when she'll pounce?

The first month of home economics was feeding eighteen-inch dolls. Young Ned is bigger than the dolls but I figure that shouldn't matter. I hold the near empty bottle the way I practiced at school. He sucks it dry and his droopy eyes flutter shut. "Move!" Irma kicks my hip. "And if you think, this is going to earn you some dinner, you're dead wrong. Go get in your bed and stay there. Next time you miss the bus you won't get off so lucky."

I scramble out of her way, dash down the stairs, get undressed and crawl into bed. I'm exhausted, but I fight sleep because I'm terrified of the nightmares. They're always the same and they're always weird. I'm half-awake when I catch Adam tiptoeing out of my room. "Psssst! Adam. Come back—I'm up."

Battered

"You looked so peaceful . . . anyway I have a surprise for you. I brought you a real, game. One somebody else made up."

"How did you sneak it past Irma."

"I used my magic powers and shrunk it to fit in my pocket. Now if I could just do the same with Irma, and throw my pants in the washer, after a few spin cycles, we'd have it made."

At first I don't get it, but picturing a miniature Irma going for a swim in his pants pocket, makes me cover my face with my pillow and laugh until I cry. He tugs the pillow from my face and pulls a tiny rubber ball from his pocket. "Voila!"

He throws the small pink ball and a bunch of metal things that look like the letter x, on the floor. He catches the ball and picks up some of the x's. "That's how you play. It's easy. Try it. The trick is to grab all the scattered jacks on the first bounce. First one at a time, then two at a time, and so on." He hands me the paper instructions.

"It has rules, and explains how to play with others so . . . But most people play it by themselves."

The truth is I hate games. I use them to keep my sanity and help time pass. When I get out of here, I plan to have a real life. One without games.

"What's wrong? You don't like it?"

"No, it isn't that. It's just everyone hates me. There are no others to play with. Besides I'm not allowed."

"You must have at least one friend at school. How would Irma know what you do at school?"

"She'd find out one way or the other. With my luck one of them would show up and knock on the door for me. Every day my life is the same. I don't get what the point is. Like what's the point of any of this? Why was I even born?"

"I'm not going to lie. I've asked myself the same thing a thousand times. None of this makes sense. The way I handle this living hell is by thinking of our lives as on hold, and in a few years we'll be out of here and hit the play button. I'm saving every cent I can so we can get out and stay out.

Hang in there, okay?" He bends down and gives me a quick hug. A sharp pain shoots through the back of my shoulder. I recoil.

"What happened? She got you again, didn't she?"

"I missed the bus."

"Have you told your teacher it's a five mile walk home?"

"Dad lied, Having the baby made her a worse monster."

"She's no monster. She's the devil and that's exactly why she'll never change. She loves making everyone's life a living hell."

"Maybe she's possessed by the devil."

"Possessed, my ass," he says. "She's not possessed. I'm telling you she's the devil itself. The old man's the one possessed—by her. Every day I try to talk some sense into him, but the more I try, the worse he seems to get. I'm beginning to think he's almost as bad as she is. I don't know what else to say to get him to turn around. I've tried and tried to reason with him, but he's so damned brainwashed."

He bounces the ball up and down, smashes it against the ceiling and grabs it midair. "How old are you now, thirteen?"

"Thirteen and three quarters," I say.

"You're so damn scrawny, I don't know if you can survive another two or three years in this hell hole. As a matter of fact, I know I can't. I'm getting close to the end of my rope. I'm out of ideas. It would be so much easier and better, if they were both dead."

He tosses me the ball and walks away.

I hate seeing him like this. It worries me. His hatred for Irma is getting stronger and his choices are getting slimmer. I know he's right. Things have to change soon but what if soon never comes?

I stay awake, most of the night. The only solution I can come up with is to run away again. I know this time it has to be for good. This time I can't get caught. I analyze what I did wrong last time, and wonder how I could have had a different result. I play out several scenarios in my head. I wonder what would have happened, if I hadn't run away. What if I had stabbed her first with the scissors, not to kill her, but enough to stop her, I probably would have gone to jail but even jail can't be as bad as this. Adam said you get three squares a day in jail. Maybe next time I'll fight back. I rack my brains for a plan.

By dawn I finally fall asleep. One senseless dream follows the other. I'm sitting beside Adam, on my school bus. When we reach my school, Adam hops off and I chase after him. Instead of books, I carry a bag of clothes, and yell, "School is out."

He yells back, "We can go wherever you want. Let's wait for a different bus. One that doesn't go home." Instantaneously we are teleported back to the exact same bus, but this time someone is sitting between us. Adam points at the person and says, "It was your idea, you tell her about it."

"We're off to find Marie."

I say, "But this bus is headed home and Marie's not there."

She takes off her floppy hat and sits it on her lap. The woman's voice has a heavy foreign accent, but her face looks like Mom's. "Let's go back and get your clothes."

The bus has no driver, but it turns in the opposite direction.

The woman points at the front of the bus. Several buses pass us, on both sides but the road only has two lanes. She sighs and says, "The problem with these buses is they all look alike and we're on the wrong one." In a split second, she transforms into a crow and flies through a nearby open window.

A person two seats ahead bolts up the aisle and slams the window shut. His black leather jacket has the words, Hells Best Angel, embroidered above a skull with wings. He walks up the aisle and sits in the driver's seat.

"Stop," I yell, "let me off this bus."

Adam's hand presses against my lips.

"Ssshhh. Be quiet."

I bolt straight up in bed.

"Shush. It was just a bad dream. You'll be quiet, right?"

I nod at him.

He uncovers my mouth.

"Did anyone else hear me?"

"I doubt it. You only screamed once before I got here, and lucky for you, Young Ned was screaming at the same time."

"Can you stay and talk to me until I fall back to sleep?"

"About what?"

"Anything. Nobody ever talks to me anymore, not even in school. I get horribly lonely especially when I'm scared or have bad dreams"

"What happened to God. The one you usually talk to?"

"Lately he seems to be too busy for me."

Adam sits in the rocking chair, and closes his eyes.

"Move your chair closer," I whisper, "I need to tell you about my plan . . . I think it's why I had the dream—Adam?"

Adam isn't listening. He's leaned back in the chair fast asleep. Even in the darkness of my room, I can see the black circles under his eyes. Maybe it's meant to be. If he knew he might try to change my mind or worry himself to death. I've given it a ton of thought and I know it's the perfect plan. There's no way I'll fail this time. I've got only this week to make it happen, because this Friday school ends.

I drift in and out of sleep, and whether I'm awake or not, I'm living my plan. It's the first thing I think of when I wake up, it's what I daydream about during every single class, and it's what I imagine every single night until Friday comes.

Friday morning, I am shaking in my boots. I've been scared every morning, every day, for the last eight years, but I'm terrified more than ever. Petrified I won't succeed.

Today is the last day I'll have to sit on the bus and sweat like a pig. June has got to be the worst month to wear two of everything to school. I hug my knapsack against my chest and sweat some more. By the time we reach the school my shirt is soaking wet.

I hide in the locker, take both shirts off and switch them for a dry one. Then I bolt outside. The parking lot, and the sidewalk facing the school, is lined with buses. The last bus to arrive pulls up to the curb and off jumps Paul Smith.

If Paul were a dog, he'd be the runt of the litter. He smokes like a chimney but isn't much taller than a window. He whistles and saunters toward me. He smells different, sort of musty. Instead of heading inside, he leans against the front school wall and lights a cigarette.

"Aren't you afraid of getting caught?" I ask.

"Aren't you warm wearing two pairs of socks?"

Embarrassed, I mumble something about blisters.

He offers me a puff. At first, I hesitate, but I need to pick his brain, so I suck it like a straw. I cough and choke until the bell rings.

He tilts his chin upwards and blows circles into the air and ignores the bell. "You're in grade eight, right?"

"Hopefully for the last day. How far do you live from here?"

"About twenty miles or more, why?"

"Do you know Bertha Smith?" I ask.

"Yep. Sure do."

"How about Martha Smith?"

"Yep."

"Do all of them know you smoke?"

"Yep." He takes a long deep puff and makes a chain of rings.

"And they don't care?"

"Why would they? All of them smoke."

"How about Minnie Smith?"

"Who? All of us Smiths are related in one way or t'other. But I never heard of any Minnie Smith. Who she be?"

I answer his question with another one. "How come you guys are always the last bus to get here?"

"Probably cuz we're the farthest away? All I know is it's way too long to go without a smoke." His dry face looks older than Adam's.

Most kids call him Coffin Nail, because he always has a smoke between his lips.

"Your bus has the Goulds written on it. Isn't that out past where I live, further out Torbay Road?"

"Your sense of direction sucks. Torbay Road is clear across the other end of town, that way," he points to his right, "and the Goulds, where I live, is over there—twice the ride. About fifteen miles from where you live. Time's up." He flicks his cigarette in the grass and holds the door open with his worn cowboy boot.

It takes me less than five minutes to empty my desk and head to the assembly. I feel bummed about being in the last row, instead of with the rest of my class, until I realize the diplomas are given out in alpha order and it doesn't matter where you sit. By the time they get past the speeches and reach the RO's it's noon.

I open my diploma after I reach my locker. Mostly B's, and a D minus in music. I throw my diploma, and everything in my locker, into a plastic bag, and race to the parking lot, spot the bus and bang on its side panel. After a loud hiss of air, the doors swing open.

A grumpy old man says, "Slow down. You've got time to eat a meal before I leave the lot."

I collapse into a seat toward the back of the bus. I'm nervous yet excited. I know everything will be better once the bus leaves. I set on the edge of my seat and crane my neck. I don't recognize one person on it. What if I get caught? What if Dad senses something and shows up? I slump back to hide from the window. The door hisses ten more times, before the bus rolls out of the lot.

Five minutes later someone taps me on the shoulder. "So who's this Minnie Smith?" Paul asks.

The Graveyard Sleepover

The space on the bus seat beside me is empty and that is exactly how I want to keep it. I place my knapsack to my right and hug the plastic bag against my chest.

"I'm related to every Smith in the Goulds, but I've never heard of this Minnie."

"That's probably because she hates smokers."

"Describe her," he says.

How am I supposed to describe a fake aunt?

"Well? What's she look like?"

I describe Aunt Patty.

"Nope don't know her."

I make up answers as fast as Paul can ask them and resist the urge to shove my knapsack down his throat, after all his gift of gab was the reason, I picked this bus. He glances at my seat, and for a second he looks as if he is going to pick up my knapsack and sit down. The thought makes me both panicked and nauseated. I curl my legs over the knapsack and sit sideways.

Juanita Ray

The only plan I have left is to get rid of Paul and if it wasn't for that, I'd be finished with my plan. My plan was to find the bus that went the furthest place in the opposite direction of my house, and board it on the last day of school.

The Goulds seems like the perfect place. This is the first I've heard of it. I knew it existed, and hopefully Dad doesn't either. It's the last place anyone would look to find me. This time I'm not getting caught and dragged back home. I'll make sure I go to jail before I ever let that happen again.

Paul taps my head. "What's ya thinkin'? Something stinkin'?"

A boy with his attitude must have gotten in trouble once or twice before. My guess is he knows firsthand about jail. He looks hard, not cute and he certainly doesn't look healthy. But he reeks of street-smart and I could probably use a little of that right now.

"I'm thinking about Aunt Minnie's homemade cookies."

"Want to know what I'm thinking? I'm thinking I can smell a lie from a mile away, and your Aunt Minnie doesn't exist."

"Well I hate to burst your bubble but she does. She lives in her own little world and keeps to herself. She's untrusting. She doesn't socialize and like I told you, she detests smokers."

"Why?"

"Because she can smell them a mile away," I say. "It is odd you both have the same last name and you both have a rare gift of smelling stuff from a mile away. Maybe you two are related after all."

"She married? Got any kids?"

I shrug, "All I know, is she's a widow and her son's been in jail since he was thirteen."

"That's another whopper. They don't jail kids. They put them in juvenile delinquent centers."

"Well it's the same thing, you're under lock and key are you not?"

"Yeah. It's called Juvenile Hall. Everyone in there is a minor. I was there once."

Ha! I knew it. "What was it like?" I ask.

Battered

"It was okay as long as you had a lot of smokes and weren't afraid. It was crammed with bullies. They like to pick on the new kids that come in, so the newbies learn to toughen up quick. Those that can't, try to find protection. The best thing is to find someone who has a younger brother, not someone who wants a boyfriend."

"What did you do?"

"As little as I could. They had activity programs, a gym, and the food wasn't the worst I've had. I was on kitchen detail."

"No, what did you do to get in there, in the first place?"

"I robbed some cigarettes."

"With a weapon?"

"No," he laughs. "I broke a soda bottle on the floor and while the owner went to clean it up, I jumped the counter, grabbed the smokes and ran. I filled a pillow sack full of cartons. Getting back over the counter took more time than I calculated. Guess I was too greedy."

"What were the others in for?"

"Why are you so interested?" Paul leans ahead.

"My cousin didn't smoke, so I know he didn't steal cigarettes. Aunt Minnie has kept the reason, a dark secret all these years."

"How do you know he didn't smoke? Kids always smoke on the sly, unless their parents are dead, like mine. I live with my older drunk brother and he doesn't give a shit what I do."

"It had nothing to do with drinking or smoking."

"I'm telling you, your cousin probably smokes. If he didn't before, he does now. It's the only way to get immune to the smell. And there's only so many shitkickings you can take, before you join the club."

I twist around and look him square in the eye. "His Dad died of lung cancer, a big lump in his throat, the size of a grapefruit. Gagged and coughed himself to death. So, he doesn't smoke."

How dare he change my story! The nerve of him. It's my fake Aunt Minnie, and her fake entire family are non-smokers. How dare he change my imagination. I squint my eyes at him.

"Ouch. Maybe I should quit." Paul chews on his dirty nails. "Maybe he stole wire harnesses from cars. Maybe he slashed tires and broke windows. Most of the kids there are vandals. They have two types of delinquents. The ones that commit adult crimes and the ones that commit kid crimes and most of them smoke."

"Kid crimes?"

"Yeah. Runaways and behavioral problems. It's not against the law for adults to run away but for a kid it's a kid crime. Bet he ran away, and she's ashamed she wasn't a good enough mother. Anyway, all this talk about smokes—I'm dying for one. No offense but I like the back of the bus better."

After the longest time, the bus rolls to a stop. More than half of the kids exit. It was stopping twice every mile but now it's stopping every 200 feet or so.

Paul yells, "Where does she live."

"By the church." Hopefully this place has one.

Only eleven of us are left on board, and eight are standing up, waiting for the next stop. When the bus breaks, across from a store, they jostle to be the first one out.

"Miss me?" His arms dangle over the back of my seat. "Looks like I get to walk you home, seeing how there's only one stop left."

One stop? My frenzied mind rifles for an excuse. "It's a really long walk. Way too far for you." Think of a better reason.

"I don't mind. I need a few smokes anyway."

"I can't walk with you. My aunt will smell smoke on me."

"I'll smoke downwind. Besides I want to meet her."

"No, she's my aunt, not yours, and a stranger to you, so there's no reason for you to meet her."

"You're wrong. She's probably my aunt too. So I'm going to follow you anyway. Don't worry I'll stay ten feet away. I just want to see who she is. I can guarantee you she's a relative of some sort."

Battered

I notice the top of a tall steeple and yell, "Look there's that church." I grab my bag and yell, "STOP THE BUS! STOP THE BUS! I MISSED MY STOP!"

The driver pulls over to the right. I jump to the ground and run from the bus. I point toward the church, cup my mouth and yell at Paul's window, "I forgot, she lives back that way."

Paul points at his head and circles his ear.

I scan the horizon and have no clue which way to go. Maybe he's right. Maybe I am crazy. I cross the road to the other side, and head toward the store.

I'm not sure what I'll need, but I know I can live longer without food than water. When I get near the store, my throat tightens. This isn't good. Too many kids are hanging around. I cross the road and walk back toward the church, until the store is almost out of sight. I climb up a bank, sit on my plastic bag, and watch the odd car go by. By sunset, half of the kids leave, but the place still seems overcrowded. Some cars pull in the lot, pick up kids, and drive off while others park and never leave.

Soon the glow of the orange sky mingles with a murky gray color. The grayer the sky gets, the more I think about home. Adam must be wondering where I am. By now he's probably at the gas station working. Yesterday, I came close to telling Adam my plan but I lost my nerve, partially because I didn't want him to be more worried or upset than he already was, but mainly because I was afraid he would talk me out of it. Instead, I wrote a note and taped it behind my dresser drawer. It's the one place Adam was bound to look. I knew, after he realized I was gone, he would look there to see if my money was missing. In case Irma found the note, and destroyed it, I gouged a heart, his initials, and today's date, on the back of every drawer in the dresser.

Once I made my plan, the locket was the first thing I snuck out of the house and the last thing I locked in my locker every day. Knowing I'll never have to take it off again, makes me happy. Never again will I have to worry about it getting stolen, or hiding anything from Irma. I pull it out from under my shirt and vow never to take it off my neck.

Juanita Ray

The longer I wait, the closer it gets to dusk but I wait without knowing why. The darkening sky makes me scared. I put my trust in God, and get up to head to the church but music blaring from near the store, grabs my attention. I sit back down and try to relax. Every now and then, a car pulls in, and brightens up everything, but once the headlights go out, it's hard to see anything at all. I guess if I can't see them, it means they can't see me.

My throat is dry. I venture toward the noise hoping the place has a garden hose. The closer I get, the rowdier the crowd appears to be. On the side of the building, an electric sign, of a mug of yellow beer, flashes on and off. The words, Smith's Bar & Dance Hall, are faded and worn. Maybe someone related to Paul owns it. I glance around, hoping he's nowhere nearby. I know this isn't the safest place to be, but I'm not certain where it's safer. I turn back in the opposite direction and walk along the ditch. The last time I walked in a ditch was the first time I tried to escape, and that didn't go so well. This time I need to do things different. The road is silent. No cars pass by. I climb out of the ditch and stroll along the roadside, like I saw the other kids do earlier.

Up ahead, a large tower and unclear shadows loom into view. I know the tower is really a steeple. Good thing I saw it during the day because it looks ghostly on the dark horizon. But nothing could be safer than a church. My eyes play tricks on me and for a brief moment it turns into a cemetery. I close my hand over my face, split my fingers and focus on the door. When I reach it. It doesn't open. There is a rusty latch locked, above the door. I tug on it but no matter how hard I try it won't open.

Headlights briefly pass across the worn siding. The crackle of glass shattering is followed by the sound of hooting and hollering.

A second later a beer bottle smashes against the steps. One chard hits my leg. I jump away and lose my footing.

The car speeds away for a short distance before it screeches to an abrupt halt. Tail lights turn from red to white. I jump off the steps and dash for the back of the church. Several doors slam.

A male voice slurs, "I'm not drunk man I saw her. She's over on the steps."

Battered

I am a visible target against the white walls of the church. The silhouette of pillars and a tree line catches my eye. My books beat against my back. Wham. My knapsack slams into my spine. My knees burn.

"Listen. Did you hear that? I told you I saw someone."

"Yer drunk buddy. There's no one here but us."

I roll off the rock and cling to the back of a tall, wide boulder.

The first voice is a few feet away, "This is a freakin' graveyard."

A second voice says, "Then what you saw was probably a ghost."

The first voice nearest me scoffs, "No shit Charlie."

An uneven stomping sound grows closer. "I love graveyards man. Charlie buddy, do ya have a flashlight in yer glove box. I'm dying to read deez grave stones. Ha-ha-ha. Ha-ha. Get it. Dyin' to read 'em?" His slurred words echo between the tombstones.

The first voice is only two feet away, "That's because you're stoned and drunk, asshole. I told you not to do both. Charlie, get over here and help me get this drunken stoner back to the car."

My breath is louder than my heartbeat. I press my hand against my mouth until they retreat. Only two doors slam. I wait for the third. I see a flashlight darting back and forth. The sound of thrashing footsteps grows closer. The light flashes across and in between the gravestones. I count five. I slither past them until I'm wedged against a picket fence. Thrashing sounds get closer. Dirt flicks at my legs. The sound of an opening zipper is followed by a splattering noise. The smell of rotten cabbage mixed with window glass cleaner, makes me gag, and for once I'm glad I learned the skill of swallowing vomit.

"Hurry up."

"Christ! Can't a guy take a whizz?" he asks, and resumes pissing.

Before he's finished, a car door slams and a second light weaves in and out of sight, stopping to rest six feet from me.

"Frankie, get your dick back in your pants. Come on. Whoa, settle down buddy, put your arm around my shoulder. You're going to break my fucking neck. CHARLIE. GET OVER HERE."

"You mean careful for me, hic! My neck, right?"

"No, I mean my neck. You're draggin' me all over the place."

All three of them are close by and they all seem equally drunk. What if I ran for their car and locked myself inside? Would anyone hear me if I blew the horn?

Screeching brakes, are followed by a loud bang. They drop their friend and run. He stumbles after them.

The flashlight darts sporadically toward their car. The squeal of peeling tires, and the unmistakable smell of burnt rubber, fills the air.

"Let's go chase them down!"

"What about Frankie."

"Fuck him."

"We can't leave him here."

After a few loud grunts, three doors slam shut.

The car squeals off into the darkness with no headlights on.

I hold my breath and listen until the road sounds silent.

The moon peeks from underneath a cloud and brightens up my spot. I gulp. My throat tightens. My heartbeat is deafening. I'm hugging a decrepit gravestone. I back away. A twig cracks behind me.

A small rustling noise comes from the direction of the trees. The lower branches of a few poke through the pickets beside me. I want to run but the stench of piss to my left, the noises to my right, the tombs in front of me, and the fence pressing against my back, leaves me riveted here.

Old bent crosses stick up out of the ground. I look to my left. The leaves glisten and the ground is soaking wet from where he urinated. To my right is more crosses, more bramble. I look up. Directly above my face, an empty rusty wire wreath hangs like a crown above my head. I jump from underneath it. I'm not leaning against the pickets. I'm leaning against a creepy wooden cross that's leaning against the fence.

Then the clouds cover the moon.

The world turns black . . .

I whisper the Lord's Prayer. My voice gets louder. I come close to yelling it. I'm not sure if it's for the benefit of me, or the dead.

Battered

I make the sign of the cross on my chest three times, hoping it works for Anglicans. Then I run straight ahead for the church. My foot catches on a plaque. I lurch forward with my hands stretched outwards. A rickety tombstone breaks as I trip against it.

"Sorry." I apologize to the tombstone first, then to God. "Sorry. Please God don't let anyone wake up."

I pick myself up and make a fast bolt until my outstretched hands slam against the back wall of the church.

I slump against the clapboard, too scared to cry. I chant, the Lord's Prayer, several more times. I remind myself God won't help me if I don't have faith. I force my mind to repeat after me, 'This is holy ground, protected ground, nothing can hurt you here.'

I inhale a deep breath, and try to relax, by imagining Mom is here watching over me. The more I pretend, the more I believe it. She could be here, if she's a ghost, she's a religious one, so why wouldn't she be here hanging out at a haunted church? Maybe she led me here.

I whisper though the darkness, "Mom. I know you're out there. Please don't leave me. I need you, and right now would be a good time to call for some backup."

Within seconds God turns on the lights. The clouds shift to reveal a blanket of beautiful stars. Maybe the stars are the souls of the dead and all the plots are empty. For a moment I forget about the graves and stare in awe at the sky.

This is the first time I've ever seen a starry night like this. It should take me all night to count these stars. Fear fades. I count them and wonder which one I saw first—which one is my lucky star? Which one should I wish on?

Before I reach one hundred, the moon fully exposes the entire area. Moving shadows catch my attention as they dance across the tombstones. It brings the graveyard back to life. A haunting howl fills the air and the stars don't matter anymore.

Twigs snap and a digging, clawing sound is coming from the picket fence. Something is panting hard. Yellow glowing eyes, dart in and out between the plots. I'm afraid to move but I'm more afraid of staying. Inch by inch I slide my hand over the ground until I feel a decent sized rock. I dig my sneakers into the ground, lurch forward, and hurtle it at the eyes. The thing snarls and shows its fangs. I hurl another rock at it. One loud yelp and it thrashes away. Maybe it smells my bloody leg.

I hold my breath waiting for the thing to return and attack me. But the only sound, besides my shaky breathing, seems to be coming from crickets. Lots of crickets. A sense of relief floods my body. A deep breath gushes from between my teeth.

I wiggle out of my back pack, take a spare pair of panties and rip the side seam apart. I pause and listen but the only sound I hear, is my breathing. I wrap the cloth around my wound and tie the ends into a tight knot.

I clutch my knapsack to my chest and scurry to the other side of the church. An old barrel clings to the right side of the church. It seems to be the best spot to hide for the night. Every five minutes, I ask myself which is better? Irma or this. I always pick this.

I rearrange my knapsack and stuff my extra clothes under the school books. I slip my torn ten-dollar bill in the envelope holding my diploma.

All I have left in the plastic bag is a roll of tape, some quarters, a Bible and a pillowcase that still smells like Marie. The day before yesterday, I made sure, to get off the bus at StayMart, and spray it with her favorite perfume. And I'm glad I did. It cost me a beating for missing the bus, but it was worth it.

I fold the pillowcase across my face, lean my head against my knapsack and shift closer toward the foundation of the church. My ears seem to pick up on every sound imaginable. Creaking, howling, scampering noises, leaves rustling, and the wind whistling, keep me on edge. I jump out of my skin and squeal when a June Bug buzzes by.

Tiny insects crawl across my arms. I squeeze my eyelids tightly together. And shove my fingers in my ears to keep the sounds out. All kinds of horrible scenarios and toxic thoughts flash through my mind. Most of them involve ghosts, bugs and blood sucking bats.

By dawn I'm a basket case. The graveyard looks eerier than it did at night. The gravestones in front of me has the name Ruby on it at the bottom

Battered

in big capital letters. Two more say Stanley an another says Cox. Some are gray concrete like my basement room, others are wooden crosses, and all of them have a weird mist hovering over them. I can't get out of here fast enough. I edge around the building, turn the corner, and freeze. A ghostly gray fog crawls over the graveyard and one of the bigger tombstones is making a mumbling sound.

Parsons Store

My nerves are tight rubber bands, stretched to the breaking point. Chills trickle up and down my spine. I cover my mouth and run back behind the barrel and cry while the wind makes a flapping sound behind me. It's my plastic bag! I left it behind. I can't believe I abandoned it. I hug it against my chest.

I count to sixty forty-eight times before the sun rises, and once it does, the fog lifts. Halfway across the graveyard a crumpled body huddles against a gravestone. It rolls over and burps. I gasp. He burps again and raises a paper bag to his lips.

He blinks at me, rubs his eyes and blinks again. I drop my rock and run as fast as I can, to get past him. He leans toward me and grabs for my bag. I kick his hand and flee toward the road.

Ten feet away from the edge of the road, I hunch over, panting for air. I tie my plastic bag to a strap on my knapsack, drop to my knees and stuff my pockets with rocks. Armed with a rock in each hand, I keep one eye on the church and walk toward the road, backwards.

Battered

Once I'm sure, the old drunk is staying put, I turn left and make my way up the road until I reach the spot where I was the day before. I climb the bank, lie back and take slow deep breaths.

I shout, "I'M FREE! NO MORE IRMA. I AM FREE!" and for the first time in my life, I feel alive and brave. I forgot what it was like to shout. It feels good. So, I shout a few more times.

I walk closer to a road sign. It reads, Ruby Line. Up past that sign, across the road to the right is that store with the beer sign.

The hot sun feels delicious against my skin. I take off my knapsack and reach for my plastic bag.

I rush to my feet only to drop to the ground. The shriveled up old man is walking up the road and he has my pillowcase! He must have found my bag.

"Twenty-four bottles of beer on the wall twenty-four bottle of beer take one down and pass it around twenty-three bottle of b—"

I snatch the pillowcase from his hand and run past him. He staggers and trips. He yells something about butts. Five feet from the store, I slow to a casual stroll.

The moment I walk inside, the clerk points at my leg. "Bet you're looking for bandages."

I point to the restroom sign and ask, "Where is it?"

"Where are your parents?"

"My Dad is down by the church with a flat tire. I fell on a broken beer bottle, probably the same one he ran over, probably from here, so can I please use your restroom?"

"Only paying customers can use the restroom." He points to a No Loitering sign.

"How much is water?"

"Small bottles are fifty cents."

"I'll take a bottle." I put two quarters on the counter. The clerk takes the two quarters and keeps one hand on the bottle, "That didn't include the tax."

I give him three more quarters. "I'll take another one for my Dad."

Juanita Ray

"What's in the pillow case? Not planning to steal something, are you?"

"Noooooo. I don't steal."

He passes me a wooden hand with a key dangling from it, tosses my change and both waters in a bag, leans across the counter and says, "Everyone steals sooner or later. You'll get this when I get back my key."

The restroom looks cleaner than our basement. I wash my hands and unwind the underwear from my leg. I wipe away the drips of dried blood and put on some clean socks. My pillow is filthier than the floor. I drop it to the ground. It clunks, clatters and clanks. A jar rolls toward the toilet. It looks exactly like the ones Irma used for her blueberry jam.

I shake the jar and take a closer look. Who would keep used cigarette butts with red lipstick stains? An old worn wallet is sitting on top of my diploma envelope. I grab the diploma and rip it into small pieces. Two flushes later, it disappears.

The first page of every book in my knapsack has my name on it. I rip those parts out and flush each piece down the toilet. I put the literature book back in my knapsack and throw the rest of the books in the big gray trash bin.

The worn leather wallet reminds me of the week before Irma came. It looks like an old version of the one Dad owned right after Irma came and it wasn't cheap. The Christmas before Irma moved in we all chipped in two months of allowances to buy it for him.

Inside the wallet, is a worn picture of a teenage girl lying on her tummy, kicking her heels in the air. She has a toddler sitting on her back. She looks young, too young to be a mother. I wonder if it's his sister and him as a baby. Maybe he doesn't know these people. Maybe they're strangers and he stole the wallet, or maybe it happened the same way he got my pillowcase. There's no way a drunk like him would own a wallet this expensive. Maybe he pretends this is his family.

Tucked inside a frayed pocket is a real looking wedding ring. In the billfold, I find an old bar receipt. The word Bar is faded and the words before it, are illegible. The date is impossible to read because most of it is missing. It's yellowed with age and the edge is tattered and brownish.

Battered

I sniff the pillowcase. It doesn't smell like Marie anymore. It stinks. The bum can have it back along with all his other crappy smelly junk.

"Hello? Are you going to take all day or what?"

I scramble to my feet, shove everything including the key into my pillowcase. I pull the door shut and turn to face the biggest lady I'd ever seen in my life.

"The key?" Her palm is the size of a baseball glove.

"Sorry. I need my bag back."

I dodge past her and hand the clerk the key. The woman behind me pants, "I ought to smack you for making me walk all the way back here for that bloody key." Her finger points past my head, at the clerk. "And I should sue you, Bob Parsons. I almost had a heart attack! You need to keep that damn door unlocked."

He hands her the key. "A walk or two wouldn't hurt you none, Mona."

"You calling me fat, Bob Parsons?"

"Nope. Calling you lazy," he ducks as she swings her purse at his ear.

Mr. Parsons is still chuckling when he hands me my bag.

I sit on the steps, fish out my change, and count it. I open the pillow to make sure I'm not forgetting anything important. Change jingles against the butt jar and falls to the bottom. While I'm reaching in a dollar drops in. I look up and a handful of pennies trickles from someone's fingers. Within two minutes, strangers have given me over five bucks and every one of them frowns at the old man three feet from me.

He's picking up a freshly discarded cigarette butt. He sucks on it until a small ember turns into a puff of smoke. He does a little tap dance, swirls, sits on the ground and leans against the corner of the store. His jaws sink inwards while he tries to suck the last sign of life out of the butt. His brows furl. He shakes the butt and puffs frantically, oblivious to anything or anyone near him, including me, but the spent butt refuses to come back to life.

He scours the ground, until he finds another one, jams it between his lips and begs an old woman for a light. She swats at him and waves him away.

I wonder if Bruce had to do that?

I go inside the store and pick out a bright yellow glow in the dark lighter. "And I need some cigarettes."

"Do ya now. Let me guess. They're for your Dad? Got an id?"

"I don't smoke. They're not for me. Honest."

"Let's see your fingers."

I hold up my left hand.

"You right-handed?"

I nod.

"Put it on the counter." I put my money in the bag with the water bottles and place the bag and the pillowcase between my feet. I slap my hand on the counter. He grabs it and examines my fingers, "Got any lemons on ya?"

"What?" I ask.

"Never mind, who do you want smokes for? I know it's not you unless you clean up with lemons or smoke with gloves on."

"That old man, out there, is smoking rotten filthy butts from the ground, so I want to buy him some clean cigarettes."

"Why? They're gonna kill him either way, germs or not. Don't get me wrong, I love Henry like a son but fate is fate."

"A son? He looks old enough to be your father."

The clerk roars loudly. "Ha-Ha-Ha-Ha. I love it! Tell you what. I sell them separate by the cigarette—this brand," he holds up half a pack, "or by the pack, any brand you want."

I ask, "How much?"

He stares out the window. "Look at him! Now he's bumming from my customers!" He glances back at me, "Fifty cents each or twenty for five bucks. Twenty should last him two weeks."

"How about three bucks for that half pack?"

"Deal, providing I'm the one who hands them to Henry."

"Who's Henry?"

He laughs, "Henry's that guy you've been eyeballing. Lucky for you he's harmless. So, we have a deal?" He reaches out and shakes my hand, "I'm

Battered

Robert Parsons but friends call me Bob. I own this joint. Need anything else?"

"No just the lighter and smokes."

"Henry, you've got yourself a stalker, and a cutie at that." Henry frowns when Bob and I approach.

He holds his arms behind his back, "You looking to kick me some more?" He takes a step backwards. I hand the cigarettes to Mr. Parsons. He hands them to Henry.

"The kid kicked ya huh?"

Henry shields his eyes from the sun and says, "Thought she was a midget, not a kid."

He holds the package toward me.

"No thanks. I'm too smart to smoke." He's stares past me, lurches for a fluffy fat cat, and it sprints straight into his outstretched arms, and the cat barks.

All my life I've only seen big dogs, big enough to warm both hands on, and never one that looks like a cat. He strokes his dirty fingers through its silky white hair, and scratches its head with his cracked uneven fingernails. Hopefully the dogs been treated for fleas.

"Did you miss me? Did you miss your buddy? Yes, you did." He kisses its forehead and hugs it tight against his cheek. The dog licks Henry's ears and slurps on his nose. He rubs the dog behind its ears and says, "You love me don't you. Yes, you do. I love you too. You and your sloppy kisses."

"I thought it was a cat."

"I didn't think you were a kid, so we both made mistakes."

"Here, you can keep the pillowcase. I took all my stuff out."

He digs inside and retrieves his wallet. He flips it open and kisses the girls picture a dozen times. He holds his obsession close to his heart and says, "This is all I care about. You can have your pillowcase back. I wasn't going to steal it. I found it on the road. Figured some school kid lost it and I'd bring it here to give to Bob, cuz they hang out here. I may not look decent, but I'm no thief."

Bob gives me an exaggerated frown, "He's trying to steal my dog. Better watch him kid, he'll steal the eyes out of your head, if you let him." Bob grins, winks at Henry and walks away.

"Hey Bob thanks for the smokes. I'll clean up the lot in a bit."

"Don't thank me. Thank the kid. She spent the coin. And be sure in a bit happens sometime in the next hour."

But Henry doesn't answer. He's preoccupied with rearranging the picture in his wallet, settling on a spot that seems to be the exact same place it was in the beginning. He lurches forward, kisses my shin and says, "Thank you, thank you, thank you so much. Thank you for not keeping my wallet."

"Maybe you should keep it in your wallet in your pocket."

"I have no pockets. Well I did before the seams broke." he hands me the pillowcase but keeps the nasty jar of butts.

"I bought you cigarettes because my brother was homeless too. I'm not sure how he got his smokes, but I doubt he scraped butts off the ground, especially ones with red lipstick stains. What if a dog peed on them?"

He rubs the dog behind the ears, and says, "You'd never take a leak on my butts, would you." The dog gives him a high five.

"What do people around here have for breakfast, besides beer?"

He mutters, "I haven't had breakfast since I woke up in a pool of my wife's blood, so I wouldn't know. I don't eat breakfast."

"Say what?"

A sandwich flies out the window, and lands on Henry's lap. He devours half of it in one bite, and gives a chunk to the dog.

"You said you didn't eat breakfast."

"True, true. But this is lunch. It'll be noon in an hour."

Seconds later Bob towers over me "You still here? Aren't you supposed to be back with your Dad?" His hands grip his hips. "What Dad wouldn't be searching for you right now? Well?"

"A Dad who plans to pick me up here, once someone brings him a spare tire."

Battered

"Henry you make sure you clean up around here and I'm not just referring to the broken glass, okay? I'll pay you for any good bottles you find. And drink some water. You look like an overbaked potato." He nods toward the garden hose. "Don't want you doing the crazy-chicken today. It's gonna be a hot one."

"Bless you Bob" He points a finger at Bob's back, "He's a good man. In the winter he lets me live in his dumpster."

Henry gobbles down the rest of his sandwich.

"The dog looks thirsty." I hand Henry a bottle of water.

"No kid, keep it."

"I can buy more. I have money. See?". I spread it across my pillow case and arrange my coins by size. A hand drops a dollar bill on my lap.

"No. I'm not—"

Henry pokes my foot, and presses his finger against his lips. By the next half hour, I have a lap full of bills and change.

"You can have it all," I whisper to Henry.

"You're a good kid but no thanks. Keep the money. You'll need it more than I ever will." He disappears around the corner of the building and reappears. His face is dripping wet.

What I thought were wrinkles must have been streaks of dirt. Henry doesn't look so old after all. If he cleaned up and shaved, he'd look like an older Drake but younger than Adam.

"You look too young to have been married," I say.

"I was sixteen, so was she. I got her pregnant when she was fifteen and we had a girl."

"So how old is your daughter now?"

He wipes a tear from his eye and so do I. "Five, but she was three when . . ."

"So you're only twenty-one or twenty-two?"

"In December, I'll be twenty-two."

"Is that father of yours ever going to show?"

I look up at Mr. Parsons. "I think I'll go check on him. Thank you for letting me use your restroom."

"You bet."

I am merely two feet away when Henry yells out, "If you lose him, or he forgets about you, come find me behind the church."

"Lose who?"

"Your father," Henry winks twice.

"That church gives me the creeps," I yell back.

"There's plenty of fine people buried behind that church. It's the safest place to be. That's where my Melissa lives. She keeps a good eye on me. And remember what we talked about. Brave eyes see better."

"Which headstone is hers?"

"None. I buried her urn of ashes in a box and I sleep beside her every night."

I don't think I could ever be desperate enough to sleep in a graveyard again. Even if Mom was buried there . . . I still wouldn't. One night was spooky enough for me, I couldn't imagine another.

"Bye. Henry."

It's a beautiful cloudless day and I've wanted to check out that Ruby Line, since I saw the sign. Maybe somebody up there has a shed or a barn.

Ruby Line never ends. The further I walk the less I see. The road stretches uphill forever, and seems to go nowhere but up. Regretting my choice, I venture back to my spot on the bank.

From here I can see Henry chain smoking. I wonder if he's dying of cancer or just trying to kill himself the slow way. I did see that 'I'm done with life' look in his eyes. I've seen that look more times than not, back in the basement mirror. A cold chill shivers down my back.

I lean my hands against the warm grass, lie back and take deep breaths of fresh air. I tilt my head toward a patch of flowers. They smell pretty. I roll over them to freshen up.

It only takes fifteen minutes for my face to start burning. I shield it with the pillowcase. Even that smells fresher. Now I'm glad Henry gave it back to me. My mind drifts back to last night and the three drunks. Maybe the church is safer with Henry there, but what if Henry doesn't go to bed until midnight? I need to find a better solution. Maybe up there in the woods would be better spot—but what if bears or foxes live up there?

Every now and then, the wind lifts the edge of the pillowcase off and I have to run and retrieve it. I roll over on my stomach, fold the pillowcase under my chest and rest on my elbows. Cows are grazing up on a far hill. If someone has cows, they must have a barn. A barn would be perfect.

I gaze at a huge pasture that stretches forever between the cows and me. It's dotted with thousands of yellow buttercups. The wind whispers like a giant fan sweeping across the massive field. The yellow flowers, disappear into the grass, then reappear after they bow to the breeze.

I pick a nearby daisy. A ladybug flutters from it, onto my wrist, crawls across my scar, and scurries down the palm of my hand. It's tiny little feet look like thin black sewing thread. I gently blow on it until it flies off and lands on a nearby beer bottle. Grass has grown around it making it look like a green lump. Looking closer, I notice bottles strewn all over the place and it's obvious they've been here for a while.

Henry must be doing okay, or he'd be collecting some of these to sell. I roll over to a different spot, to spy on him.

He looks like a puppet, bobbing up and down, picking up beer bottles. Am I watching my own future unfold? In two months, I'll be fourteen. In six years, I'll be his age. I know I'll never go to school again. Which means, according to my teacher, I'll never get a decent job.

And then there's the winter. Not sure what I'm going to do when the snow comes. Maybe I can find a library and hang out there all day. Maybe I'll have to ask Henry to share his dumpster. It's bound to be better than my back yard was. At least snow gusts can't whip you in the face.

Henry looks drunker than ever. He wavers left and right as though he's dodging a pile of wasps. He must be playing with the dog, but . . . I don't see the dog anywhere near him.

He staggers some more, clutches his chest and drops to his knees.

Alice from Nowhere

Henry slumps to the ground, motionless. I shake him. His eyes are bulging out of his head and his face looks like a balloon ready to burst. He grunts, groans and goes limp. I scream at the top of my lungs. Some person pulls me away and rips off Henry's shirt. "Go call 911. NOW." The smell of booze from him almost knocks me out. Bob pushes past me and races toward Henry. Inside the store is empty. Bob must have dialed 911 but just in case he didn't, I make the call. My fingers shake. My chin trembles.

"911 state your emergency."

"There's a . . . a—"

The operator interrupts me. "Do you need fire, police or ambulance?"

"Ambulance. There's an old man — I mean he's a young man. He needs medical help."

"Do you see any blood?" the operator asks.

"No. I think it's his chest."

"State your location."

In that moment, I realize I don't know where I am.

Battered

"State your name and location,"

I drop the phone.

Bang. Thud. Clunk.

It knocks against the side of the counter, sways in the air and hits it again. What am I thinking calling the police? Bob runs back inside. I point to the phone and run from his store. There's a small crowd around Henry. The drunk person from the bar is still there giving him CPR. I wonder if the booze from his breath will give Henry an urge to start drinking again.

A siren wails in the distance. The urge to see what happens to Henry is overwhelming but what if Dad reported me missing and someone recognizes me?

The sirens are deafening. Cars pull over to the side of the road. The first vehicle to barrel into the lot is a police car. I dodge through the crowd but I'm not the only one walking away from Henry. The guy who smelled like booze is leaving too but not one car is moving on the street because more sirens are sounding. Crossing the road is the easy part but seeing Henry or what's happening is impossible, especially when a foghorn sounds and a fire truck blocks my vision.

I move further down the bank until I see two firemen disperse the crowd and three others make their way to Henry. One fireman has a satchel while another has an oxygen mask and tank. They bend over Henry and all I can see are their butts. The ambulance arrives last. Medics rush to join the firemen. When I finally get a glimpse of Henry, he's strapped to a gurney and disappearing into the back of the ambulance. It heads away from the Goulds, while the fire truck and the police leave in the opposite direction past the church.

The church! What if Henry doesn't come back? What if he dies? What do I do now? I have no choice but to wait and see what happens.

I grab a pencil and flip to the inside cover of my literature book.

Questions About Henry
1. Do you ever get a bath?
2. If yes where?

235

He probably uses Bob's hose.

I chew on a blade of grass and wonder how a bum like him could have such a nice looking watch. I've seen his watch before. It looks exactly like one I saw on the front cover of a magazine, at the doctor's office, back when I got my ears checked. Henry's must be a cheap copy . . . or else he stole it.

1. Where did you get the watch?
2. How did your wife di—

My hand stays frozen.

"Juanita? Is that you?"

My pencil lead breaks. An electric shock gyrates through my chest and arms.

"What are you doing here?"

I look past them and ask, "You're alone right?"

"What are you doing here, so far from home?" Samantha asks again.

"Well, I have this aunt and she—"

"You ran away, again didn't you?" Karen says.

My nose tingles and burns. Henry told me earlier today, to hold those tears hostage, and that's exactly what I try to do. But it's hard work.

I manage to fake a brave face and shake my head no. I don't speak because I know if I talk my voice will break.

Samantha shields her eyes from the sun. "We live up there now. On that road." She points toward Ruby Line. "Waaaaay up there on a farm. We ran out of hamburger buns, for our barbeque. Want to come to the store with us?"

"I'll come with you but I can't stay too long, because I'm here visiting my Aunt Minnie." That's when I notice there's a police car parked in front of the store. "Maybe I shouldn't. I'd rather stay here."

"Then I'll wait with you." Samantha pulls ten dollars from her pocket, gives it to Karen, and says, "Don't forget to buy some ketchup too."

Battered

"Karen can you ask the clerk, what's happened to that homeless man. The one that got put in the ambulance?"

She raises her eyebrows and says, "No weirdo. I don't think so," and jogs across the road.

"How did you get here?" Samantha hugs me. "I am so glad to see you!" She hugs me, leans back and studies my face. "Karen's right, isn't she? You ran away again, didn't you?"

I put my finger up to indicate I need a minute. My lip quivers. When I try to speak, I can't. Each time I try to talk, my voice breaks. I pluck some blades of grass and tie them into knots.

When Samantha tries her grass blades break. "Wow you're fast. You make it look so easy. How long have you been practicing that?"

"Seven or eight years."

Karen pants and thrusts the paper bag at her sister. "You can carry it up the hill. Oh, and I bought gum, anyone want some?"

We blow bubbles while we walk up the lane and Samantha chatters about their new home, I kick rocks while I listen.

"What happened to your leg?" Karen points at my wound.

I shrug.

"Who cares about her leg?" Samantha says, "I want to hear what happened, period. You just disappeared from school. Start back there, the last morning we rode the bus to school together."

"The guidance counselor tricked me and sent me back home with Dad."

By now, we're only halfway up the road and they're asking me how I got here. We take a shortcut through a large open field of tall grass. After a mile it leads to a glade of trees. Within one-eighth of a mile, we squeeze through a chained wooden gate and follow a short trail in the woods. By the time we reach their back yard they're prying about where I slept, but lose interest as soon as we reach the clearing.

The best aroma ever, curls past my nose. "What's that smell?"

"It's a barbecue. We're having burgers and dogs," Karen says. She grabs the bag from her sister and runs to an older lady with a stern looking face.

Juanita Ray

The sounds remind me of the park we went to back when Marie disappeared, and it's every bit as big. The place is swarming with noisy people. Several blankets are splattered on the lawn. Most people sit in folding chairs, while some others stand in small clusters. The smell of burgers and charcoal drift through the country air but when the wind changes, it's laced with a putrid odor.

"When did your Dad buy this place?" I ask.

"He didn't. He fell off the wagon again." Samantha puckers her lips downward. "This is our foster home. The same one as before. Come, I'll introduce you to Mrs. Ruby, before we eat."

I shake my hand free from hers and step back behind the trees.

"Wait. Where are you going? Stop," Samantha tugs at my hand.

"You can't just bring me here to eat. I'm a stranger."

"She won't mind I promise.".

"Promise not to tell her anything about me."

"I won't. Well . . . I have to tell her something."

"Please don't say I ran away." She laughs and skips toward Mrs. Ruby. While I wait, my nose follows the stench. It's coming from a huge red barn across the road. How can they stand the stink? A large sign, with the shape of a cow, reads, Westvale Farm. In that moment I know there's no better place than the church.

Dry branches crack under my feet as I shift from foot to foot. Samantha returns, smiling from ear to ear "Don't be such a nervous nelly. Mrs. Ruby said she wants to meet you."

"Does that mean yes or no? Or is it a maybe?"

"She said yes silly and asked to meet you."

"What is she's just being polite? Can you ask again?"

"No." She yanks me out into the clearing and when she does Mrs. Ruby and I lock eyes and although the smell of food is irresistible, my nerves get the better of me. "I can't. What if she doesn't like me. I think I should go."

Samantha grabs my wrist and pulls me out toward Mrs. Ruby. I pull back. She giggles, "You're too skinny to win a tug of war."

Battered

My shoes turn into concrete blocks. My chest cramps from front to back. Deep breaths feel shallow. Breathe, Juanita, breathe deeper.

Luckily Mrs. Ruby is busy talking to someone and Samantha is too hungry to wait. "I'll introduce you later. Dogs or burgers?"

Should I stand or sit. Where do I wait? I choose the tree furthest away from everyone and sit under it. Samantha motions for me to come closer but I pretend I don't see her. Maybe she lied about getting permission. Maybe I'm not welcome. I scan the tree line for my exit.

Half of me wants to leave but the other half wants to stay, not because I'm hungry but because I have no where better to go. Samantha squats down beside me. A soda pop can, is bulging out of each pocket, a bunch of napkins are clenched between her teeth and each hand is carrying a plate, loaded with enough food to last a week. A mountain of egg salad, is squashed between a baked potato and a chicken leg. A hot dog smothered in ketchup sits on top of a cheeseburger.

"I figured you were starved and Mrs. Ruby said to pile up your plate because you look skinnier than a toothpick. I put salad dressing on your hot dog. It's under the ketchup. Mrs. Ruby makes it from scratch. You should try that first."

We watch Karen chat, a mile a minute, to Mrs. Ruby who combs her fingers through her gray hair, folds her hands across her blue plaid smock and turns to scrutinize me. I don't detect even a hint of a smile.

"She's a good foster mom and the man over there with the red plaid shirt is my foster dad. He's really nice too."

I whisper, "Are you sure she said I was allowed to eat here?"

"Yes. We can go ask together if you don't believe me." She reaches for the hotdog and shoves it in my hand. "Eat."

The wiener has a slit down the middle that's stuffed with cheese and it's wrapped in a bacon strip and despite feeling full after three bites, I finish the most delicious thing I have ever tasted.

Everything looks temping but I doubt I can manage another bite of anything. "This is way too much food. Will it be okay if I save it for later? To eat at Aunt Minnie's?"

"No. All the plates scraps go to the pigs. But I can make you a new plate to go."

"Pigs as in real pigs?"

"What other kind are there? Want a second plate?"

I pick at a piece of egg and say, "No. I'm too full. Honest."

But I nibble a little bit here and there in case I don't get a chance to eat for a few days. While I munch, Samantha tells me her Dad started drinking again, shortly after I disappeared. "He's in the Rehab Center now."

"Did he have an accident? Did he hurt anyone?"

"No. He wasn't driving. He got drunk and told off our social worker after she said he hadn't dealt with his guilt about not saving Mom. According to her, if he had, he would accept that it isn't his job to save everyone, like you. Anyway, it's not so bad this time. At least he didn't lose his license."

"What happened?"

"Remember how he was going to get the social worker to help you? Instead of filing an investigation, she told him what I just told you, and called your Dad. When my Dad found out, he got drunk, phoned her up, and told her she was a lazy cow, a stupid idiot, and a few other choice words. He also told her to stop playing shrink and to go get a lobotomy reversal," Samantha giggles

"Next thing I know, she shows up and we're packing for here. Oops. I'd better shut up, Karen's coming and she doesn't like to talk about it. She kind of blames you."

"What are you guys yapping about?" Karen kneels between us.

"Sleeping," Samantha says, "just where Juanita is going to sleep tonight." She turns to face me, "Where did you sleep last night, I know you have no Aunt Minnie here or anywhere else. Is it the same place you're sleeping tonight?"

I don't want to tell her. It's not their fault I was caught, last time, but I'm not sure who I can trust, certainly not Karen. "I was thinking about the recycle dumpster behind the store."

Battered

"You're sleeping outside?" Karen coughs ketchup all over her shorts. A mustard stained, paper plate blows past me, and settles against a broken branch three feet away. I ignore Karen, scoop it up and toss it in a nearby trash bin. Then I pick up another and another . . .

Samantha and Karen gather up the unused plates, forks and condiments from the picnic tables. Most of the people are leaving and by the time Karen and Samantha carry the condiments in the house, the crowd is gone. I stick out like a sore thumb, just like the empty chip bags scattered across the lawn. A gust of wind blows some empty paper cups against the tree line. I catch them and stack them in a pile. For a split second they turn into clay pots and I'm back at Hollikan Nurseries.

A rock whizzes above my head, hits the tree beside me and scatters leaves and twigs across the ground.

"GERALD!" Mrs. Ruby's voice sounds harsh. She jumps to her feet. Instantly she looks slimmer, still plump, but not as big around the waist. Her features are stocky and slightly masculine.

"KNOCK IT OFF."

Her hair is barely long enough to gather in a short ponytail. She shakes her finger at Gerald, and then curls it up and motions me over.

Samantha runs my way, slips her hand in mine and says, "Mrs. Ruby told me to bring you over to meet her."

I force one foot in front of the other until I am two feet from her constant stare. I avoid her eyes, and concentrate on the swollen feet planted in front of me. She lifts my chin, forcing me to look up at her.

"Thank you for the food. It tasted great."

"Thank you, and you're welcome. Do you think you could help me bring these containers in the house?" Her bird-like eyes are searching my soul. I'm uncertain of how much of me she sees, but I feel stripped naked.

Karen and Samantha speak in unison, "We've got it!" and follow Mrs. Ruby into the house with armfuls of dishes. The house is a long white bungalow with two porches, one on each end. Part of me wants to stay but most of me wants to go. I step toward the trees.

A tap on my shoulder makes me jump two feet. Mr. Ruby coughs and mumbles an apology. "Stella told me to keep you here and I could sure use a hand to help fold up these chairs."

His soft-spoken voice is kind and caring. His smile is gentle and genuine, but I'm tensed up and nervous.

I fumble with the chairs while he drains the cooler and collects the blankets. I'm almost finished when his red plaid sleeve takes the last chair from my grasp. His giant hand reaches toward me, "Hi I'm Cyril Ruby, pleased to meet you."

"Thank you so much for the food. Well . . ." I glance around. There are no more napkins, no more abandoned plates, no more excuses to stay, so I say, "Thank you again . . . I guess I'd better be getting back to Aunt Minnie before she gets all worried." His watery eyes look sad but kind. His tanned rough hand is as big as my face. I shake it awkwardly. He laughs and rubs the top of my head. If he had a red hat and a beard and mustache, he would make a good Santa, except his silver hair is clean cut and he's barely overweight. I look into his eyes and for a moment I think how lucky the Matthews girls are, then I say, "It looks like Samantha and Karen are busy, so please tell them thank you. It was really kind of you and Mrs. Ruby to feed me."

"Don't move. I'll get them so you can tell them yourself."

He jogs, toward the house bellowing, "Stella! Stella!"

I glance toward the trees. I'm not sure if I can find my way back through the shortcut. Maybe I should wait and see if Samantha can walk me back— or I could take the road. At least I know where it ends up.

The stench of cow manure gets stronger as I pass the front porch and head down the driveway.

"Alice. Alice—Alice, get back here," the voice is stern. I don't turn to see who's in trouble—I'm just glad it's not me.

"Alice, turn around. Get back up this driveway."

This Alice must be following me. I stop and turn to look.

I see no one but Mrs. Ruby, pointing from the porch.

"Yes you! Get back here this very minute!" She is definitely pointing at me.

Why is she calling me Alice? She curls her finger toward herself and slowly reels me in, until I'm standing at the bottom of her front porch steps. My heart thumps faster.

"Come up here."

The lump in my throat is too big to swallow.

She pats a space to her left, on the porch swing. "Sit down."

Even though her voice is gentler the second time, I'm still petrified. Her face is a mask. I can't read it.

"For the third time, sit down Alice. I don't bite."

The swing has a space big enough for five of me, so I sit at the far edge.

"Where did you think you were going?"

I wait for her to say something else. She's remains quiet.

"I beg your pardon?"

"Tell me where exactly were you planning to go?"

I mumble an excuse about Aunt Minnie being a worry wart.

"Where does this Aunt Minnie of yours live?"

"Just past the church." She raises her eyebrows quite high. "And past the police station." I'm guessing the police station has to be somewhere past the church, because that's where they came from earlier today.

"Alice, that's way too far to walk especially all alone. Let me have Mr. Ruby drive you—Cyril!"

"Stella I'm right here." The screen door creaks shut. "Scoot over Alice. That's my side." I edge toward Mrs. Ruby. He sits next to me.

I want to tell them my name isn't Alice but I don't want to get Samantha in trouble. She must have lied, about my name, why else would they call me Alice. "Who told you my name?"

"Why?" Mrs. Ruby asks. A surprised look flickers in her eyes. Is this a test? Did Karen tell them who I really was. What if she's stalling because she called the police? "The girls told us you ran away. Where did you run away from?"

"Nowhere." They are stalling. Are they sending me back? I want to die. I tell myself, no, this can't be happening to me again. Panic prickles every cell in my body. "Thank you Mrs. Ruby, but I have to go and I'd rather walk to Aunt Minnie's. I like fresh air and starry skies."

"The only place you're walking is straight into this house." Mr. Ruby holds his arm in front of my chest to keep me from rising. Mrs. Ruby pats my leg. "You must be frightened to death sleeping by that bar. It's not safe for anyone, especially a young girl like you."

Mr. Ruby shivers, "She slept there by herself?"

Mrs. Ruby answers, "Yes and then hung out with Henry all day who was half out of his mind from dehydration."

They continue to talk about me as if I'm not here.

"Well, well, it is a small world after all," chuckles Mr. Ruby. "So you're the girl Samantha told us all about when she first moved in with us. We prayed for you every single day, not just on Sundays."

Mrs. Ruby pats my leg again, "Yes, but I prayed more than once a day." She wipes her eyes with her dress collar. "Imagine you, showing up here out of nowhere. Well you'll be safe now and that's all that matters."

I shake my head to clear my ears. Their kindness hurts my feelings more than some of Dad's ordered beatings did. "You mean you didn't call the police. You're not sending me back?"

She wraps her arms around me. I feel awkward but thankful.

"Alice. Why would we send you back to such a place? We plan to protect you. Keep you safe here with us. You can live here for as long as you want, how would you like that?"

"Why would . . ." My voice breaks. Why aren't they calling the police? Something has to be wrong.

"No more lies okay?" Mr. Ruby's voice is as soft as a feather.

"Why the Goulds?"

"I don't know. It seemed far enough away."

"How did you get here?"

"I took the wrong bus on purpose. A bus to nowhere."

Battered

"Is there any place out there you could go? Do you have any place you could call home?"

"Nowhere."

"Alice that's all we ask. Honest answers to honest questions."

I swallow a huge lump and say, "Okay . . . The truth is my name is not Alice it's—"

"Oh yes it is." Mrs. Ruby's voice is firm, "You slipped out of a dark hole into my tea party and I don't care what anyone else calls you, but to me you're Alice and if you're going to stay here, that's what I plan to call you from now on. Alice from Nowhere."

A Wild Stallion

Here I lie in this strange bed, sandwiched between both girls, wearing pajamas that are clearly two sizes too big, but it sure beats sleeping in a graveyard.

"How did you know to come here?" Samantha asks.

"I didn't. It just seemed like the right bus to take."

"You took a bus to nowhere?"

"According to Mrs. Ruby I took a bus from nowhere."

I'm too excited to sleep. The longer I stay awake the more my thoughts drift to toxic. What if Karen rats me out? What will happen when I get sent to school? What if Dad called the police? Maybe I'm safe until school I am almost drifting off when Mr. Ruby taps on the door.

"Rise and shine. It's breakfast time."

Karen and Samantha grab their clothes and head for the bathroom. I wait for them to return, but they never do.

Battered

I comb my hair with my fingers for the fifth time, waiting to be told to come out of the room. Waiting to be invited for breakfast. Maybe they forgot about me.

The door busts open. "Hurry. We're not allowed to eat until we pray and Mrs. Ruby won't pray until you join us."

I follow Samantha to the kitchen and hesitate in the doorway. At first everybody is chattering then there's a dead silence.

"Alice, sit here by me." Mrs. Ruby pats an empty seat beside her.

I'm not used to a real breakfast or sitting with a family at a table, so I don't know what I'm supposed to do after she prays. I clasp my hands on my lap and stare at all the food. There are platters of fried bologna, bacon, sausages, hash browns, toast, pancakes, mixed fruit and whipped cream. On each plate, there are already eggs. I look at the heaped platters, and wonder who gets what? I watch what the others take, but they all take something different.

"What are you waiting for Alice? Grab some grub before it's all gone," Mr. Ruby's eyes twinkle, as he nods at the platters.

I feel embarrassed and ashamed at my awkwardness, and although I'm hungry, I'm too nervous to eat. I nibble on a piece of toast Karen tosses on my plate.

"Karen next time please pass the platter. Everyone share a pleasantry from the past, so we can give thanks this fine Sunday morning, ladies first," Mr. Ruby nods at Samantha. She points at her full mouth and pokes Karen.

"It's okay if you're not hungry Alice, more for me!" Gerald whispers with a grin. He seems to be Ryan's age.

"It's not that she's not hungry, she's shy, so let her be," Mrs. Ruby snaps at her son. "I'm sorry dear, carry on with your story, sweetheart."

I feel uncomfortable, and squirm in my seat as Karen finishes up. Do they expect me to be next? Do they know I am younger than Samantha or will Samantha be next? Am I imposing on family time? Should I ask to be excused, or just sit here until they tell me to leave?

Everyone has something pleasant to say and it seems to be over until Mrs. Ruby nods at me. "Go ahead Alice."

Juanita Ray

I try to remember something pleasant, I can share, but I can't.

My heart pounds faster. I sit in a theatre inside my mind, watching a movie from the past. No meals, stolen bread, sour milk, freezing hands, her fists and feet—I fast forward to the end.

Counting was pleasant at times, but who wants to hear about that? Maybe something nice happened in the yard, think, just think! My throat feels dry but I'm afraid to reach for the milk in case I spill it. My palms are too sweaty to be trusted. I'm so nervous I'll mess up and I don't want to have to leave this table. Being here in front of this food, listening to a bunch of chitchat and hearing so much laughter feels so weird, yet I like it. I don't know how to participate any better than I knew how to join conversations at school. My chest feels tight. I don't belong somewhere nice like here. I belong nowhere.

Mrs. Ruby's eyes are drilling a hole in my head. I'm afraid to look up, afraid she'll see me for who I am. A stupid klutz who has nothing good to say.

"Excuse us for a minute." Mrs. Ruby pushes her chair away from the table. I flinch. "Alice, come with me."

I follow her down the hall, into the bathroom. She takes a seat on the closed toilet, and brushes my hair. I feel awkward. "Did you bring a brush?"

"I don't own one and the comb back home belongs to the bathroom."

"You must feel hungry? Surely you're not full."

I feel full all right. Full of confusion. I'm not sure what the right answer is. I say, "I don't know."

She asks, "When was the last time someone brushed your hair?"

Is she asking me when is the last time I brushed it?

"I don't have a brush," my voice cracks.

"Why didn't you use one of these?"

"I wasn't sure if I was supposed to leave the room and I . . . I'm . . . I . . . don't know what I'm supposed to do or use."

She dampens a face cloth and hands it to me. "Wipe your face Alice." I wash, rinse the cloth, and hang it back in its place.

Battered

"Take a seat," she points at the tub. I sit on the edge while she remains on the toilet. "This is Cyril's reading chair so we can't stay here long," she smiles. "Sit on this end, closer to me." She leans forward and pats the part of the bathtub closest to her. I reluctantly scoot my butt along the edge that is across from the toilet. She looks deep in my eyes, scanning from one to the other.

"Alice, I don't know what's happened to you and I don't want to because, I have a strong feeling that if you told me just this much," she holds her thumb and forefinger an inch apart, "my heart would break in half." She pauses and wipes her eyes with her apron.

"When Samantha and Karen came, they made themselves right at home. I couldn't keep them out of the fridge if I wanted to. They helped themselves to everything, just like my boys do. Once they had their homework finished, they watched TV, and argued over which channel to pick. That's normal behavior. I want you to do the same."

I jerk and cower as she raises her hand toward my face.

She blinks, and gently brushes my bangs from my eyes. "Maybe it will be easier if you just pretend this is your home and we're visitors. That means you have a right to everything here and the right to do most of the things you want. Try to imagine that okay? You even have a right to pick the channel you want to watch, one night a week, just like the rest of the family and that's a good thing because there are seven days and only six of us. You make seven."

She waits for me to respond. I don't know what to say. It sounds like she's planning to let me stay for a while, but I can't fathom why.

"Alice, what are you thinking about this very second?"

"Why are you being so nice to me when I didn't do anything to deserve it?"

"Because God sent you here and you most certainly do deserve it, Alice. I want you to act like you are part of this family. Will you do that? Please?"

I say, "Yes, I will try to do that," because that's what she seems to want to hear, but I know there is no way I can when I don't even know what family is supposed to mean. How can I pick a TV channel to watch, when

249

I haven't watched TV in years and I don't even know what channels there are?

"Alice I can see your nerves are like frayed wires and your voice is so strained, all I can hear is your fear. There is nothing to be afraid of here. I want you to stop holding your breath. Breathe slowly in through your nose and out through your mouth."

She puts her hand on my chest. My heart panics and races faster. "I want you to stop over thinking. I can see your mind whirling. Just listen to this one question and answer me as honestly as you can, straight from your heart. Ready?" Her hand moves to my shoulder. "If you could have one wish granted what would it be? Take your time and think about what matters most to you."

"Never go home again. Ever again."

Mrs. Ruby smiles, "I'm looking for a good thing to start, not a bad thing to stop. Bad things won't happen around here. What would be your wish, for something good to start?"

"To find my sister Marie. I didn't get to say goodbye or a bunch of other stuff I should have told her and nobody knows where she is or if she's dead or alive."

Mrs. Ruby looks sad, "How about your brother, the oldest one, the one Samantha told us about. Would you like to see him instead?" I think about it. Part of me wants to say yes but a bigger part of me says no. "Alice tell me exactly what you're thinking. Think out loud."

"I miss him and I do want to see him but I'd be afraid Dad would follow him and find me. So, to be safe . . . I guess . . . I would have to pick . . . no," I try to keep my lips from quivering. I blink repeatedly. "I don't want to talk about family anymore . . . is that okay?"

Mrs. Ruby sighs, "Alice your eyelids look like hummingbird wings. It's okay to show your feelings, sweetheart. How about we pretend you are an orphan and have no family. Now what would you wish for?"

I don't have to pretend or imagine anything. I've always felt like an orphan. Figured God was responsible for me and at times it felt like he'd given up and abandoned me too. For a minute, the screen is blank because if I were a real orphan all my problems would be gone. I look her in the eyes and say, "I would just want to be treated fair."

Mrs. Ruby rolls her lips together and stares hard at me for a full two minutes. Then she looks down.

More silence . . .

"Alice today is Sunday. On Sundays, Cyril and I try to take a break and Samantha and Karen usually visit their Dad. Do you have any friends anyone you want to see today?"

"Are we supposed to go away on Sundays? Is that your day off as a foster mother? I mean do you close up?"

"No," she laughs, "on Sundays we try to make the day special, go somewhere, visit others, or just relax at home. Do you know any friends or have anywhere, around here that interests you?"

I shake my head no.

"Not one friend?"

I shake my head again.

"The girls told me you didn't know they were living here, so why on earth, of all places to come, would you pick this town? Of all of the buses there are, why did you pick the bus coming here?"

"I really do think God picked it," I answer. "I fell asleep one night while I was praying and the next morning when I woke up I just knew what to do." I leave out the part where I dreamt about Mom.

"You don't know a single soul here?"

"Just Henry. He was at the store." I tell her about Henry but leave out the part about the church.

Her eyes glisten over. "How did you find the girls?"

"They found me, I was writing a list of questions I wanted to ask Henry, when he got back, and they just called my name."

"What kind of questions. I know Henry better than most."

"You do? Do you know if he's okay?"

She smiles. "He's fine but he won't be back in town today. He was extremely dehydrated and they want to keep him in for observation."

"I know what my one wish would be, if I had one. I wish I could help Henry and help him find his daughter."

Mrs. Ruby dabs her eyes. "Don't we all. But nobody but Henry can help Henry. I'll tell you what. That seems like two wishes to me but maybe I can help you with of them. Today I plan to bake a cake. You can help me and while it's baking, maybe I can answer some of those questions you have about Henry."

"How do you know Henry?" I ask.

"Everybody knows Henry. The Goulds is a small place, and the world can be cruel, especially the newspapers."

The half-open door creaks when Mr. Ruby taps it. "Well now Stella, you can't keep her all to yourself. You're going to have to share her once in a while." He's chuckling but his eyes are tainted with worry. "Is everything okay in here?"

Mrs. Ruby's eyes brim with tears, "It's going to take quite a while for her to get accustomed to a normal life, never mind us."

"Why is that young lady?" Mr. Ruby smiles, sits beside me on the tub, and slings his arm loosely over my shoulder. I swallow hard. I have a huge lump in my throat and my voice is pinned underneath it. I squirm to create a little distance between Mr. Ruby and myself.

"That bad huh?" he smells under the arm of his shirt. I can't help but laugh along with him.

"Alice you have a beautiful hearty laugh. You know we could use a little more of that around here. Now both of you get out of my reading room and go eat some breakfast. I put your plates in the oven."

I can't eat everything on my plate and when Mrs. Ruby tells me not to scrape the plate into the trash, prickles run down my back. I freeze by the garbage can. She must expect me to finish it. "We don't throw away potato skins or scraps. We give those to the pigs. Use that silver bucket over there in the entry."

I look at Mrs. Ruby amazed, "You really do have pigs?"

Mr. Ruby walks into the kitchen and reaches into the fridge. "We love pork and speaking of pigs, I am going to make room for one of these cookies." He passes the plate toward me. I hesitate and eyeball the food left on my plate. He shoves it to one side, "No matter how full we are, nobody can resist Stella's cookies. And the pigs love it when you don't finish your food."

I smile at the thought of not having to eat what I don't like.

"Stella, see how beautiful her smile is? Maybe I can borrow her for a bit and see if we can conjure up a few more of those. Or is that out of the question. What do you think Stella?"

"Go on Alice. Cyril will show you around while I clean up. But don't keep her for too long. I promised her we'd bake a cake."

We start with a tour of the barn. The smell is nauseating. I gag while he laughs, "That goes away with time." When I ask where the cows are he tells me they have acres and acres of land on both sides of Ruby Line.

The house is surrounded by enormous grazing fields and a cluster of small buildings. The dairy business is across the road from the house. It's there, in a giant barn, I meet my first cow.

We collect eggs, feed chickens and dodge a clutch of fluffy yellow fur balls, with toothpick legs, chasing each other in circles. It's hard to tell what chicks belong to what hen.

"Where did the baby chicks come from?"

"Eggs we didn't eat."

Mr. Ruby drives through a field toward the duck pond. We pass a goat ramming its horns repeatedly into the fender of an old truck. He warns me the best way to avoid being butted by goats is to stay clear of them or give them something better to butt.

He throws some feed to the ducks and says, "These ducks are opposite to that goat. They're as docile as they come."

The ducks stopped by during migration but became so spoiled they stayed and turned tame. Between more showing up and babies being born, the mud hole became overcrowded. Mr. Ruby had to build a second pond and join it to the first one with a trench.

We hop on the tractor and ride to where the cows graze and finally venture over to some hayfields. "Is this your first time on a tractor? Because if it is, you look mighty comfortable up here."

I tell him there was a broken old tractor in our back yard at Heart's Delight. When I was four, I used to make meatballs and find rusty old cans to store them. I would pretend the tractor was a store and try to sell the cans to my brothers. It is one of my better memories. One I'm not afraid to share with him. One I should have remembered for this morning at the breakfast table.

"Meatballs made out of what?" he stops the tractor.

"Worms and mud, for fishing bait."

"Ha-ha. A little entrepreneur. Did you sell many?"

"No. They didn't want to buy them so they stole them instead."

"How do you know they stole them?"

"I just knew it had to be them, so one day I filled the cans with mud and left out the worms and they didn't like that one bit."

His cheeks crease with dimples. "How did that go over?"

"That's the day my brother, Ryan, almost drowned. They were looking under rocks for worms. Bruce, he's older, told him not to throw heavy rocks over the bridge but he wouldn't listen. When Bruce told him to let the rock drop, he wouldn't let it go and fell into the river. It was over ten feet deep and Ryan couldn't swim."

"I take it Bruce saved him?"

"No. He told him tough luck and said he was going to the diner to get some fries and left him bobbing up and down in the water."

"Oh my goodness, did he drown?"

"No. Whenever he hit the bottom he'd push off and come up for air until a friend, eating at the diner, saved him, and pulled him to shore."

"Did you get off with your no-worm trick?" he laughs.

"No such luck. Later that day, they pelted me with my own mud balls. I tried hiding behind the tractor, but it didn't help much. I was out numbered," I grin.

"Take the wheel," he says.

Battered

"What if I crash?"

"You can't crash a tractor."

I drive a crooked line across the field but when we get near the house, he takes control and parks on some grass, under an apple tree.

"Are you sure we should park here? Won't it ruin the grass?"

He kicks the lawn. "I can do this all day and it still grows back. It's half weeds anyway. Mother Nature is tough. She can take it."

As we walk through the door, I ask, "Do you just have boys?"

"No. We have two daughters—"

"Dad, I need to talk to you for a minute." While Alan talks to his father, about the cows Mrs. Ruby tells me about Henry.

"Was he okay?"

"He was half out of his mind with dehydration, but not now."

"Did he remember meeting her at all?" Mr. Ruby asks.

"Oh he remembered Alice alright. That's all we talked about," she raises her eyebrows at him, "her and the church."

"What church? The Ruby church?"

"Yes. St. Matthews."

"What about the church?" Mr. Ruby's fork full of food hovers in front of his lips.

"We can talk about it later," Mrs. Ruby looks my way and shakes her head. "Alice, oh Alice, oh Alice. How bad can life be that you'd rather sleep with the dead."

Mr. Ruby chokes on his food and rushes to the bathroom.

Whenever I was at the table back home the only thing to listen to was scraping forks or Irma's yelling. But meals are different here. There's not a mean word out of anyone's mouth. They talk about friends, animals, cows, food and fairs and apparently, there is a large fair going on now and we're heading that way today.

Mrs. Ruby has been baking all week and the counter has been covered with preserves and pies. At first, I'm embarrassed to ask what a fair is and by the time we reach the fairgrounds I don't have to. It looks like a circus. Exactly like the circus Aunt Sally took me to when I was five.

Juanita Ray

While she carries a pie somewhere, Mr. Ruby takes me over to the pony rides. My first job is to cut up the apples and feed pieces to the ponies while he walks each one in a circle.

Everything is going perfect, until I kick over a bucket of apples. An olive colored hand scoops up the pieces and tosses them back in the bucket. I take some out of the bucket, and brush off the dirt before putting them back. An older boy above us sneers, "Horses eat grass and roots all the time. You don't need to wipe them off."

He looks shifty. I doubt, given the chance, he would ever return Henry's wallet. I turn my eyes from the older boy and use my sleeve to brush more dirt from the apples. The younger scrawny boy, kneeling beside me, says, "Hi, I'm Gordon."

Gordon seems to shadow me from that moment forward. When I venture from booth to booth searching for Mrs. Ruby, sure enough, Gordon is trailing close behind. The older boy seems to be following me too. I'm more than glad when we head back to the farm, because something about that other boy gives me the creeps.

At one point, I ask Mr. Ruby who he is.

"I can't remember his name but he's a good kid. Always volunteers every hay season. Want to help corral the cows?"

It takes weeks for me to learn how to corral cows. Too slow and dusk would pass, and cows get spooked. Too fast and the milk would sour if they ran. Some grazing fields are one-fourth of a mile away from the barns and although it takes a couple of weeks, I learn how to head them back without spooking them, or provoking a nearby bull. By midsummer, I'm an expert at rotating the cows between pastures.

Tonight, I can't wait to lift the chain over the last fence post and get these cows into the barn and visit a herd I like much better.

As soon as I latch the last of the three barn doors, I climb the tree, grab some apples, and run like a bullet up the road. I push through the thick shrubbery, lean against the fence and crane my neck past the maze of brush but the horses aren't here yet.

Battered

The first time I heard the grunting and snorting, I thought it was a wild pig, until I heard the weirdest sound. I can't even imitate it. Maybe I could if I could squeal and play the bugle at the same time. The stallion, who made that sound, always pins his ears flat against his skull, has his tail do a rapid twitch and then he bolts. He reminds me of my old cat Crowley. He'd always flatten his ears, and flap his tail before he ran off.

But horses are different than cats. They always show up the same time every evening, and they don't bolt unless there's a good reason. I tried coming at different times, and discovered when I arrived an hour early and stayed quiet, they always stopped, stayed and grazed.

After a few weeks, the stallion's ears go from flat to being upright and stiff. His roar becomes a neigh sound. Now he sounds like he's laughing and whistling at the same time.

But no matter how quiet I am, once he senses me, he pauses, curls up his upper lip, snorts, and gallops off with his herd of mares.

It's been awhile since they've been here. I tried taking apples and cutting them up into small squares and tossing them as far as I could toward the area where I first saw them, but day after day, I sat and waited for nothing. The day I decided to give up on them, and not come back was the day they showed up again.

Now I come here every sunset, right after we finish baling hay, and sing the same two lines of a tune, and hum the rest. They don't seem to mind that I don't know all the words. They show up for their apple treat every time.

For weeks I bribe them with larger chunks of apples, until the stallion responds by moving away from his harem of mares and eating from my hand. He won't let any of the mares approach me. Whenever one tries, he snorts a reprimand, and nickers as he nibbles. I love feeling his soft throaty voice vibrate on my fingers. It becomes my favorite pastime, and my second favorite is baling hay. But now that we are in the middle of hay season, it's harder to spend as much time with the stallion.

I'm glad that hay season is nearing its close, only because I'll have more time for the horses. It's bittersweet because I'll miss the fun we have in the fields. The past two months have been nothing but fun. We've been cutting hay for one month solid and tonight is one of our last nights left. Gordon, the boy I met at the fair, is working by my side.

He wipes his sweaty brow. "It's your first hay season, right?"

"Sure is. Have you done this before?"

"Last year was the first year I volunteered."

I rake the sun-dried straw into a pile and wonder how many bug homes I'm destroying. I lean on the rake, wipe my brow and say, "How come? Why would so many strangers volunteer?"

"For the hayrides. Tomorrow when we start tying and lifting bales on the wagons, loads of kids will dribble in from everywhere."

"Why wait for the last day?"

"To go on the wagon rides. The bales are heavy and it takes a few of us to lift them so we do work hard. But we get first dibs on the rides because we've been here all season. The main reason I volunteer is because Mr. Ruby makes it so much fun," he laughs and dives into the pile, "and because he's the nicest man on earth."

"And he's nice like that all the time, no matter what."

Samantha and Karen rake their piles toward ours and we spend the rest of the day hay diving, raking and diving again.

We go home exhausted. Neither one us wants to do anything but sleep. Even chatty Karen can't manage to keep her eyes open.

Two days later I'm in my room being outsmarted by a very evasive fly. I try to smash it flat, but I can't. I slap the rolled-up magazine on the dresser, miss and throw it against the wall. I flop on the bed and cover my face with my pillow. I want to kick myself for picking wagon rides and not the tractor. How could I be so stupid? I should have known better when Gordon said something about kids dribbling in from everywhere to lift the bales and go on wagon rides.

I should have known he'd show up.

Cuffs and Cops

My brain feels like a wasteland littered with debris—scavenged by toxic thoughts from my past. It's hard to envision a bright future when the same nightmares that haunted me for years, have returned. Maybe if the girls hadn't gone back home, maybe if they were here, I'd have someone to tell but the truth is I trust nobody now.

The fluttering curtains dance around my windowsill enchanting me. It's as if the wind is telling me to celebrate my freedom. I remind myself how big my bedroom window is compared to the postage stamp I had back in the basement. I can actually climb in and out of this one, which I prefer to using the door. It reminds me of life before Irma, climbing the fence to Sharon's house and other freedoms long forgotten and although I have a nightstand with a reading lamp, I can't seem to break the habit of standing by the window, and reading by the light of the moon.

Sleep got better. Mr. Ruby thinks it's because of all that fresh farm air. I've gotten use to the stench. When Samantha use to open the window, I'd cringe. Now, I sleep with it wide open.

Juanita Ray

Usually my nights are dreamless, but when I do dream, it's always in the form of an old nightmare, back to haunt me. It usually plays out like a movie, when I awaken it stays on pause, but when I drift back asleep, it resumes. I dream mostly about water and being abandoned and standing alone in the middle of the ocean. I watch my shoes drift away, as I stand frightened on a rock, knowing I can't swim and no one is there to save me.

I guess it's better than my nightmare about flying and crashing into the closet. During those times, I lie awake and try to stay that way, until floorboards creak, signaling dawn is almost here.

Today is one of those days. I can tell, by the creak, it has to be close to five o'clock. I kiss my locket, hurry into my clothes, and sneak outdoors, just in time to see Mr. Ruby sauntering down the driveway.

My presence startles him. "You're so quiet! You almost gave me a heart attack! I didn't even hear the door shut."

"That's because I used the window."

He smiles and nods, "Looks like you're an early bird like me. You know the early bird always gets the worm." He winks and squeezes my shoulder. He's wearing black gaiters, bibbed jeans and looks more like a fisherman than a farmer. "You remind me of our old cat. She never left the house through the door. She always liked the window better."

Mr. Ruby chuckles and messes with my hair. "Looks like it did the first morning, you spent at the house."

We laugh together about that first morning. My hair looked bad but the rest of me looked worse. I was wearing the same clothes I wore when I ran away and I had specks of toilet paper lint, stuck to my face, because that's what I used to dry it. Real towels hung from the rack but I wasn't sure if I was allowed to use them.

I used my finger to brush my teeth. Back then, I had no grooming tools, so I finger-combed my hair.

"Thought we threw away that finger brush."

"We did. I didn't use my fingers."

"Well it looks like a rat's nest, so what did you use?" He plucks at my tangled hair.

"Nothing. I left my brush in the bathroom and I didn't want to wake anybody up. Is it okay if use that hose to wash my hands?"

"Yep. Fill your boots." He sits on the milk stool and yawns. "Can't beat this time of day. Nothing better than solitude, but," he yawns again, "I like it better with you here. We should make this a morning habit." Oddly enough, I find Mr. Ruby's soft voice comforting. His nature never changes. He's always sweet. Always kind. Maybe I like him so much because he's good with animals—good with me. And because I knew little about my parents, I wanted to know everything about him and Mrs. Ruby.

"Can I ask you something?"

"Sure," he says.

"How come you and Mrs. Ruby take in foster kids?"

"We're slowing down on that, and you're not a true foster kid yet, so you don't count. Samantha and Karen were just short-term returns. They lived with us some time ago, so we took them in, again, as a favor."

"Thank you for taking me in too."

He pulls the stool beside the cow, "You're a whole different story. God dropped you into our laps. He blessed us with you. Now let's see if we can put a little more country in you."

Mr. Ruby and I have a great time in the barn. His blue eyes have a constant twinkle. He tells me how his mother worked the farm by herself for years after his father died.

"How did he die?"

"A minor flu but back then if you got it you were gone."

"How did she look after all those cows?"

"A year after he died, we lost most of them to Bangs disease."

"How many cows are here at Westvale now?"

"Seventy-three if you count the calf born last week."

"What do you do with all this milk?"

"Sell it to Central Dairies."

"How did you meet Mrs. Ruby? At school?"

"The six of us were homeschooled until my two brothers and I were old enough to run the farm. I was twenty-two, Stella our housekeeper, was twenty-three, just a year older than me." How can two housekeepers be such different people? "You had a housekeeper too?"

"Yes, and another at age twelve, when my Dad died. Her name was Minnie. I was the oldest son. But I had three sisters. Grace was ten, Pearl, God rest her soul, was six, and Isabel was three, when I was born. My father, Alan, was a good man, so was my grandfather. He started the Ruby church. He, my father and mother are all buried there and Pearl too. She died exactly a year after Mother did."

"It had a lock on it."

"That's because it's a cemetery now." His eyes look dusty. He nods and wipes the corner of his eye. "Seems to me you picked a fine spot to sleep." He squirts me from the cow. I dodge but the second squirt gets me. "It doesn't get any better than this. Warm milk fresh from the cow." He squirts some inside his thermos cap and hands it to me. "Try it, you'll love it."

I reluctantly take a small sip and pray I don't puke.

———+—+—+———

Rocks skip up the lane scattering pockets of dust in the air. Gordon walks past me, twists his body into a pretzel and fires another against the next roadside tree. I catch up and walk beside him. His swing is angry. He hurtles another at a nearby boulder. It bounces toward me. I dodge it and catch up with him again.

"When people don't slow down after you call them, it's because they don't want you around. Get it?"

"Who shit in your cornflakes?"

"Where did you get that expression?"

"Bob Parsons—Anytime I have a frown. Well . . .?"

"Everybody and nobody. I want to be alone, I hate me, I hate you, and I hate everybody."

I want to say, you live way down there, if you wanted to be alone why come up where I live? Instead, I ask, "What happened? I can tell something bad happened . . . I've got big shoulders and I'm really good at keeping secrets."

Battered

He looks at my shoulders with dubious eyes. His voice is filled with mistrust, "Your shoulders are skinny and for your information, I don't have any secrets. Leave me alone. Didn't you hear me? I said I hate everyone. That includes you. I especially hate you."

"Nice! If you're trying to hurt me, forget it. It's going to take a lot more than that because I've heard that one all my life, from a person four times your size."

He glances at me out of the corner of his eyes. They look dull.

"When I'm sad, or mad, I go to a secret spot. Want to see where it is?"

His face looks like he took a swig of vinegar. "Not really."

He follows me anyway.

"Gordon, promise me you will keep this place a secret too. I haven't shared this place with anyone before. It's a magical place that makes worries go away—at least for a while."

"Why are you sharing it with me?" he asks.

"Because you're obviously good at keeping secrets."

How did you find this spot?"

"I heard a snorting sound."

Gordon stops abruptly, "I don't hear anything." He cups his ear.

"No! I found this place after I heard a snorting sound."

He scoffs, "Most people would expect it to be a wild pig and run."

I smile and pat the fence. "I come here when I find it hard to cope. Sometimes I still feel all the restrictions I had at home, even though they're gone. So, I do things, like climb through the window and come here to sit on the fence. Just little things I couldn't do before, to prove to myself I'm free from the past."

"Does it work?"

"Sometimes. But it's like I can't stop looking over my shoulder. This probably sounds weird to you, but I feel such a wild-crazy-free feeling just standing outside our fence looking in at the yard."

"Naw, that doesn't sound weird at all. I feel frozen in place sometimes, when I don't want to walk through a gate."

263

"I had that a lot before too, but we didn't have a gate, just a driveway. If I ever own a house, I'm never building a fence, as a matter of fact I don't even want a house and I'm never living in one with a basement." I pull away some lower tree branches and make my way toward the second fence. Gordon hesitates. I reach for his hand to pull him through. He jerks away as though his fingers were burned.

"Are you sure none of the snorts weren't from wild pigs?" He takes a step backwards.

"Yes. Pigs have a different snort. If you want to hear the difference, come over after dinner, when we feed them scraps."

"Thanks, but no thanks." He looks left, then right. "When do they come? From what direction?"

"Never at this time of day. I mean I trust you, but the horses have to trust you too. You can't just show up all of a sudden or you'll scare them off. There's little things the horses expect you to do before they trust you and they only come at a certain time."

"What kind of horses?"

"I don't know, just wild ones. A stallion with a bunch of mares."

"Have you ever wondered what happens to the boy babies? Like what the stallion does to them?"

"No, I never actually thought about that at all, but can you imagine riding one of them. It would be better than riding with the hay bales!"

"What's wrong?"

"Nothing."

"You looked like you were going to vomit or something."

I love riding in the back of the truck watching the long trailer filled with hay swerve back and forth on its hitch. It's better than the stack wagons. The wind isn't as hard on my face and the smell of hay—my mind jerks to an abrupt stop. I hack at the apple.

"And I thought I was in a bad mood," Gordon says. "Where did you get the pocket knife?"

"From Mr. Ruby." I stab my knife into the fence post, "Why don't I show you where to toss these apples."

Battered

For the next three days, I make him practice throwing apple pieces until he gets the toss just right. We sit together on the fence and listen to birds chirping and the wind rustling through the trees.

"My secret to getting them to come out from the trees is I sing a special song. They hide until they hear it,"

"What song?" he waits for my answer. I feel I'm being tested.

For some reason I am not ready to share it. Instead, I watch his shoe. Gordon is using his heel to scrape at the fence, making the fence sway. I move my foot in front of the fence post.

His startled look, turns to shame. "I have a friend who buys me things and gives me money."

"So?" I hold my breath and wait for the rest of his story but he clams up. I know I haven't earned his full trust yet so I wait a few minutes before I say, "I ran away the last day of school and nobody in my family knows where I am."

"That's not a real secret." Gordon looks at me expecting something better. "Why did you run away?"

"I wouldn't have had to run if I had a driver's license."

"Funny. Ha-ha-ha." He says without laughing.

I still can't seem to talk about my past to anyone and he's no exception. I'm not sure what he wants to hear. I have plenty of memories but struggle with sharing any. I break the silence by saying, "I'm not good at talking about me, so let's head back. I need to help Mrs. Ruby do some of her chores."

"The other day, when you were angry, when you stabbed the fence post, what was that about?" he asks.

I turn away. He runs to catch up. As we walk, I stare toward the tool shed over in a field, halfway between the house and us. I force my mind to go back to last Saturday, the last day we baled hay in the largest field. Everyone who had ever helped all year long showed up for the last baling. It was late afternoon, when my pitchfork went missing and I took a shortcut through the field to the tool shed to get a replacement. When I reached the shed, I stumbled smack into someone that was lurking around the corner.

He was about my age, maybe a little older. His shape looked familiar. When I heard him zip up his pants, I tried to back up but I tripped on a pitchfork. He turned, pounced forward, grabbed me, and pressed me against the barn. He shoved his hand over my mouth and groped my chest. I opened my mouth to scream but it came out muffled. He laughed and told me I was going to like this, as he pulled at my pants. My first thoughts were, no, this can't be happening! Not to me! Not here!

Before he could get my pants down. I bit his hand and kicked at him until he stumbled away in shock, threatening to kill me if I told anyone. I flew through the field as fast as I could, yelling, and waving at Mr. Ruby, but he just waved back. By the time I caught up to him, he was busy talking to someone. I was out of breath and sick as a pig.

All I could do was vomit. He instructed someone to drive me home in the baler. I had dry heave after dry heave. I've tried to block out what happened, but since that night, I've spent my dreams dodging hay bales, running from another monster.

The memory still makes me nauseous, but for some strange reason I tell Gordon about it.

Gordon looks startled, "Well, who was it?"

I ignore the question.

"What if you get pregnant?"

"He didn't get that far. Let's not talk about it anymore okay? I'll bring you back here tonight but meet me outside the house so we can walk together."

Mr. Ruby is walking up the driveway heading for the house.

Gordon points and says, "Go. Hurry. Tell him."

Then he breaks into a run and jogs down the road, out of sight.

"I see you made a friend for yourself," Mr. Ruby catches me as I trip over my own feet. "Where do you guys hide out all day?" his eyes are twinkling.

"It's a secret," I smile.

"Ouch! Keeping secrets from me? That hurts," he laughs and tousles my hair. He scoops up his Sunday paper and heads to the front porch swing.

Nobody is at home. The boys, are off somewhere, and Samantha and Karen haven't even dropped by for a visit in weeks.

I find Mrs. Ruby on her hands and knees scrubbing the bathroom floor. She pants as she tries to clean around the toilet. I offer to help.

"Go do something fun," she smiles, "you'll have plenty of time to scrub floors after you're married. Take the bus, go shopping, go make some friends, you need to be a child while you still have the chance." I watch her, watch me, for the longest minute. She looks a little worn and tired. "Why not take the bus to town and treat yourself to something at the mall? Mr. Ruby is going to town this afternoon if you want to ride along." I shudder at the thought of going to town. What if someone notices me? I'm so used to confinement, just walking up the road or going to the barn feels like a huge treat.

"Alice, oh Alice, I wish I could change that look in your eyes."

"I'm sorry," I say.

"Don't be. It's not your fault. My goodness, where does the time fly? It already lunchtime. I made some sandwiches earlier. They're in the fridge, and for dessert we can have hot apple pie with ice cream, but first I have to clean up."

"I'm not hungry," I say.

"Are you not feeling well enough to eat?" she looks worried. I can tell there is more than lunch on her mind. Something is bugging her. Something she wants to say but is holding inside.

She heads to her bedroom without waiting for my answer.

While she bathes, I scrub the other bathroom. I know she has more work because of me and I always try to sneak in at least two extra chores every day to make it up to her.

I finish before she gets out of the bath. I change the water, grab a different scrub cloth, and scrub the hall and porch floors.

"Alice. Please get up off your knees. Get up this minute. You are not here to work! You can help with dishes and that's it." I detect a note of anger in her voice.

"It was just to pass time. You usually bathe longer. I didn't expect you to be ready so quick." She seems upset at something and I think it's me.

"I want you to be normal like other girls, and fight for what you want. I want you to enjoy your life." Her voice softens. "It'll do you a world of good. Do it for me. You've missed out on most of your childhood already. Alice, I just want you to be a kid before you grow up. You don't have much time left and God knows when it goes, you can't get it back. I won't let you miss what little time is left of it. You need to learn to be a little more selfish."

"Stella, she doesn't know how and there's nothing she wants more than to please you." Mr. Ruby stands in the doorway and scratches his head.

"It would please me to see her have at least a year or two of normal childhood. Maybe we need to foster another girl so she can learn how the rest of them act," Mrs. Ruby sighs. "She thinks she has to earn her keep. I want her to accept that she's here because we love her. It breaks my heart to see her try so hard. There's no need for it."

Mr. Ruby smiles and winks, "Maybe she likes helping you. Maybe something that simple makes her happy." He messes up my hair. "I see a change in you, every day. Little by little, you're coming out of your shell. You're doing good."

Mrs. Ruby says, "Yes she is, but one day I want to see the smile on her face go all the way to her eyes, like yours does. Well . . . now might be as good a time as any to tell her. You haven't mentioned anything to her, have you?"

Tell me what? My heart fears the worst.

"No." His voice is faint but gentle, "Of course not. It should come from you. You're the one who prayed the most, and you're the one who cried the hardest, so it's only right you be the one to ask."

"Let's do it over pie. I made your favorite, cinnamon apple. Have a seat Alice."

At the table, she clears her throat. "Samantha and Karen won't be coming back here anymore. Their Dad has recovered and they have returned home for good."

Battered

They exchange looks. The kind of look two students exchange at school, when the principal asks, 'Who wants to go first?'

Mr. Ruby clears his throat. "You've seemed sick with worry lately and we didn't want to upset you but there is an issue, and important issue we need to discuss. The only way we can protect you from—"

Mrs. Ruby sighs. "Sounds like the boys are back a little early. Alice, get two more plates. We'll have this talk another time."

Relief floods through my body. I have no clue what they wanted to talk about but whatever it was made them nervous and that's not a good sign. I reach in the cupboard for two plates while Mrs. Ruby gets the pie out of the oven.

Mr. Ruby's voice sounds louder than normal. "Come in."

I know it's not Alan or Gerald, when an unfamiliar voice says, "We understand you are harboring Juanita Rose."

Pricks roll across my skin. I haven't heard that name in months.

The air catches in my throat. I momentarily freeze and in slow motion watch Mrs. Ruby drop the pie, as it splatters across the floor, mingled with fragments of white and blue ceramic. A few chards embed into my ankle.

The voice walks toward me, "Are you Juanita Rose?"

I gulp and say, "I'm Alice." In that moment I hate my real name.

Several police officers glance at each other, look at me, then at a piece of paper. "Looks like we found her."

One of them seems to know the Rubys. While they talk, I eye the open door.

The trees seem so far away, and as I reach them, an arm winds around my waist and pulls me backwards. I kick and scream.

Mrs. Ruby yells, "No. Alice, No."

But I don't stop . . . I break free.

Half way down the front lawn, the same female officer closes in on me again. I slide past her legs and grab her ankle. She swerves but only stumbles. I know I won't make it. I head left toward the apple tree and run in circles. For a brief minute, it transforms into a ping-pong table. I blink my eyes trying to get the tree to reappear.

Wham!

All I can see are her uniform buttons.

My eyes go blind and slam shut. Everything from my chest up burns so bad, I can't do anything but cough.

"Please don't take me home, please, I'm sorry, I'll do whatever you say, just don't take me back home."

She grunts, pushes me inside, and slams the car door.

"Please come back. Please. Let me ou-ou-outtt. Ple-e-ease . . ."

My desperation ebbs away, and a fear, greater than any I've ever known, consumes me. I know I'm done. There's no hope. They're bringing me back. I kick the door repeatedly, until I'm too exhausted to lift a foot. I hyperventilate when I hear the click of a lock. Someone scoops me up. Convulsive sobs catch in my throat.

The officer stands me up and holds my shoulder. "Be good, okay."

I stutter and babble an answer, even I can't understand.

The female officer, standing with the door ajar, seems to be crying. I tell her I'm sorry for kicking her. She turns her back to me.

A gruff voiced officer says, "She doesn't look fourteen. You sure she's not ten or eleven?"

"She's was scrawnier when we got her." Mr. Ruby says.

Mrs. Ruby dabs her eyes with her apron. "Yes. She was worse when she first got here. Nothing but pale skin covering bones. Malnourished."

An officer taps his walkie-talkie.

"Still waiting for instructions."

The female turns around and blinks her red eyes. "A kid doesn't act like that for no reason, I say we don't notify the parents and we bring her to Juvie. Look at her wrists—the cuff burns. The kid would have chewed her arms off before she'd let us bring her back home." I keep my eyes closed, while the cuffs come off my hands. I bolt upright, run to the kitchen and grab a knife. I press it against my chest and threaten to stab myself if anyone comes closer. I am terrified but desperate. The wobbly knife won't stay still.

Mrs. Ruby clutches her chest and screams at me, "No Alice!"

Battered

The officer's voice is as cold as ice, "You can stay. Don't move. Just put the knife down."

"You promise?"

"I promise."

"Swear on your life," I sob.

"I swear on my life and every life here. I'm going to come and take away the knife. I'm not going to touch you. I promise." The police officer takes the knife from my limp hand. Her shoulders drop. My entire body is shaking. It feels like I'm dying. "I don't care if this costs me my job but we're not bringing this kid back."

"I agree. Based on the knife trick, I vote for Juvie."

She points her finger at me. "You have two choices. You can behave and go to Juvenile Hall or misbehave and go home. Which is it?"

I crumple into Mrs. Ruby's outstretched arms. Her cries are barely audible. Her face looks stone-cold. "Alice you'll be back I promise. We won't stop fighting for you. Do you hear me? So be a good girl and do whatever she says. Promise me."

Tears flood my face. "Please don't let them send me back home."

"Alice your home is here and always will be."

"I can't breathe very good. A black hole is swallowing me up, suffocating me. I'm scared . . ."

The last thing I remember is a floating feeling, a stab in the arm, and eyelids heavier than lead.

A Missing Statute

A finger pokes my ribs. "Got any smokes?" My eyes jerk wide open. I am half-awake but confused. Where the heck am I? I sniff the air and smell concrete. Concrete! I bolt upright.

The clamor of voices blend with the clatter of footsteps. Nothing looks familiar, not even my clothes. I'm wearing what looks like a janitor's jumpsuit, lying on a striped mattress. There are two cots in this room and a strange girl is sitting on the edge of mine.

"You have the same uniform as me."

"Yep. We're Cinderella's gone bad. Got any smokes or not?" She twirls my hair with her finger, sniffs it twice and says, "Nope. Guess you don't smoke."

"Amy back off." A guard bangs on the iron rods, waves a baton at her and turns away. Amy walks to the railing and makes a rude gesture at the guard's back.

"I saw that!"

"I swear she's got eyes in the back of her freaking head," Amy grumbles.

Battered

"Where am I? Is this Juvenile Hall?" I ask.

"No. You're at the Ritz."

She bends over checking my socks and shoes. "The Juvie Ritz. You got no smokes, not even a butt!" she sounds utterly disgusted.

"I don't smoke."

"Neither do I," she says. "What are you in for?"

"I ran away two months ago and the police finally found me."

"Who ratted you out?"

"Ratted me out?"

"Yeah. Someone had to call the cops on you. How else would they find you? By the way. I'm Amy but you already figured that out unless your name is Amy too. That bell means it's chow time. Get your lazy butt up. Let's go."

"I'll pass. I'm not hungry. I'll stay here." Amy's right. But who called the police? The Rubys? If they didn't, who did?

"Like you get a choice! You best move your butt before you find a baton crammed up it."

We walk single file into a room with rows of steel tables and benches bolted to the ground. Amy tells me it's to hinder chair fights. "It's to protect the furniture because it's more expensive to replace the tables and chairs than it is to mend the broken bones."

I find out she's been here four years.

"Next year I get transferred to the woman's correctional facility downtown." Her voice has a bragging tone to it, as if it's some sort of accolade.

"Is that a good thing?" I ask.

"Not initially. I'll be a small fish in a big pond. I'm collecting smokes for then. To get 'em on your side, ya need to have a bribe."

We each are handed an identical tray of food.

"Thank you," I say.

Amy knees me and hisses, "Shut it! You grunt or nod when you take your tray. The nod means you like it."

"Thanks. I get it. I'm good at nodding."

Juanita Ray

She knees me again.

Most of the girls look tough and mean. I wonder if they looked like that when they first arrived here, or did mealtime make them that way? "When did they bolt everything down?"

"Two years ago."

"But all the trays are the same. What did they fight over?"

"Mostly turf. Follow me and keep your eyes on your tray."

"Ooohhhh, sweet catch."

I ignore the cat calls and count how many times the jelly jiggles. But I don't count the times I try to scoot my seat closer.

Amy growls. I can feel more than one set of eyes glued to me.

"This is the worse grub on the planet." She moves the mushy mashed potato around with her fork. "It looks like baby vomit."

I take small bites. It's not as bad as Amy thinks. My guess is she never was forced to eat real vomit. I squirt a line of ketchup down the center of the bologna, roll it into a cigar and eat it in three bites.

"You done?" Amy asks.

I nod.

"Thanks!" Amy takes my muffin without asking.

"What happened to don't say thank you?" I ask.

"Thanks, means it's mine now. Thank you means you're a suck." She smells the muffin before biting it, "What duty you on?"

"Duty?"

She lifts my sleeve and twists my paper bracelet.

"Suicidal, are we? Bet it's not dish detail," she grins. "Keep it covered," she looks around, "you'll be a target or end up in isolation. Trust me I know. Been there, done it."

A loud buzzer rings. Like cows on a farm, we're corralled back to our cells. A guard waits impatiently by the door. She puts the baton against the opening preventing me from entering. Instinctively I flinch. She points her baton down the hall to my right and taps the bars.

"Proceed to that gate."

Battered

At the gate, a frozen faced male guard has his feet spread eagle. He propels me into an office. The name plate, defaced by fresh graffiti is littered with deep indentations, swirls, that only steel wool could have made.

The name plate, Cecelia Downs -Warden, is hardly legible.

"Getting along with your cellmate?" Her smile is warm but her ice-cold calculating eyes measure my every move.

I nod.

She brushes something only she can see, off her desk. "Looks like you're here, until we hear from your parents."

"Pardon?"

The woman laughs loudly, "Are you for real? Did I hear you just say pardon? Now that's a first." She flips through a file and chuckles, "Pardon? Girl you won't last a lick with that attitude."

She reads for a while. Her chuckle turns solemn.

"I think we need to get you out of here," she mutters.

My heart drops somewhere past my ankles.

"But I-I-I don't want to leave. I like it here. Please. I can scrub floors. I'll do all the dishes, I'm not suicidal, I promise. I made a mistake. I was desperate."

"Now your sounding normal. That word, mistake, isn't a first."

"Please don't send me home."

"Relax. Out of here doesn't mean the institution, it means Ward B. At least until I figure out where to put you and while I'm working on that, I'll put you on—I can't put you on dish detail. They'd probably drown you, or worse. Tell you what, I'll take you up on that scrubbing offer." She presses an intercom and a guard appears. "Bring her to Jimmy and have him rig her up with a bucket and a mop."

She leans ahead, lifts up my sleeve, and taps her fingers on the yellow bracelet, "The only thing I want touching these wrists is rubber gloves. Make sure you wear them. You never know what you'll find on these floors."

To my right is a short hall. At the end of it I find a bathroom with several cubicles and an unmarked door, which leads back to the break room I just

275

cleaned. A disturbance is happening in the hall. Footsteps sound outside the door. It bursts open

"She's here," the guard announces, "scrubbing the toilet." He listens to some chatter and studies me with locked eyes. "Let's go."

The guard folds his arm and taps his fingers on his elbows, "You might have all day, but I don't. Let's go."

He leads me back to the warden's office, and pushes the door open with his baton.

The warden motions for me to sit. Her voice is curt. "I hear you cleaned the entire west wing—the break area. We have janitors here, and they won't take kindly to you trying to steal their jobs." A loud exhale escapes from between her lips. "So why have such a radical reaction to going home? I read the report twice and it appears the police brought you here as an interim solution. They need some time to investigate what's going on at your father's house."

I break out in a cold clammy sweat.

"Nothing's going on. I'm a rotten stupid kid who belongs here."

She sits back and studies my eyes. "Humor me with a little game I like to play. It's called role reversals. Let's pretend you are me and I am you. If I told you the housekeeper treated me badly and my father allowed that to continue, would you believe me?"

"No. I mean yes. Yes, I would, because nobody makes up stuff like that."

"I beg to differ. Any father would, at the very least, have fired her. No man puts a housekeeper above his children."

"How about a girlfriend."

"Now that could be a different story."

"She ran away from her husband to live with us."

"Maybe the husband was abusive. Maybe he deserved it."

"Well he wasn't because he got the two boys for being nicer and she lost them for being mean."

"Women who abandoned their children usually forfeit custody." She closes my file and pushes it away from her.

Battered

"She didn't abandon them. They moved in too. But she kept them locked in until they escaped back to their Dad."

The warden's phone beeps. She presses a perfectly shaped, shiny nail, on a matching red blinking button. "Ms. Lolita has arrived," says a nasally voice.

"Good. Send her in."

The door opens and a tall slim woman wearing a gray and black suit enters. Upon the warden's nod, she takes the seat beside me. Her perfume loiters between us.

"She doesn't belong here. God knows I've seen my share of every type of bad and this one doesn't fit the bill."

Ms. Lolita clears her throat and nods her head, "I tend to agree. Until court, I could place her temporarily with the Rubys."

"The court—How long before the hearing?"

"The parents get at least a ten-day notice, no more than twenty."

"She said she doesn't want to go back to live with the Rubys."

I interrupt the warden, "I didn't mean that home, I meant the other home. The one with Irma and my father."

"Why not?" Ms. Lolita is quick to fire the question at me.

"Because she hates me."

Ms. Lolita laughs. "I've heard that one a time or two before."

"Me too. And I can't keep track of how many times."

"It's not funny. What if you send me back and I—and I die. What happens then? She hated all of us. My sister said she's worse than the devil and my brother said she is the devil."

"The wicked stepmother story. You're not our first Cinderella."

The more they disbelieve me, the more deranged I get.

"I don't believe I introduced myself. I'm Ms. Lolita, a social worker for the government. My job is to keep families together—not destroy them. First things first. Tell me about your father."

"There's not much to tell," I mumble.

"According to the police report you made suicidal threats," Ms. Lolita opens the file, flips some pages and points to some typing.

The warden searches my eyes, "It says you said, 'shoot me' to the officer. Is that correct?"

"I don't remember saying that." I shrug twice.

The warden lifts her eyebrow. "Hmmm. How convenient. So let me see if I got this straight. Police officers witnessed you threaten suicide at the Ruby residence, but you can't go back to your proper home because you might die. Is that correct?"

Beads of sweat cover my face. I can't breathe. "Maybe I'm sick. Maybe you should lock me up in a mental hosp—" My voice breaks. She opens a drawer and shoves a box of tissues under my nose, spins her chair to face the water cooler behind her and spins back with a cup of water. She places it on the table and slides it toward me.

"You look like you could use some." She fills two more cups and slides one toward Ms. Lolita.

As I'm about to swallow I choke. Water spurts over her desk.

The paper cup topples. My eyes are jumping from their sockets. Ms. Lolita leaps from her chair. I instinctively protect my head. She pulls the file from under my face and holds it above the desk.

Drip. Splat. Dri-i—i-ppp. Splat.

"I'm sorry. I'm so sorry." I rip tissues from the box. The water devours them and continues to flow toward the warden's phone. The warden spins a full circle, snagging a roll of paper towels from the credenza behind her. She unrolls several, sops up the mess and slides the drenched towels into a trash bin.

She overlays a few on the desk, wipes it again, takes the file from Ms. Lolita and places it on her side of the desk. Ms. Lolita is still standing with her mouth hung open. "Did you see how fast she cowered?"

"As a matter of fact, I did. Lightning fast."

Ms. Lolita clears her throat, inspects her shirt and sits beside me. "If you had a say, what would you do about you?" she asks.

"Me?"

"Yes, where would you rather stay if you could choose anywhere in the world?"

Battered

"I would rather stay here."

"That isn't an option Ms. Lolita is asking if you'd rather stay with the Rubys or a temporarily placement elsewhere."

"I like it here." I lift my knee against my chest and twine my shoelace around my index finger.

"Please look at me—Why not the Rubys?" asks Ms. Lolita.

"They might come get me." I say and untwine the shoelace.

"Who might get you?" She nods at my knee. "One of the Rubys?"

"Yes. I mean no," I say, and drop my foot from the chair to the floor

For a split second I misunderstand the question. "I was talking about my father. Dad and Irma will try to get me back because I made Irma a promise and they want to make sure I keep it."

The warden and Ms. Lolita exchange concerned looks.

Ms. Lolita leans toward me. "What promise?"

Air catches in my throat. "I want to stay here because this place has guards and it's locked up." I glance at the guard by the door. "It's safer here."

The warden stands up and says, "Sweetheart the guards are to protect us and society, not you, or the inmates." She leans across her desk and asks, "One more time. What promise?"

"That I wouldn't tell anyone."

"We are not anyone. We decide your fate, so I strongly suggest you break your promise." She sits back down and sighs. "Do you know what we do for the children that keep secrets?"

I gulp. "What?"

"Nothing. If they tell us nothing, how can we do anything but send them back to their proper home?"

"Do you have to tell them who told you—if I tell you?"

Ms. Lolita pats my hand. "No because what Mrs. Downs said a few minutes ago, was the absolute truth. We are not just anyone. Our job is to listen to the truth, and I'd like to hear exactly that from you. This is your last chance . . . tell us everything you've kept a secret about your past."

279

Juanita Ray

This is your last chance. That's the last words my counselor said before Dad came in and took me. Is he here, spewing out a bunch of lies, like he did last time?

I look Ms. Lolita square in the eyes and ask, "Where do you want me to start?"

"How about we start with the day you ran away. No better still start with the day you made the promise."

"It was the day Irma got served papers about being an unfit mother. I had a scarf—"

Ms. Lolita says. "Stop. I thought your mother was deceased?"

"She is, but Irma had two boys she beat and locked up and I helped them escape and Mr. Hogan—"

"Ms. Lolita, would you agree it might be better if Juanita started with her first encounter with the housekeeper?" The warden flips through the file and adds, "Irma, correct?"

"I agree with Mrs. Downs. We would like you to start your story with the first day you saw Irma doing something wrong to you or anyone else. You can leave out all the nice stuff. We don't need to hear about that, just yet."

"There isn't any nice stuff to tell, and the first day something bad happened was nine years ago."

"And . . ." Ms. Lolita's voice trails off.

After one hour, Mrs. Downs pulls the box of tissues toward her and blows her nose then passes the box to our side of the table.

Ms. Lolita hands me a tissue and asks, "And at this point you're still living in Stephenville?"

"Yes."

"Juanita, I need to compartmentalize the incidents and by this I mean— you seem to be focused on the physical abuse but I can already identify occurrences of emotional abuse and neglect. So let's start with neglect first. Neglect means ignore things."

"Like when she ignored us knocking on the door when we were freezing outside in the blizzard, the day the school closed?"

Mrs. Downs murmurs, "No. That's child endangerment."

"Let's talk about breakfast. What did you usually eat?"

"Breakfast was always cereal. Soggy cereal."

"Lunch?"

"Runny blueberry sandwiches but on weekends cereal happened at eleven so it was considered lunch too."

"Dinner?"

"Not always."

"Did she ever humiliate you?"

"That was harder than being hungry and skipping meals."

"How did she humiliate you."

"She shaved parts of my head and . . ."

"What places did she hit you and did she ever hit you with anything other than her hand?"

By the time I finish with all of the objects she used to beat me, I am exhausted.

The warden raises her eyebrows, "Revoke parental rights?"

Ms. Lolita nods. "At the very least."

They make multiple phone calls to various places and discuss statutes and laws.

"Nothing? Nothing to cover a situation like this?"

After three minutes of silence, Mrs. Downs hangs up and says, "We have eighty-two Acts and not one covers this. What do you know about this new Human Rights Commission?"

"Well it was only formed this spring, and Gertrude Keough is the commissioner. Whatever code is in the statute was written by her late husband and Joey Smallwood, but I heard it didn't do anything much but address wage issues."

"Maybe I'll call her."

"I'm not sure it will do you any good because I read a piece in the Evening Telegram, where they interviewed her, and apparently she admitted to knowing next to nothing about the code—"

"Really?"

"—or human rights. I'm not certain she's the right one to call."

Mrs. Downs smiles and says, "What harm can it do? . . .Yes. I'd like to speak to Gertrude Keough . . ."

"We have a situation here and I thought you might be able to help." I bite my nails while she tells her about 'the problem'.

Two or more minutes of silence pass before she says, "Then they need to revise them. All I know is she's got to go somewhere and it isn't here and it isn't back to her father . . ."

"Not possible . . ."

"Well if you come up with anything call me back."

She dangles the phone, and studies my face. "How can a little girl like you cause such a big problem? Whatever am I going to do with you?"

"Can I live with my brother?"

"You said your brothers were missing," Ms. Lolita's snaps.

"You said to tell you the bad stuff. But I have two more. The oldest is Adam, and Ryan is the youngest, I think he joined the air force or army, I'm not—"

The warden taps her pen on a paper pad and says, "Okay now it's my turn to ask the questions. We're going to need a list of all siblings, missing or not. Let's start with this Adam. Where does he, live?"

I think for a second before answering, "He was living at home but he said he would only stay there until he knew I was safe."

"Does he know you're safe?"

I shrug.

"Who was born after Adam and where is he?"

"Bruce, but he was kicked out."

"Was Bruce a good boy?"

I shrug.

I know a few stories about Bruce. Some good . . . some bad. Bruce was seven, outside playing street hockey when the minister walked up to him and announced, your mom is dead. Bruce flipped out, beat him with the hockey stick, and called him a big fat liar. When he found out it was true, he went crazy, and Dad had to keep him away from the funeral.

Battered

The warden taps her pen harder. "Well?"

"Adam knows more about Bruce, because he's the oldest."

"You said the oldest was your sister?"

"Yes but Adam is the oldest one now. My sister disappeared."

"How do we get hold of this Adam?"

After I give her his college information, she asks, "Was he aware of the fact you were planning to run away? Did you tell him you were running away to the Rubys?"

"No. I didn't know the Rubys. I didn't have anywhere to go, I just ended up in the woods by their house."

Ms. Lolita turns her chair at an angle toward me, and states in a matter of fact voice. "It wasn't preplanned between you and the Matthew girls? You just appeared out of nowhere like the Rubys claim?"

I nod. "What will happen to me next?"

She glances at Mrs. Downs and says. "Some sort of court hearing—but after most court hearings the kids end up back here."

"That's okay with me."

"No, it isn't. Most cases we see are delinquents from poverty— and most people don't torture their children—they just can't afford them—like widows or unwed mothers, but you're fourteen and your father is well off . . ." She brushes imaginary crumbs off her skirt and shakes her head.

"Well my father was a widower, does that count?" I smell the ugly scent of fear in my nostrils. My voice cracks, "Can the judge make me go back because he can afford me?"

Ms. Lolita smile is a sad one. "I would be lying to you if I said no. The problem is, we all have a lot to figure out. And what you've told us, is the complete opposite of what was filed in the missing person report."

"Who filed a missing person report?"

"Your father did."

"They lied on the report. They always lie. They lied in Stephenville, they lied to my school and they even lied to my Grandma." Any tears I have been holding prisoner, break free and flee down my face.

I feel exhausted . . . defeated. "Then where do I belong?"

Ms. Lolita's voice comes back into focus, "Juanita, where can I find your brother? The oldest one? Preferably a location outside of the home?"

My fingers fumble to open my locket. Finally, it unsnaps and a scrap of paper falls onto my lap. Adam is my last piece of hope. I hand her the scrap of paper.

"This is his home number?"

"No. For Trades School." I knead my fists into my eyes.

"Juanita, put your hands down. And look at me."

The warden looks blurry. She tilts her head at Ms. Lolita and says, "They'll have his date of birth and with any luck a forwarding address or a job posting."

Ms. Lolita jots down the number and hands me back the scrap of paper. The warden reaches under her desk and hands me my bag of clothes, opens a door to a toilet room and says, "Change."

"Change for what?"

"A road trip. If you didn't have to go to court to get here, you don't have to go to court to get out. But let me check something first. My area of expertise is addressed in the 1968 Statutes, and she's outside of the realms of those, unless I slot her under 84-1, special cause for detention, but she's not a transient." She pulls a large document from her bookshelf, flips to the middle of it, tries another and says, "Nothing in the 1971 or 1970 statutes either." She pulls out a third book labeled 1969 Child Welfare Amendment Act. "Ms. Lolita, page 414 of the Act, Section 2-1 states, we have the right to apprehend a child without a warrant if we have reasonable grounds for believing that child is neglected. The problem is the police were investigating a missing person's or abduction report. However, Section 11-3 (a-i) gives us the right to take the child into custody and detain her in a receiving home or according to 11-3b or with the guardian or person whose care the child was found in at the time of apprehension. And because this has turned into a case of child neglect which falls under the Child Welfare Act, I would adhere to Section 11-3b and return her to the Rubys."

We walk to the car in silence and Ms. Lolita is quiet for the entire ride. She's lost in her own thoughts, and that's fine by me, because I'm talked out too. When we pull up to the farm, Mr. & Mrs. Ruby are standing on the porch smiling. After the initial excitement subsides, we sit in the living room with somber faces. It feels like a funeral—my funeral. Ms. Lolita is the first to break the silence. "It's going to be a tough one. He can afford the best attorney."

Mr. Ruby who is always the calm and quiet one says, "So can we, if we have to."

A cloud of dust floats into my room. Standing beside a maroon car, a skinny hippy, with long hair, is holding his nose. He's probably looking for work, and if Mr. Ruby hires him, he won't last a day. I flick an ant from my windowsill, close the latch, and flop face first on my bed.

Moments later, the floor boards outside my door creak. I lift my head waiting for a knock. The door knob rattles slightly followed by a clawing sound.

"Oh Juanita, oh Juanita, oh Juanita I call your name."

I whip the door wide open, "Adam! I can't believe it's really you." I fly into his arms. "Oh my god, I saw you get out of the car but I didn't recognize you. All week I've asked God to send you. All week I prayed you would find me before I had to go to court."

"Well God must have a telephone and he must have called the government, because they called me yesterday afternoon and gave me your phone number and address."

"Thank you God!" I shake my head in disbelief.

Adam chuckles. "Oh, you are most welcome."

"I just can't believe you're here. You grew your hair. And a mustache. And a goatee. You hardly look like you."

"Get dressed into something nice. I'm taking you for a surprise."

"What surprise?"

"Oh, you'll see," he grins, "wear something flattering," he winks and closes the door.

I scramble into some different clothes. I'm beaming from ear to ear when I enter the kitchen.

"Now that's more like our girl," Mrs. Ruby wipes her eyes on her apron. "Now you look more like our Alice." My smile widens.

"Did you even change? You look like you're wearing the same thing."

I grin at Adam, "Well I'm not. This top is a different color."

"Come Alice." She kisses my face and says, "Have fun."

Mr. Ruby shuts my door and taps the car hood. "Adam, bring her back to us safe and sound."

"You bet I will. That's my job!" Adam honks the horn, rolls up his window, and reverses out the driveway.

"I hope your shoes are clean," Adam grins.

I grin back, "Define clean. I live on a farm."

"Geez, Juanita, how the hell do you stand that smell of cow shit. That would drive me bloody nuts."

"You get used to it."

"No way. Not in a thousand lifetimes. Not ever," Adam waves his hand in front of his nose "They seem nice. They treat you good?"

"Really good. And they are nice. Really nice."

"My God Juanita I cannot believe you're in my car." He grins at me. "Do you have any idea how privileged you are? I don't let just anyone ride with me. You're only the second person I've had in that front seat. This is my pride and joy. Rebuilt her from the chassis up."

"Where are we going?"

Adam is humming a tune, his hand tapping to a silent song only he can hear. He smiles and says, "Shopping."

At the end of Ruby Line, he turns left.

My eyes widen, my heartbeat accelerates. "No! Please don't go that way."

"I have to. I'm bringing you to a mall. A very nice mall."

"What if they see us?" My voice sounds small—smaller than I like.

"Who?"

"Them." Fear floods my body. I press my hands against my belly. It feels like a bunch of twisted vines are growing inside of me.

"What's wrong with your stomach?" Adam asks.

"Nothing. I just feel nervous."

"Juanita, listen to me. Those son of a bitches won't hurt you again and I can't wait to see both of them locked away."

"What do you know about what's going on?"

"Apparently the Government set a hearing date."

The more I massage my stomach, the sharper the pain get.

"What's going to happen to me?"

"I don't know. There's no laws in place for something like this. They said it was an unusual case. It's pretty serious though. The law was made back in 1964, but even under that old law it looks like Irma isn't the only one to face charges. The old man's got a couple coming his way too, and then those pricks won't ever get their hands on you again. I can't count the nights, I'd sit on your bed and wonder if you were alright. I was worried out of my mind. They told them you ran away because you failed at school, but I knew different." He swerves to the right and pulls into the parking lot of a large plaza. The parking lot is near empty but Adam parks at an angle across two spaces at the far end.

"What are we shopping for?"

"For clothes for you." Adam grins and flings his door open.

"For court clothes?"

"Stop thinking about court. You're here because no sister of mine is going around looking like an old maid. Especially when I have some special friends, I plan to introduce you to. I want you to look great. Let's find you something more trendy, other girls your age wear."

His laugh, sounds devious, a sure sign Adam is up to no good. I never thought I'd miss Adam's practical jokes as much as I did and at this point, I don't care if the joke is on me.

"Honestly Adam, what are we doing here?"

"Remaking you into the kind of girl any guy would die to date. I am here to dress you in the kind of style that makes other girls jealous. I am here for your beck and call—at your service Madam."

He's wearing a white windbreaker from a decade ago and the same pants he had on before I left. I doubt he knows squat about style but this is my first real shopping trip and I'm thrilled to be able to pick out something new. But a dreadful preoccupation of court smothers any anticipation that seeps through the cracks. I catch myself constantly looking over my shoulder. Part of me is expecting Dad to appear and whisk me away, while the other part wonders why Adam is doing this. He's up to something awful.

"Did you have to park so far away?"

Adam twists his mouth into a weird grimace. His left knee cap flops erratically with each step. He lisps, "Yeth. And I can move my car across the road if it takes longer than I think to cheer you up." He continues to distort his facial features and writhe his body down the parking lot, toward the entrance. Tears run down my face.

I'm not sure if the attention we're getting is from my loud laughter or his outrageous behavior but the looks on some of their faces makes me laugh harder.

"Adam you need to stop. People are gawking at you."

"And that's exactly why I can't stop." His voice sounds warbled. "But, if I stop, they're sure to think I'm making fun of the handicapped."

"You really do look handicapped. Practice much?"

Adam laughs back, "Whenever I can," and limps inside.

He flails down aisle after aisle, pulling clothing from racks. It reminds me of the old days when he did the weekly laundry and for the briefest second, I miss those days.

He insists I try on everything he picks out but nothing is good enough. It's not like him to be so picky. I try on a dozen more outfits before we find an ensemble that makes his eyes light up. The stranger in the mirror widens her smile, as she models her clothes. I don't recognize her. Her eyes are sparkling and she looks like a normal teenager. The kind a boy might want to ask to a movie.

"I don't look like me."

Battered

"Yes, you do. That's the real Juanita. The one you've been hiding for eight years. God, I wish Marie could see you now. You're the spit out of her mouth. Did you enjoy yourself? Have fun?"

"Yes, I did. Thank you for all of this. One day I'll pay you back."

"One day you most certainly will and sooner than you think." He rolls his eyes in circles, then up toward the back of his head, limps to the car and tosses the bags in the back seat.

Most of the ride home is quiet. He glances over and winks at me. The kind of wink that says, 'wait and see what I've got in store for you.'

But nothing weird happens. He's got nothing up his sleeve but his arm. When we get back, it's dusk. Our goodbye is awkward for both of us. We never hugged much and I have had to hide my feelings for years. Or maybe they got smothered by my fear. I want to tell him how much I love him but the words are caught inside of me, so instead I tell him how much I love my clothes.

Inside I race straight to my room and try on my burgundy ribbed top and hip-hugger jeans. I turn around and face the same girl I saw a few hours earlier and for two hours I stare back in the mirror and try to get to know her.

Reunited

Mr. Ruby taps on my window twice before I wake up, tumble outside and race to catch up. He's already at the barn.

"Alice. Did we ever tell you how different the world was when you were gone? How much we missed you?"

"No but you showed me when I got back. I saw it in your eyes." I scoot my stool beside the cow.

He smiles. "It's great to have you back but we've noticed you've withdrawn deep inside since you got home. When you first came your eyes look like they do now. Scared but determined. Your smile melted our hearts but what really made us fall in love with you was how you appreciated the nothing things, how hard you worked, not because of the work, we loved how hard you tried to give us what you could. How you expected nothing in return. And that's what makes Stella worried about you. She wants you to have everything. Be a real part of our family. She wants to protect you, and so do I, because we love you, like a daughter."

"I'm sorry," I say. "I-I-I . . ."

Battered

"It's okay Alice. It takes time to open up a closed heart and we're willing to take all the time you need." He dangles a bucket in front of me. "Alice, I don't know if there's any milk left in that udder but if there is you should make sure it lands in here."

I stare at the white puddle on the ground. I gasp, let go of the cow and move away from the milk stool. I trail behind him to the house and try hard not to obsess about the court hearing but it's impossible.

While Mrs. Ruby fills the table with food platters, I run to the bathroom and barf. My appetite is non-existent. The more I move the food around on my plate the more the past haunts me. I hardly eat a bite but Mrs. Ruby saves my breakfast in the oven. She does this for three days straight. I sit and stew until it drives me crazy. The only thing that helps me past it is scrubbing anything dirty.

"Alice, you been cleaning the same section of the floor for an hour not that you should be scrubbing it at all," Mrs. Ruby shakes her head and motions for me to get off my knees.

I pick up the bucket and feel around for the dirty cloth before I toss the water down the toilet. Two years ago, when I cleaned the basement bathroom, I accidentally dumped the cloth with the water and flooded the downstairs. That was the only time I understood exactly why I got a beating. I still hear her voice keeping rhythm to the belt lashes, "Never-slash-flush-slash-cloths-slash-down-slash-the-damn-slash-toilet-slash-you-stupid-slash-ugly-slash-idiot." Since then, I always check more than twice, to make sure there are no rags in the water.

Today as I dump the bucket of dark water down the toilet, I get that flashback. It's not the only flashback that's haunted me lately. Going to court has conjured up a bunch of old best-forgotten memories, that I wish I could flush down the toilet. Over the past few weeks I've relived so many parts of my past, it feels like I time travelled backwards. I want those memories to stop but they won't because I'm so afraid Dad and Irma will trick the judge.

Mrs. Ruby's shadow falls across the sink. I dry my hands, try to smile at her from the mirror, but instead a huge sigh escapes.

291

"Alice, you look so troubled. Tell me, what's on your mind?"

"Am I easy to forget?"

"No far from it. Even Ms. Lolita said you were the only girl she ever brought home after work."

"She didn't ever bring me home with her."

"She meant figuratively, that she couldn't get you off her mind. She also said you have a tendency to think you have to work to earn your keep, even at Juvenile Hall. I don't know how to fix that unless I ground you from chores, and I would but I don't want to ever ground you from anything or make you feel punished. Anyway, the government just sent us a letter and payment for your foster care. Even though that's not why we have you here, it's a good reason for you to stop working so hard and start having some fun."

"But they didn't pay you since June, when they didn't know I was here and you fed me and—"

"Alice you're missing the point. We enjoy having you here. We should pay you for the joy you bring us—but they did give us a clothing allowance for you. Here," she hands me an envelope.

I hand it back.

"Alice, I thought you and Adam could go shopping. You must need new school clothes. It's almost September."

I stare at her in disbelief. If I had a videotape of Adam shopping, she wouldn't let him within a mile of the house. "How about you keep it and we go shopping together another time?"

"Alice I'm too old for shopping, especially for a teenager. Beside have you forgotten Adam will be here, soon? You need to get ready it's almost eleven. Off you go. Scoot."

At eleven o'clock, Adam's maroon Chevy pulls up into the driveway. I dash toward the car and hop in.

"Hot! Damn! You look like a million bucks!"

One look at Adam's face tells me he's up to something evil. When his eyes sparkle this much and he chuckles for no reason, he's planning a trick. He tries to wipe the devilish grin from his face, several times, but he can't.

Battered

Even if someone chopped off his head, his body would still give him away. He can't keep still. He's lurching and rocking in his seat. It's as though he can't get to wherever we're going, fast enough. I expect him to eject through the windshield any moment. He is so emerged in his secret plans, he hardly says anything to me, and that's not like Adam. He chuckles to himself for five more minutes.

"Care to share the joke?"

"Oh, I'll be sharing it fully, shortly," he laughs hysterically.

"Where are we going? Adam, hello, anybody home?" I'm a little nervous. I suspect this joke might be at my expense.

"Never mind, you'll see where soon enough," he slaps his leg and howls aloud. He presses his lips together. "Juanita how was your week?" He tries to wipe the smirk off his face but fails miserably. I can tell he isn't the least bit interested in my answer. He's preoccupied with something or someone else.

"Oh, not bad, I just killed two neighboring drug dealers and stole their dog."

He stops laughing and pulls in front of a hydrant. In front of it is a bus stop. The day I missed the bus, the wheel chair, me wanting to jump in front of a car, it all flashes in my mind. It's then I realize things have changed. I don't want to kill myself anymore and I'm thankful I didn't because I want to live.

"Juanita, it's time to get serious. We're almost there."

"Where?"

Adams face is solemn. "When we get there, I want you to sit in the car and wait for me okay. No matter what I say, don't disagree with me. Just play along. If you don't know the right answer just smile and say nothing."

"Is this about Marie? Am I going to see her?"

"No." Adam's tone is matter of fact and his eyes are somber. He drives at a snail's pace, past the bus stop and pulls off the road. "Stay here, and no matter what happens, smile and agree with what I say."

He dashes to the house, doesn't bother to knock, flings open a screen door and struts in. Five minutes later, I'm still waiting, and sweating like a

293

pig. I open the car door, keep it ajar with my foot and lean my head against the backrest. Between the dark leather seats and my knit top, it feels like a sauna. My face is flushed from the heat.

When Adam finally reappears. He's grins excitedly. His dark eyes have a mischievous gleam. I know that look. He is absolutely up to zero good. He leans against my door, extends his hand, yanks me out of the car, wraps his arms around me, and whispers in my ear, "You are a knockout. They are going to love you!"

"Who?"

"My new family, the Greens, I board here. This is where I live now."

"Why are we whispering?"

"Because we're under scrutiny," he whispers back.

We pass a white picket fence and walk through a white iron gate. Along the stone path, gnomes with flowers growing from their heads, smile at us. The one and one-half story, is mauve with white trim. The lawn is immaculately edged. It looks like Adam's handiwork. There's an open porthole type window near the loft area. A set of female fingers tap impatiently on the ledge. I cup my hand over my eyebrows, to shade out the sun. A blonde head with sharp features, glares down at me. Her eyes are stone-cold.

"Are you sure this is okay?" I ask.

Adam hugs me, "Don't be foolish, of course it's okay. You're invited to stay for dinner."

"Well I guess it's safe to say the invitation didn't come from the blonde."

Adam eyes gleam. "Where is she. Is she looking?"

"Up there. The one shooting death rays from her eyes."

He smirks at me. "Do you have any idea of how much I missed you?" He hugs me close and kisses my cheek.

I wrap my arms around him. "I missed you too. Thanks for finding me."

"Now, don't look up. Just look at me. Is she looking at us right now?" Adam asks. "Whisper the answer in my ear."

"Probably," I say. "I don't know. You won't let me look."

Battered

"Give your big brother one more giant hug and a kiss." Without hesitation, he lurches his lips toward me and gives me a quick peck on the cheek. He whispers in my ear, "Is Angela still looking?"

I look up to see the blinds swinging violently. "Not anymore."

"Are her blinds open or closed?" he asks.

"Both. They're clanging back and forth, banging against each other."

"Good, very good! That's just great! Don't look up anymore, this is just perfect," Adam gloats.

"What's perfect?"

"Having you here!"

And for a minute he looks halfway genuine.

Adam wraps his arm around my waist and propels me to the front door. As we approach, the door swings ajar. A short, plump, sweet looking woman brushes her gray hair from her damp forehead and wipes her hand in her apron. As I attempt to shake her hand, she pulls me toward her. I find my face smothered in her chest. I'm about to collapse from suffocation when she releases her deadlock hold on me. Her smile reminds me of sunshine.

"Juanita, this is Mrs. Green," Adam smiles.

"My, my, you are absolutely gorgeous. My, oh, my, just in time for dinner, don't be shy, come in and have a seat," Mrs. Green steps aside and yells at the staircase, "Angela come down to eat."

A white crocheted cloth, embroidered with yellow daisies and green leaves, covers a square table. Steam rises from the largest bowl of beef stew I have ever seen. Green peas and bright orange carrots float in dark brown gravy. A plate of butter-glazed buns hovers in front of my nose. Adam sniffs the bread and passes the plate to my right. He chuckles and says, "Have one, my little sweetheart," and gives me another peck on the check. He brushes my cheek and comments on how much he loves me the way I am, but he'd like to see me gain some weight.

I'm full before the bowl is half finished. I stop eating, tell Mrs. Green, it's delicious, and push my bowl away. She smiles and adds another scoop to it and says, "Don't be shy. Eat up."

I loosen my belt and unbuckle my top jean button trying to make room for more. Somehow, I manage to eat most of it.

Throughout the meal, the girl from the window, gives me ice-cold looks. There is no Mr. Green at the table. He's sleeping in the living room recliner. His snores plug the large gaps, between the terse words, Angela flings at Adam.

Close up, she looks not much older than me, and doesn't have a shy bone in her body. She asks me several questions, ranging from farm life, to the school I attended. She cocks her head sideways, "So . . . where exactly did you meet Adam?"

"Oh, I can answer that," Adam hurriedly butts in, "I didn't meet her anywhere. I drove out to the farm and picked her up." He smirks as he compliments Mrs. Green on being a great cook.

Highly agitated, Angela tosses a dirty look at Adam, "What I meant to ask was how you two first met?"

"I can answer that too," his smirk gets bigger until it breaks into uncontrollable laughter. I feel like a small fish that's about to be swallowed by a shark.

Angela's jaw is tight, "I am asking her. She can talk for herself can't she?"

"Actually, no she can't because she does not remember how I met her and I do," Adam raises his eyebrows up and down.

Angela folds her arms against her chest, "Go ahead. I'm listening. This should be good. Was she drunk?"

"No. That's not a very nice comment to make about my baby sister. You see, I met her when she was one week old. That's when Mom brought her home from the hospital!" Adam ducks the bread roll aimed for his head. His shoulders are shaking, despite his fake serious look.

Angela twists her napkin into a ball puppet, proceeds to wring its neck and throws another bun at Adam.

"You're an idiot."

Adam's eyes glitter like diamonds. "Thank you. I wanted another bun. How did you know I was just about to ask you to pass me it?" He dips it in his gravy and proceeds to eat more stew. His grinding jaws fail to hide his smirk.

Angela's scowl transforms into a relieved smile. "She's your baby sister?" Her ice-cold attitude melts into a puddle of mush, "So you're Juanita! I never would have thought it! I have heard so much about you! Come here. Let me give you a big hug!"

She tosses Adam a smug glance, "Now it's my turn buddy boy. Juanita, come up to my room. We have so-o-o-o-o much to talk about."

"Oh no Angela, she can't you see. I have to get Juanita back to Mrs. Ruby by three o'clock." He points at the wall clock, "It's half past two and it's a half hour drive."

"Adam, don't you, 'oh no Angela' me! Nice, try buddy." She nods at me and adds, "she's not going anywhere yet."

"No, no Angela, she has to get back on time or Mrs. Ruby will be worried to death." Adam grins nervously. "You see; I can't risk her being late, she has strict rules to follow until the trial."

Angela folds her arms tighter. "No Adam, I don't see."

Adam smiles, "Well Mrs. Green, we have to leave now. Thank you for the meal. Leave the dishes for me and I'll do them after I get home. I should be back in an hour." He gives Mrs. Green a loud kiss on the check and walks toward Angela. She circles, keeps her back to him, as he tries to face her.

"You can play hard to get all you want, but it won't get you anywhere," he laughs. "We'll talk when I get back."

Mrs. Green says, "It was lovely to finally meet you Juanita. Adam you bring her back anytime."

"Yes. Don't be a stranger," Angela's voice is right behind us. "If Adam doesn't bring you back soon enough, I'll have Mom drive me to come get you myself."

Adam glances over his shoulder and smirks, "She has restrictions. I'm the only one permitted to pick her up."

Angela mimics back, "I know until the trial. You know, Adam Rose, there'll come a day after the trial, and I guarantee you, that day will come sooner than you think. A day of reckoning."

Adam rolls down the car window and blows her a kiss.

"Thanks a bunch," I say to Adam, "I'm surprised she didn't stab me with her fork."

Tears fall down Adam's cheeks. "I know," he laughs, "Juanita that was perfect. Too perfect."

"What was perfect?" I ask.

"She believed you were my girlfriend."

"Well I'm glad one of us finds it funny."

For half an hour Adam can't wipe the smug look off his face. Occasionally he bursts into laughter, slaps his knee, and gleefully talks to himself. "Same time, next week. Okay?"

"That depends. Are you bringing me back to Mrs. Greens, or will I be a pawn in a different game?"

"Oh it does depend," he grins impishly, "on if I get back and find my bags packed."

Mr. Ruby is on the porch, pacing. He taps on the window and Mrs. Ruby pokes her head out the door. "Adam would you like to join us for tea?" she asks.

"No thank you. I have an urgent matter to attend to at home. Maybe next Thursday after the trial," he says.

The moment he leaves, fear returns. I watch the tail lights until they disappear. Adam is the only person I truly trust. Dad is the person I mistrust the most and the trial is my biggest fear. My stomach churns. Thursday? I don't want Thursday to come. I stifle an insatiable desire to run away. I know better than to try running away from the government especially while this is going on. I have a ton of questions and nobody to ask. The main one is what happens after Thursday? Where will home be? This would never have happened if I kept my mouth shut and lied to Samantha. Maybe her sister called the police. Who knows? All I know is I don't trust fate, any more than I trust Dad, and I don't feel safe.

I run for the bathroom and hover over the toilet. I throw up everything I ate, and just when I think I'm done, dry heaves keep me on my knees for another five minutes.

Both Mr. and Mrs. Ruby are waiting outside the bathroom door. "How do you feel?"

"Like I busted a bunch of blood vessels in my head."

"Oh Alice, whatever are we going to do with you?" She ushers me into the living room. Mrs. Ruby clears her throat, but it's Mr. Ruby who speaks first. I half-listen. All I can think about is the trial. I can picture Irma at the stand denying everything and my spineless father agreeing with her. I knead my bloated stomach. Waves of nausea slap against my throat. I run to the bathroom and upchuck the last remnants of stew.

After five minutes of dry heaves, I head back to the living room.

"Are you okay?"

Do I look okay? "Yes. I'm okay. Just not okay with Thursday."

"Alice everything will be alright. I hate seeing you fret like this. We love you so much. And we can't wait to change your name," Mrs. Ruby smiles gently.

Did she say change my name? Change my name to what? Back to Juanita?

Their eyes are glowing. "We've fallen in love with you Alice. We want to adopt you. We want you to be our daughter. Alice Ruby."

The Crown vs. Rose

The majority of the next few days are spent in the bathroom flushing meals down the toilet. I wipe my face and return to the living room. It's Wednesday and Ms. Lolita is here prepping me about tomorrow's trial. My stomach rolls like a twig on the ocean. She opens a folder and preps me on the types of questions I will be asked, but before she's finished, I zone out. My mind is swirling too fast and my stomach is rolling with nausea.

When I return from my third vomiting spree, Ms. Lolita is talking to Mrs. Ruby, in a hushed voice. "Section 41-3 stipulates the offense must be within the past six months and it appears the defense is focusing on that time limitation. It may be a tougher battle than we anticipated." She sees me and raises her tone and talks about the weather. She hardly utters five words and I'm back doing a fourth face plant in the toilet.

Mrs. Ruby sits on the tub and says, "Ms. Lolita has left but she wants you to see a doctor, the same one that took care of you in Juvenile Hall. He's agreed to see you without an appointment."

"What happens if I'm too sick for court?"

Battered

"If the doctor says you're too sick, then you're too sick."

Mrs. Ruby hands me my coat. Her face seems to have new wrinkles and I know I'm the one responsible for aging her. But she seems to age more after we arrive at the clinic. The stuffy office smells like Henry did. Rows of metal chairs are, a foot apart. And half of them are covered by small children with snotty noses.

Mrs. Ruby browses through the Farmers' Almanac for twenty minutes. My name is called two minutes after she picks up a gardening magazine.

The nurse hands me a jar and instructs me how to pee in it. Then I wait, and wait, and wait . . .

After he comes in the room, he asks how long I've been sick. Because I don't know, what would be the best answer, to get me out of going to court, I tell him the truth. He seems concerned that I only weigh ninety-eight pounds but I know I assure him I was much thinner four months ago. I use one hand to keep my paper gown together while he helps me get on the gurney.

The cold gurney gives me goose bumps. The thin paper rips as I slide my butt further down toward the end. He guides my feet in steel stirrups. I feel like a sacrificial lamb at the slaughter. The doctor presses hard on my stomach while he shoves his gloved hand between my legs deep inside me. I expect him to reach my tonsils any minute.

"Relax."

My fists clench into tighter balls.

After ten minutes of pure humiliation and personal trespass, he quietly says, "Get dressed. Your foster parents are waiting for you."

The door closes. Weird lubricant oozes from me. I see no tissues or paper towels. I remove my gown and use it as a wipe. I don't know what the point is, of what just happened, but I do know I feel violated and totally insulted. The hall has three doors and none of them have an exit sign.

A nurse gives me a sucker and leads me in the opposite direction, to the waiting room.

I hand the sucker to the nearest kid and instantly regret it when they fight over it. The mother throws it in the trash bin. Mrs. Ruby is profusely thanking the doctor, shaking his hand and smiling from ear to ear. I glare at the sucker in the trash bin, maybe I should retrieve it and shove it up her nose. Mrs. Ruby blows into one end of a tissue and dabs her eyes with the other end. She clutches a piece of paper in her other hand, presses her lips against it and holds it to her chest.

She smiles, "Alice you are sick. We need to fill a prescription."

Elated she hugs me twice.

"That doctor was rude to me. I don't like what he did."

"Let's talk about it outside. In the car."

I purse my lips together. Why tell her anything? What's it going to change? Halfway home, my tongue comes out of hiding.

"Do you know he put his entire arm up my privates?"

Mrs. Ruby pulls the car to the side of the road, jumps out and slides into the back seat. She folds her arms around me.

"I am so sorry Alice. I wasn't thinking about the exam. I was only worried about the results. I'm not the one who ordered the tests. It was Ms. Lolita, not me. We have no control over these things, the government owns you, and we have to do what they tell us. Until your court hearing our hands are tied, but God pleasing, if all goes well, once we adopt you, it will be our say . . ." her voice trails off and she blows her nose into the crumpled tissue.

"What do you mean by if all goes well?"

"Alice they've never had a case like this one before so there's no telling how it could go. All we can do is pray and wait."

She doesn't say another word until we reach the house. "Alice you have to trust us. We can't help you if you don't trust us. If you'd just tell us what's troubling you, we would fight day and night to fix it."

How can I tell her I don't want to be a problem or cause them anymore problems? Why should they work hard for me when my own father wouldn't? How do I make all of this go away?

Mr. Ruby comes from the pantry with my knapsack. It's full of apples. When I ask how he knows, he winks.

Battered

He tells me one of his favorite moments is watching me scour the grass looking for bad apples to steal, and his second favorite moment is watching me scrub them clean.

"I don't spray them with insecticide. There's no need to scrub them."

"But I saw you out there with the hose hooked up to the green container of bug spray."

"That bug spray is long gone. I use it as a handle. Keep meaning to pick one up but keep forgetting. We're still learning about each other, aren't we? We have plenty to learn about you and you have much to learn about us. Years ago, I learned the best way to find something out is by asking. If you could get comfortable with asking questions, and trust that our answers will never hurt you . . . you would see there's nothing to fear—nothing you can't ask. Alice the truth is, you'll never find a safer place on earth than here, at home with us."

Asking questions is something I never got to practice with Irma or Dad. It wasn't tolerated. Any questions I asked, were answered by a guess from me or in a pray to God and most of my questions never got asked. They remained questions. If I was in a dilemma, there wasn't anybody to ask for advice. Adam was already worried sick about me, so I couldn't burden him anymore than I had. I tried to figure out what God would want me to do. And it's hard to change old habits and learn new rules when the old ones are still embedded deep in my brain. I've been trained to be a loner, not a team player. It's hard to be something you're not.

"It's hard for me, because . . ." The right words are impossible to say. They dance in my head but my tongue won't co-operate. I swallow hard and ask for permission to visit the horses.

On the long walk to the hidden fence, I think about his words. and forget to sing my song. But when I reach the fence I see the horses are waiting for me, eager for apples. The stallion hangs his head over the fence to greet me. His eyes look like a human is hiding inside of him. Like he's sifting through my soul. I wonder if he can sense my pain. I whisper, "Can you take me with you?" He nods and makes a throaty snort as though he is saying yes.

Juanita Ray

In that moment, the urge for freedom overwhelms me. I want to ride one of the horses so bad and I want to ride to nowhere. I want to go with them, be part of the herd. I don't want to be owned by the government, and I don't want to be Alice Ruby either, because the Rubys are too good for me. They don't deserve my problems. Eventually I'll do nothing but disappoint them, just like I disappointed everyone else in my life. I think about how much I wanted a family, different parents, and now that I get a chance for that I'm too useless to embrace it. Maybe Irma was right all along. Maybe I am simply worthless.

The stallion trots backwards, expecting some pieces of apples to be pitched his way.

All that separates me from the herd is a tattered old fence with three rotted planks and about twenty feet of grass. They don't seem curious about me. They accept me as part of the scenery. They trust me. Why can't I trust the Rubys like that? Maybe they never had a human mistreat them. Maybe that's why they're so good at trusting. If reincarnation is a real thing, I want to come back as a wild horse. Maybe then I could learn to trust too.

Dusk follows me home. The house is lit up and I know the Rubys are waiting to have that talk with me. But tomorrow is Thursday and I don't want to talk to anyone. I climb in my bedroom window, put my shoes under my chair, take my medication, and wear my clothes to bed.

I wake up to a beautiful morning, the kind that makes you want to stay outside for the entire day. It's not until I hop out of bed, I realize what this dreadful day is. I shut my window and crawl back to bed.

Tap. Tap-tap.

"Stella is having a real rough morning. Her nerves are getting the best of her. Do you think you can help me make her smile?"

"How?"

"By showing up at the table."

Mrs. Ruby looks terrible and Mr. Ruby doesn't look much better. His jokes are thin and forced. Mrs. Ruby makes a weak attempt to smile at each bad joke he makes.

"How big is this farm?"

Battered

Mrs. Ruby glances at Mr. Ruby. "Over 400 acres. Why?"

"How did the police find me here?"

"Alice, we called the government about you."

My fork clatters on to my plate.

"This is the only way we could legally adopt you and it's illegal for us to keep you without authorization. We'd lose you. It's more complicated than you know."

Her answer is confusing. Why would she risk sending me away? Why couldn't things stay the way they were?

Her eyes have dark circles and her nose looks swollen and sore. It's like I aged them. For a few minutes, the solution to this mess seems to be to run away from it all. If I was gone, they would be much better off. Adopting me won't make anything better. It won't change my past or who I am. I'm too broken to love.

"Alice how are you feeling about today?" Mr. Ruby smiles and adds, "be honest."

"I would rather go lick the barn clean, than have to face Dad and Irma."

Mrs. Ruby's smile stretches across her entire face.

"Ha! Good girl. You did it Alice. See that smile?"

Her smile fades. "Alice don't forget to take your medicine. Today of all days, we don't want you getting sick. Not today."

The ride there takes forever. The medicine helps control the nausea but it doesn't stop the fear, and at this very moment fear is wreaking havoc through every fiber of my being. It stalks my every move, and as we climb the steps to the Justice Department, my feet are heavier than blocks of lead. My shallow breathing turns into a full-on panic attack. My heart crunches into a tight ball. The closer we get to the door, the louder, and faster it beats.

I've counted many things in the past, footsteps, creaking boards, belt slashes but never my heartbeat. It's deafening. The door opens. My heart beat sounds like a war drum, racing so fast, I can't keep up with the counting pace.

305

Ms. Lolita pauses, takes me to one side, and says, "The judge will want to talk to you. Probably in private. I know it's painful for you to talk about your past but I need you to be brave. You'll be under oath. It's imperative you tell the judge the truth about everything. He wants to hear it from your lips not ours. A lot is at stake here. Your life—your future, and the repercussions could affect others—" her eyes flash toward the Rubys "—be brave."

"What will happen?"

"Anything could happen."

"Will they go to jail?"

"Probably not."

"I mean if he's charged."

"The Director of Child Welfare has applied to the judge for a declaration of neglect. This hearing is for that application. If all goes well the judge will make an order. Typically to bring you into a receiving home, a place where they examine you physically or mentally, but neither will apply to you."

"Mentally?"

"They didn't envision your entire situation when they wrote the Act. A large portion of Section 10, was written for delinquents and mentally defective children. The rest was written for children without parents or parents that abandoned them, or parents who were too poor or sick to care for them. However, there is one small sub-section, just two lines long, where the interpretation of a neglected child, is applicable to you. It addresses unlawful assault, cruelty and neglect. And although you have no bruises, you did have five sibling witnesses. But technically, you are considered a runaway."

I glance around for the Rubys. They are sitting on a bench, having a deep discussion with a man.

"What will happen to me if we win."

"If he declares you neglected, or declares offenses have been made against you, he can return you to your parents, return you to the Rubys, or make you a temporary or permanent ward of the court. But all three scenarios, would fall under the supervision of the Director."

Battered

"Don't they get punished?"

"According to Section 34 if found guilty."

"What kind of punishment?"

"The maximum fine is two hundred dollars."

"What if they include the rest of the family?"

"They won't. But if they did, the fine would stay the same."

"What about prison?"

"If they don't pay the fine, or can't afford to pay it, the maximum sentence is two months."

———————

This place resembles a giant church. A man in a large robe walks in, and everybody stands. This must be what judgment day feels like.

Mrs. Ruby's damp hair clings to her forehead. Sweat beads drip down Mr. Ruby's face. The floor swirls, and goes in and out of focus. I pray for it to swallow me up.

———————

Two full days pass before I can get out of bed. I am overwhelmed, drained and confused. I pull the sheets over my head and sulk. I continue to wallow in self-pity for another hour before I pull the sheet away and notice my knapsack hanging on the hook. The horses! I haven't given a single thought to feeding the horses. I can tell by the gospel music playing down the hall, that it must be Sunday. But where did Saturday and Friday go? Getting dressed, I find it hard to keep my balance. I feel ashamed and lazy. I tell myself, go do something useful. I get the scrub bucket and start filling it up. I figure if I'm on my knees scrubbing, and pass out, I won't have far to fall. Mrs. Ruby appears out of nowhere.

"Not today Alice, just rest and try to relax."

I hear tires crunch to a stop. I drop the bucket in the tub. Shivers creep down my spine. Mrs. Ruby sucks in a quick sharp breath and whispers, "It's okay Alice. It's over. There's nothing to fear." She disappears as quickly as she came.

"Alice you have a visitor," her voice calls from the porch. "A nice visitor."

Adam is standing there, and I'm so happy to see him, I leave without saying goodbye to anyone.

"Bet you're happy that the court case is finished."

"I'm relived more than happy. How about you?"

"I'm pissed. I can't believe the old man got off so easy. They should have thrown his sorry ass in jail. At least they took away all of his parental rights. And as for Irma, that pisses me off even more. They should have locked, that thing away, and thrown away the key."

"So, at this very moment, am I an orphan or what?"

"No Juanita. You have a parent. A very special parent. The crown owns you now, your highness. Speaking of special, I'm taking you to someone very special."

"Who is it this time? Wait! Is it Marie!"

"I tried. But it's like talking to a brick wall. I don't get it. Maybe she needs some more time. I just need to work on her."

"She doesn't want to see me?"

By the time we reach the main road, Adam has repeated the same answer, in three different ways, but my brain is still waiting to hear a different answer.

"What's wrong with the Rubys? They're a perfect family. People would give their eye teeth to have them for parents. How you stumbled into the arms of one of the most predominate families in the Goulds—or half of Newfoundland—is beyond me."

"They already have daughters. They don't need another one, especially like me."

"What do you mean like me? What's that supposed to mean?"

"I've only known them four months and look at the trouble I've caused so far? I want to live somewhere where people don't try to love me, but I don't want to live with anyone mean who hates me. Just with someone who doesn't care."

"Then Marie would be perfect for you."

"Then why doesn't she see that?"

"Because all she sees is the past. She has issues with it, and she can't ignore all of them if reminders of the past are sitting right in front of her face. Have you ever heard the expression opening up a whole can of worms?"

"Yes I have."

"Then look at it this way. There's a big can, inside of Marie, and the past is the worms."

"Just say it like it is. She doesn't want to see me. Period."

I lean back against the car seat and close my eyes. A road bump, jolts me and my purse falls to the floor. I reach to get it, and gag. Something is choking me. My locket is caught on my belt. The chain snaps. The locket pops open. Staring at me from a tiny picture, is Marie and Mom, and the locket they're in is about to get broken apart. It's caught on the belt buckle, Adam bought me. I untangle the chain, slip the locket from the buckle and sit back up.

"She's scared stiff of any relationships. She won't even get married. She was engaged to a guy for six years and flaked."

"Then why can't we live together like a real family. I'm older now. I could do chores. Earn my keep."

Adam blinks. His nostrils flare open. His chest caves in as air fills it. "Juanita, we're not back in the dark ages. Finding a home has nothing to do with being a slave or earning your keep. No matter how hard you worked, Marie wouldn't change her mind because she's not ready, and the truth is, she'll never be ready."

"Ready for what? It's not like I want to marry her."

"Marie's compartmentalized her life —"

"There's that word again. What's that mean?"

"If you let me finish, I'll tell you."

"Tell me what compermental, or whatever you said means."

"It's compartment," he points his finger at the glove box, "like compartment box, but you add alized to the end after the t. And what that means is she's made glove boxes for every aspect of her life. She did it years ago. It's how she got over the anxiety of having a painful past. It's how she

309

survived. And," he sighs, "she didn't bother making a glove box for you or anybody else."

"What about a back seat."

"What back seat?"

"If her life's a car, what about the back seat or the trunk?"

Adam laughs.

"I'm not joking."

"That's exactly what I'm laughing at."

I cross my arms, and decide not to talk to him for the rest of the drive. One minute later I ask, "Fine, can you at least explain it, like it is, in plain English, without the glove boxes?"

"I need to work on her. She has trust issues."

"So do I, but I trust you, and you're her brother too, so she should trust you like I do."

"We don't exist. We're intruders into her fabricated life."

I raise an eyebrow at Adam.

"Her closest friends have no clue she has a brother or a sister." His eyes are sunken. His voice sounds tired. "You know I expected her to be excited about the news, and I didn't expect her to be this damaged, considering she only had to put up with Irma for a year or two. And as for Dad, she hates the hell out of him. As far as she's concerned, he's dead. He died when Irma came."

"Well I have to agree with the dead part. When did you talk to her?"

"After the court hearing."

"You're telling the truth, right?"

Adam snaps in my face, "Of course I am. My point is it's not just you she's shutting out. It's all of us. She hasn't told a soul she has siblings."

"Adam don't lie. What exactly did she say when you mentioned me? Word for word."

"If I tell you word for word, everything she said, right down to the last detail, will you promise to drop the subject? At least for today?"

"Yes. What did she say?"

"The past has no place in my life."

The Aftermath

Adam pulls into an apartment complex, stops halfway in front of a long carport and lurches to the left. He cranes his neck and slowly backs into the narrow stall.

"Who lives here?" I glance around and recognize nothing.

"Someone very special," he chuckles.

"Adam, no. Not again," I say and cross my arms.

He chuckles some more, "This time, I'll let you be my sister."

"Gee that's awful nice of you. Thanks."

We walk into a lobby and go up the elevator.

"You look nervous. Is this your first time in an elevator."

"Yes."

"Well get used to it because you'll see a lot of this one."

Adam stops at a door at the end of the hall and fumbles for the correct key. Before he can insert it, the door flings open.

"Hey you. What took you so long. I missed you buddy." Two arms that belong to Angela Green, wrap around his neck. After they smooch for five minutes she hugs me, "How are ya? Come on in."

"Welcome to my bachelor pad," Adam laughs.

"Not for long," Angela waves her finger in his face.

"That's right. So I'd better make the most of it."

"Did you tell her?" She raises her brow at him and tilts her head at me.

"No, we talked about the past instead."

For the better part of fifteen minutes, the past continues to dominate the conversation.

"Cheer up," Angela smiles. "It's over now."

Adam nods and says, "That's right. It's the past. It's over. Better things lie up ahead."

While Adam and Angela play some more kissy-face I check out Adams décor choices. The only piece I recognize is his trunk.

"Do you still have your bird card collection in there?"

"No," Adam laughs. "Angela relocated it to the bottom dresser drawer. She's claimed the trunk as her hope chest."

"A what?"

She says, "You know a dowry chest. Things for the future."

"It's called a hope chest because she hopes I'll marry her."

"Listen mister, you're the one hoping. Not me."

"You marrying me is a given. But you are right, I am hoping— hoping to get the family back together."

"Oh, it'll happen. Just wait and see." She smiles, "Anyway, Juanita, anything I buy for after we're married goes in the hope chest, and doesn't come out until after our honeymoon."

"Speaking of honeymoons, who's going to tell Juanita where we're going for our honeymoon, you or me?"

"Camping here in Newfoundland, right Adam?" she twists up her nose. "But guess what we'll be camping in?"

"A tent?"

"Not just a tent. A tent in the snow."

Battered

My eyes bulge. "You're joking right?"

"If my woman can't handle winter camping, she has no right to be my wife," Adam smirks.

Angela's eyes twinkle, "Maybe it's because your lives have been one hell of a storm. I think it's his way of initiating me into the Rose clan."

"You know Angela, the name Rose means nothing to me. Green is a good family name. I should change my name to yours."

"Adam Rose, I have no intentions of marrying you and keeping my maiden name. So, you can forget that one right this minute. Besides, family is what you make it, and we don't have to make it the same way your Dad or Irma did."

"Adam is wrong. The Rose name means something. It means pain, suffering and living life on a bed of thorns. It's a bad omen."

"There you go Angela. Juanita's right and that makes me right."

"Knock it off guys. For the last and final time, I'm not keeping my maiden name and neither are you." She turns to me and shakes her exasperated head. "You know, sometimes your brother drives me absolutely nuts. The deal is I get to plan the wedding and he gets to plan the honeymoon. And the name I choose to take is part of the wedding planning. Compromise is the key to any good relationship, right?" Angela looks at me and winks.

Angela dangles her arm across Adam's shoulder, while he flips pictures of the park. Winter never looked like that out back.

"You know, of all the times I've gone camping, I've never been camping in the snow. Who knows, maybe we'll get to go ice fishing. The only reason I didn't go before was I was waiting for the perfect female to take, so she could keep me warm, but I guess Angela will have to do."

Angela punches his arm, "You better watch it, buddy. I still have time to say no."

"In the snow? But you'll be freezing. After the winters we spent outside? Are you insane?"

"If a person can't survive the tough times, what good are they? Besides, if you could survive the freezing cold outside of a tent, without anyone to cuddle up to, I think we'll do just fine. She'll be cuddling me the entire time. We won't be roughing it. I have insulated sleeping bags and a propane heater and that's more than you ever had. All the bears will be hibernating, no mosquitos, what more could you ask for?" He pulls Angela's face toward his, kisses her square on the lips, and says, "It will be our first official adventure together as husband and wife. Who knows what adventure I'll plan for our first anniversary?"

Is Adam trying to obliterate those horrid memories? Change what winter means? Is that how? Bury memories under new ones?

"I have a funny feeling, being a Rose will be enough of an adventure in itself."

Adam bows and says, "Welcome to the world of Roses, where life is one giant misadventure."

Angela pats my knee, "I'm saving your brother you know."

"From who?"

"From himself."

"Come here. You've got to see this."

I follow her into a room. She closes the blinds, shuts the door and says, "What do you see?"

"Not much, it's too dark."

Her silhouette turns on the lamp.

I laugh, mostly because I'm lost for words. The ceiling has a trail of purple glowing footprints, from one end to the other.

"They're Adam's footsteps," Angela folds her arms and shakes her head. "Don't ask. Trust me you don't want to know."

"How did he get up there? Did you help him?" I ask.

"Hell no, I had no part in it. This was his man cave phase. Do yourself a favor, if you date someone who does this, run."

"I will and I won't look back!"

I nudge Adam and nod at the door. "Is it okay if you leave to drive me home? I have to get back to feed the horses." I can sense Adam and Angela want to be alone and by their quick response, I know I'm right.

Battered

On the way home I try to talk about Marie but every time I bring her up Adam switches the topic to Angela. That's when I know Marie, Adam and I will never be a family under one roof. Like Marie, he broke his promise. Maybe it's time I stopped wanting a family. Maybe family isn't the best thing for me, and the truth is I wouldn't recognize a good one if it slapped me in the face. The biggest slap in the face is Marie turning her back on us. The Marie I knew valued family above everything else. She always thought things through thoroughly. Maybe she's smarter than the rest of us. Maybe she knows something we don't.

Adam asks me one final question before I get out of the car. "What do you think of her."

I can tell by his eyes it doesn't matter what I think. He's smitten.

"Lucky for you she's nice."

"Why do you say lucky for me?"

"Because you look at her the way Dad used to look at Irma."

Adam points at the Rubys. Their gray hair glistens under the porch lamp. Sitting on the porch bench, hand in hand, smiling at each other, they look like the perfect couple. "I want that," he says.

It still feels strange to see someone, without a belt, waiting on a porch for me. It feels uncanny to have someone care about how I am, how I feel. It's hard to soak in the kindness, because kindness makes me feel awkward and uncomfortable. It's too drastic a change for me. It's like taking a feral cat and expecting it to trust your dog when it licks it.

The truth is, instead of feeling good, their kindness hurts. I'm not sure why being treated good still makes me squirm and cringe. Maybe it could be that it shines a brighter light on how bad my own family mistreated me, or maybe it's just because I'm too messed up. After being treated so bad, for so many years, it's hard to accept the extreme opposite. Years ago, I had to turn off as many emotions as I could, to survive. Love was never part of the equation. When I would think about how much other kids were loved and how hated I was, it made survival unbearable. I learned to accept the lack of love, knowing love was my kryptonite. The Rubys think it's conditioning, and with time it will go away. I suspect it's a bigger part of

315

me, bigger than they'll ever know. Whatever it is, I know it's but a small portion of a big aftermath.

Normally this time of day Mr. Ruby is in the barn, Mrs. Ruby is baking and I'm feeding horses, but today the three of us are sitting in the living room because we 'need to have a talk'.

"Alice while the court case was ongoing, we were scared to death for you. We were so afraid we would lose you. It broke our hearts to hear all those stories of what they did to you. Why didn't you tell us about it?" Mr. Ruby's eyes are riddled with pain.

I glance back and forth between them. They're both crying. Words catch in my throat. I wait for one of them to say something else but they both wait patiently for my answer.

Mrs. Ruby's voice is soft. "Alice why didn't you tell us? Why didn't you talk about what they did to you? Why not let us know?"

"You said if you knew just a little, it would break your heart."

"And it did but we would have rather heard it from you."

"I didn't—I don't ever want to break your heart. There was nothing good that would come from it and I didn't want anybody to pity me or think I was making up stories or see me as nothing but a liar."

Mr. Ruby takes a deep breath and says, "Pride and fear are not always our worst enemies. True warriors have learned to survive the most challenging obstacles because they made fear work for them. You have that gift. But until you learn to manage your fear of trusting people, it will hinder every path you choose to take."

Mrs. Ruby nods her head in agreement. "Our fear is you won't take the time to learn to trust us. Time to prove we can keep you safe here, and time for you to learn to love us like a daughter."

I can't think of one past wound, as big and hurtful as the huge pain that's flickering across my chest. It hurts to know they may be right. I can't stand the pain—can't stop my chin from quivering.

Tears flood down Mrs. Ruby face, and everyone joins in. The crying lasts on and off throughout the day. Part of it is over my past and part of it is something I can't figure out, but I know it has to do with me fearing the future. They can't seem to fathom that I need to earn my keep, and it's crystal clear I'll never be able to work hard enough to pay them back for loving me. Truth is I'm more scared of love than Irma. And the thought my sister could change her mind makes me want to keep that door open.

Mr. Ruby pats my knee. "Don't worry, we can afford to send you to college or you can stay and work on the farm, raise some horses, whatever you want your future to be, is what it can be."

I try to picture that future but it looks bleak because Marie isn't in it. My future looks like broken pieces that can't be glued together, and them adopting me is a quick fix to major surgery. What if Irma is right? What if I'm too rotten to be anyone's daughter? I'm not blind. I can see the pain in their eyes right now and the cause of that is me. If they didn't know me, they wouldn't be crying today, they would look like they did on the day I met them.

My siblings are scattered all across the country like fragments of debris from a nuclear bomb, and no matter how strong a survivor I feel we each are, all of us are damaged—maybe beyond repair. All of us are shell shocked, licking our individual wounds.

I stay awake long after the others sleep. Slivers of past moments rear their ugly head, and remind me I am still a victim. I think about the time Dad approached my bed. Something about him scared me. I remember him sitting there, giving me my first hug in years. Then he kissed my cheeks. I remember trying to squirm away but he wouldn't let me go, not until I threatened to tell Irma.

He did nothing wrong, but I simply didn't trust him. Maybe if I had hugged him back things would have changed.

That night, that moment replays in my dreams. I toss and turn trying to shake Dad off. I threaten to tell Irma. My voice yelling, 'I will tell Irma', jerks me awake. I realize it's not Dad but someone real I am wrestling with. Someone is on top of my blanket, covering my mouth. I bite his hand as hard as I can. He jumps up and disappears through my window.

I rush to the window and slam it shut. The slam is so loud it awakens the Rubys. They both rush to my room, and flick on the light.

"Her nose is bleeding. Cyril, grab a wet towel. Alice, tilt your head back."
She pinches my nose, another trigger that reminds me of my past. Mr. Ruby
returns with a towel and some ice, kisses my forehead and leaves us alone.
Mrs. Ruby stays in my room and hums softly as she wipes my face. She
looks worried and tired. I pretend to be asleep until she leaves, but it's
almost dawn before I drift off. I awaken to birds singing, and fear ripples
through me until I am fully awake and realize I am not back home in the
basement.

I skip breakfast, go for a long walk and decide I don't have to hide the
truth anymore and choose to tell Mr. Ruby about what happened last night.
I find him in the barn, milking a cow.

Someone else is in the barn helping him. The cows block his upper body,
but when he turns, I see his hand is bandaged. My heart skips two beats. I
walk around the cows, so I can see his face.

Nearby, a pitchfork stabbed into a bale of hay, calls my name. For one
minute I consider plunging it through his chest.

The last time I saw him was by the tool shed and last night wasn't the
first time I've bitten his hand.

He smirks and waves. He knows I haven't told the Rubys about his
attacks against me because he knows he probably wouldn't be standing here
on two good legs, if I had. I watch him raise his finger across his throat as
if to slit it. He points at me and then holds his own lips shut and motions
to slit his throat again.

Mr. Ruby is humming, milking the cow, oblivious to my plight. I
rethink telling him my secret. I know it's impossible for him to protect me
day and night. There's too much to do and he has to sleep sometime. What
if Mr. Ruby believes him and not me?

I resist the urge to run. Instead, I turn and walk away until I'm out of
sight, then I bolt. I don't stop until I'm at the fence where I feed the horses.
I jump it. I don't check to see if they're nearby. I don't care if they stampede
me. I run through the clearing to the edge of the field. I am standing at the
edge of a drop, wondering what would happen if I hurtled myself over it.

Battered

I slowly back away from the edge. Out there, somewhere, there has to be a safe place for me. The trees rustle, twigs crack, and goose bumps crawl across my arms.

That old familiar smell of fear fills my nostrils. I frantically scan the ground for a large rock.

"Thinking about jumping?"

"Gordon you scared me to death!"

"They won't be back," he sighs.

His words make me angry. I want to say, who died and made you lord-and-master over the horses? Instead, I bite my tongue, count to ten, and ask, "Why not?"

"They ran right through last night. Didn't even, stop to eat apples. It's as if they were wigged out."

"You were here?"

"I hid in the bushes and waited for a long while but they never came back." He plops down beside me and plucks at some weeds. "What were you doing? Waiting to get trampled to death?"

"No, but it's a thought," I say. "How many other times have you hidden in the bushes, without me knowing?"

"I get here before you do most days," he admits. "That's why no one hears me. I tried your song once, but the stallion knew it wasn't you and stayed right here where you're sitting. He made the mares stay back in the trees until you came and sang."

"So, they didn't bolt when you were hiding before?"

"Nope."

"Then that means they'll be back," I say.

"I don't think so. Maybe they have a second home, somewhere else. Sort of like you do now." Gordon chews on a blade of grass and says, "I heard about your horrible life."

"How?"

"Everyone knows. This is a small place. It's hard to keep secrets here."

"Well you seem to be doing just fine, you're like a secret hoarder," I scoff.

"I can't believe that woman did all those awful things to you. They should have hung her. Why didn't your brothers stop her?"

"How do you know all of this?"

"My other uncle is a lawyer. He was at the court hearing."

"My brothers were barely older than me and were too busy trying to survive themselves. It's hard to outsmart a monster."

"Was your father poor?" he asks.

"No. Far from it, why?"

"Was he a drunk?"

"No."

"In social studies, my teacher said abuse stems from poverty or addiction."

"Well your teacher is dead wrong. Abuse stems from messed up minds. There is no excuse for it—not poverty, not anything. It's some sick mental disease that some get and some don't. The problem is nobody wants it to be true. Nobody wants to report it. They don't want to swim in dirty water. I bet more kids die from abuse, because nobody believes them, and they're too afraid to run. Running away, when you're petrified and desperate, takes bravery, it takes courage, and when you're told you're despicable every single day, bravery is hard to come by. You run away when there's nothing left to lose. When I ran, I ran for my life."

"In social studies I learned that running away is related to shame and weakness, so what are you ashamed of?"

Gordon's question unnerves me. "Your social studies teacher?"

He laughs and says, "Seriously. She said that."

"She's repeating some crap someone made up, or published after they interviewed runaways—who returned home, because they ran away in the heat of the moment. The real runaways—like me—won't get interviewed, so nobody knows why we really run."

"Why not?"

"Because real runners, the ones who run to survive, work hard *not* to be found. And we never go back home or get interviewed, and nobody gets to know our side of the story. Bad parents never tell the truth—never the whole truth—they never take any blame."

"Never? Then how do their stories get told?"

"The real ones don't. If the real ones get caught, and get interviewed, they're like prisoners of war. They get told what to say."

"How do you know that for sure?"

"Because that's who I was. All my life I was brainwashed not to talk. I ran, got caught, got sent back home and was brainwashed even more."

"Weren't you scared?"

"Of what—the parents or running?"

"Being alone. Getting hurt."

"Nobody could hurt me much more than—I was scared lots, but thinking I might be killed on the streets didn't enter my mind, because the odds were if I stayed, sooner or later I would end up dead anyway. It was my one chance at survival."

"How did you make it out? Like, how did you do it?"

"The first time was a disaster. I guess you get better at things, if you plan them, or try them a second time."

"How did you know it was the right time to run?"

He reminds me of myself and all the questions I asked God years ago, when God was too busy to answer.

"Try asking God. I think it helps, especially if you have problems talking to adults."

"I don't trust adults, and I especially don't trust God." He picks at his shoelace, lowers his eyes and blurts out, "Have you ever had sex with an adult?"

I try not to look shocked. I know if I do, he'll clam up, but it's impossible to look anything else, so I close my eyes.

"You look disgusted."

"No Gordon, that look is called tired and confused. Maybe you're not seeing right, or looking for something that's not there."

He sucks in a deep breath, "He's a family friend. He paid me for chores, like sweeping and gardening. Somehow, the chores changed to showing him my genitals for money. Then he gave me a raise to keep it a secret. He said I owed him and it was time to pay him back. He said the money wasn't free." Gordon gulps and talks faster.

"Things got more and more out of control until one day there was nothing disgusting left to do. I feel so ashamed for not stopping it." Gordon punches his gut.

"And . . .?"

"After I stopped going there, he lied to my uncle and said I refused to mow his grass after he'd already paid me in advance."

Gordon punches his chest twice. "My uncle asked if it was true and when I said yes, he blew a fuse, and told me to get my butt over there, so I did."

"Did you ever try telling them the truth?"

"Would you have the guts to tell anyone if that was happening to you?"

"No. Because I'd be terrified that nobody would believe me."

"See? We're not so different."

Inside my guts are rolling like ocean waves. I can't comprehend what he just shared.

He exhales slowly and stares at me with a face full of shame. I try to think faster. What am I supposed to say? I know about running away. I can talk about that. "It doesn't take guts to run away. It takes fear, a lot of fear. And it takes guts to turn that fear into bravery."

His eyes widen, "Fear?"

"Yes fear. Not shame. Fear of losing yourself, or killing someone for the nasty things they do. And fear turned into bravery is a powerful weapon. There comes a time you have to stop waiting to be rescued, and save yourself. It's the right time to run, when the fear of the unknown is safer than what you're enduring."

"You're not judging me? Not disgusted?"

I have no clue how to show him I'm not judging him. I know I need to get him to open up more, but I don't know how. I don't want to pry, but I can see he has a lot on his chest. I see the animal in his eyes, that same trapped look that stared back at me for years from my bathroom mirror. I've seen glimmers of that look, revisit my own eyes lately.

Battered

"There's a phone number to call for help, but I don't know it. I think my neighbors called it years ago, back in Stephenville but after they came by, Irma got worse."

"Who calls a stranger and tells them this stuff? Where do you start? My bum hurts . . . he likes boys . . . he likes me . . ." his voice fades into the wind. "No one would believe me if I told them. They wouldn't want to believe me. People think he's such a great guy being a priest and all."

"A priest? Is that why you don't trust God?"

"Yeah. You're disgusted right?" Gordon gets up to leave.

"Yes, I mean no, not at you, at him. That's like double disgust because he's like a devil in disguise. That's like an arsonist becoming a firefighter, it's just so much worse than just being a pyromaniac. Can't you tell anyone?"

"I just did," he retorts. "You!"

"I meant someone like an adult."

"Can you tell the Rubys some pervert is masturbating by the barn and trying to assault you? Can you tell anyone anything? You're not accusing a respected adult of anything. He's just a scumbag. His word isn't any better than yours is, so what's your excuse? What are you going to do about it? Put up with it? Run away? Now imagine if that was a priest that everybody loved and respected."

"I get it. My fight was against my family. Yours is against society. And you run when you know you can't win the fight."

"Can you help me run away?" his voice lowers, "I'm too scared to try alone. But I know running away is right and would fix it."

I find it impossible to say no to his big desperate dark eyes. I take a slow deep breath and say, "Fine, but be back here by dusk. Bring enough stuff to last a week. Make three to five small trips, to avoid suspicion. And, don't bring more than you can easily carry under your arm or in a knapsack. You have to carry, what you bring, by yourself."

"What kind of stuff?"

"You'll be hungry, thirsty, lonely, scared and cold. Plan for that."

"You're exaggerating, right?"

"Far from it, and wear comfy walking shoes."

The rest of the day is a slow blur. Mrs. Ruby doesn't know I'm helping her set the table for the last time.

I tell her I'm not hungry but that's normal for me lately. I make an excuse about needing fresh air. She insists I take some water and some sandwiches with me. I thank her and give her a long hug. She drops a fork and bends to get it, frustrated she mutters at the mess on the floor. I get a paper towel and dampen it to clean it up. She points to a spot I missed. This moment reminds me of the time in the cellar when Marie knew she was leaving, when I was obsessed with the quarters I dropped, just like she's obsessed with the spot on the floor.

I take the time to wipe it properly, and although I'm still uncomfortable with hugs, I give her two good ones because I know this is goodbye and I don't want her to have the regrets I had with Marie's goodbye. I remind her how grateful I am she saved my soul and how her and Mr. Ruby are the best people I've ever had in my life. And it's then I think, maybe I'm making a huge mistake.

"Alice, my love, what would I ever do without you."

Oddly those words hurt worse than any belt buckle in the face. It's too extreme from my past. Too hard to handle.

I'm afraid to look back when I close the door. I walk toward the apple tree. If I go, who will feed the horses? I turn the corner, and bang into Mr. Ruby.

"Alice, be careful," he catches me as I slip. I remember how many times Irma tripped me on purpose, just to have an excuse to beat me. Wasn't a family like this what I always wanted?

"Yeah be careful." A bandaged hand taps my shoulder.

Mr. Ruby asks, "Have you met Juanita?"

"Yes sir. Back during hay season."

The screen door opens. "Alice are you sure you're not hungry?"

"Yes, Mrs. Ruby."

"Stella set another place at the table. This boy worked like there was no tomorrow."

Battered

I shake the jerk's hand off my shoulder, count to thirty, and climb into the house through my bedroom window.

He's helping Mr. Ruby to get to me. He knows I won't tell.

I grab a spare lightweight blanket from my closet and stuff it in my knapsack. I grab my Bible and my money. I change into the clothes Adam bought me, twist my locket around my neck and make sure the clasp is secure. The last thing I toss into my knapsack is the empty spool that Adam turned into a weapon. Then I climb out my window and walk away.

My first stop is to say goodbye to the stallion, but he's not there.

I glance at my watch. It's six o'clock and Gordon should be here by now. I don't give him an extra minute, I turn and walk away, relieved to be alone.

"Slow down, just a little, you're killing me."

I turn to face Gordon. How do I tell him I've changed my mind and I don't want to be responsible for him? I open my mouth, press my tongue against my lower teeth, and force the words up my throat. "Gordon, you need to turn around. You're too young."

"Too young for what?"

"To run."

"But I . . . I want to save myself."

His defeated, broken look kills me. I groan and say, "Maybe you should turn around and go back—"

"Go back to what? You have more to go back to than me . . . if I go back, I'll stab him with a knife," Gordon looks more frightened than serious. I recognize fear better than most do, and his eyes are brimming with it.

"Fine. But you'd better keep up and don't ask me where we're going because I don't know."

"Wait. You don't know where we're going? How are we supposed to get anywhere?"

"There's a big world out there, so we'll end up somewhere. The question is could somewhere be worse than here?"

"Never." His eyes are filled with fear and bravery.

"Then somewhere is our destination."

We climb the fence to the field. The knoll turns into a hill. The hill turns into a cliff. I look down and feel instant fear. "Remember when I told you I didn't despise anything? I forgot about one thing. I really hate heights."

"Did you fall when you were a kid?"

"Actually, I did. Repeatedly."

"Where?"

"Mostly in my nightmares. Sometimes in real life." I step back and adjust my knapsack.

Gordon pulls his off and pats it. "I filled it with food."

"What about water?"

"Water's free."

I scoff, "You try telling Bob Parsons that." I scan the contents of his knapsack. "I don't see a blanket."

"A blanket?" Gordon looks stumped.

"Where do you think we're going? Florida? Nights get cold."

"I never thought about nights. I only thought about leaving. Besides, I don't mind the cold all that much."

"If we fail, next time you need to plan ahead, okay?"

Gordon nods. He pulls a beef jerky and some bubble gum from his pocket. "I brought stuff, so I'm not completely useless."

"Stuff doesn't make you useful. Actions do."

The road starts to bend downhill. I twist back and soak in one last look at the barn. But the barn doesn't bring me the joy it once did. All I can see is that creep scoffing at me. I blink my stinging eyes. "What if we went back? Teamed up and told the truth?"

"The Rubys might believe you but who would ever believe me? I live with people who do drugs and are always drunk. Who's going to save me from that?"

I remember wishing, praying for someone to save me.

"This is what you want right?"

He nods.

"You're not going to be sorry if the police catch us?"

"I'd rather be in jail anyway."

326

"They put kids in Juvie not jail"

"There's one in St. John's so maybe we should head that way. You're from there, been there, it's nice, right?"

"I'm the wrong person to ask about St. John's. I spent the majority of it confined to the basement and barred in the back yard."

"If it gets cold, we can share your blanket, right?"

I raise my eyebrows at him.

"I think I'm gay, so I'm pretty safe."

"You're too young to be anything," I laugh.

"Not too young for some people," Gordon mutters under his breath.

He looks scrawny and scared. Six months ago, I looked like that.

"I'm sick of living in fear. I hate being afraid, and I hate him, but most of all I hate me."

His words hit home. I kneel in front of him. "Be brave. Fear cripples us. Find the courage to like you. Don't ever let any other person define the real you. People don't have the right to define us."

I brush the debris from my knees and hold his hand. We walk along the dirt road until it forks. To my far right is a well-worn path. "Maybe we should follow the horse trail," I say. I jerk my head toward his knapsack. "Did you bring anything other than junk-food? Anything useful, like apples or a compass?"

"I bought a radio," Gordon says. He stops and tugs back and forth on his knapsack until it breaks free.

"Does it work?"

He turns the knob left, then right until the static disappears and a station tunes in.

"Yep. I even brought spare batteries. I love this song. It's called 'Runnin' Away'. Have you heard it?" He turns up the volume and bobs his head to the beat.

I listen for a bit. "No. What's it about?"

His mouth hangs open. "Are you for real? It's about wearing out your shoes running away."

Juanita Ray

I laugh, "Just for the record I don't plan to keep running away for the rest of my life. This time will be my last time. Besides, I like these shoes, so find a better song."

Static pops and crackles, as he races back and forth across the radio bands. "Give me that thing." He hands me the radio. I twist the knob and find the perfect song. "Now this is more like it."

'. . . winter, spring, summer, or fall, yeah all you gotta do is call and I'll be there, yeah, yeah, yeah you've got a friend . . .'

Five songs and eight commercials later it starts to rain. Gordon taps me on the arm. "I have just one question." He tugs at his hood. I reach back and yank it from under his knapsack. "What will we do when we run out of batteries?"

"Batteries?"

"Yeah. My radio runs on batteries."

"Can you sing?".

"Nope. How about you?"

"My music teacher gave me a D minus. But we can sing if we want, because nobody can hear us, and our hearts don't have ears."

Two hours later a steep cliff looms in the distance and before long we are standing at the base of the rugged stark hill.

"Isn't that the place from History class, where Marconi received the very first transatlantic wireless signal? Where they fought the last battle of the Seven Years' War?"

The only war I knew about near this area, was the one I lived through, and it was eight years, not seven. "I wouldn't know. I spent History class at the dental office."

An eerie sense of unease, grapples with my gut. Is this an omen? Is it a sign that I'm walking towards seven years of trouble?

Am I feeling hesitation . . . or fear?

The truth is, I've learned to trust fear. Fear and I are finally good friends.

Without me, fear is nothing, and without fear I wouldn't have survived. Fear has kept me safe more times than I can count. But the most important thing fear has done is make me brave. That's something only fear can do.

Battered

And yes, this hill looks scary, but somewhere up there is a path, that leads to my future.

It's hard to imagine the future when you're standing in the middle of nowhere not knowing what lies ahead, but whatever it is, has to be better than the past. But what if it's not?

For extra insurance, I make myself a promise. A promise to never stay in a bad situation. The moment it happens, I'll walk away and never look back. It's a promise I'll keep for years to come. A promise that impacts the rest of my life.

About The Author

Juanita Ray, a dual citizen, born in Newfoundland Canada, is a well-educated, retired entrepreneur who has had several successful careers, and earned multiple certificates and awards. She is married to her soulmate Scott, and together they live at 'the jungle' in Southern California, with the horde, a 6-pack of dogs, 150 small birds housed in an outside aviary, and a 6-pack of adopted outside semi-feral cats (one loves to crash photo shoots), who have spent the last decade drooling while 'guarding' the aviary. Her newest rescue is a misfit Siamese cat with a dissociative identity disorder.

Juanita's hobbies include photography, creating music, writing lyrics, and painting everything in sight. Her favorite tools are drills, hammers, and her 10-inch miter saw. Her lifelong passion for animals has never waned. Neither has her allergies to cats and dust.

Juanita wants to thank you for reading this book. She invites you to leave a review online and share what you thought with others. Keep in touch with her by visiting the following websites, or sending her an email.

AuthorJRay.com
ToxicThoughts.com
Twitter @toxicthoughtsbk
Facebook @ToxicThoughtsSeries
Twitter/Facebook @authorJRay
SmorgasbordPublications@gmail.com

STALKED

the trials and successes of a child marriage

JUANITA RAY

TOXIC THOUGHTS

a true story series

Printed in Great Britain
by Amazon

20046741R00195